# TRADITION
# ALIVE

The icon depicted on the front cover is from a series of frescoes done by Sister Joanna Reitlinger (1898–1988) in 1947 for the chapel of St. Basil's House, Ladbrook Grove, London. St. Basils, now closed, for many years was the home of the fellowship of St. Alban and St. Sergius, an ecumenical community of Anglicans, Orthodox, and others started in the late 1920s and still existing today in the United Kingdom. When the fellowship center was moved to Oxford and St. Basil's House closed, these wall paintings were installed in the chapel of the monastery of Christ the Savior in Hove, a monastic house of the Anglican Community of the Servants of the Will of God. Sister Joanna, who lived in the Russian emigration of Paris from the late 1920s until the end of the war, had as her spiritual father and teacher the great theologian Fr. Sergius Bulgakov. A trained and gifted artist, she was asked, along with Leonid Ouspensky and Fr. Gregory Krug, to learn iconography so that the Orthodox communities in France might have icons for their churches. Along with her colleagues, she became an important figure in the contemporary renaissance of icon painting.

The chapel of St. Basil's house had two series of icons on its walls and all were dedicated to the memory of Fr. Bulgakov, who had died in 1944. The upper level depicted scenes from the Book of Revelation, views of the heavenly Church, the Kingdom of God present but yet to come. It is from the lower level, namely the historical Church throughout the world, that the icon represented on the front cover was taken. Each of the four icons from which this was selected depicts a gathering or assembly of saints from a particular local church or region. In this fresco, the saints of Russia (gathered before the Sarov forest, hermitages and cathedrals of Moscow, and Kiev-Holy Wisdom) are Seraphim of Sarov; Tikhon, bishop of Zadonsk; Prince Alexander Nevsky; Alexis, metropolitan of Moscow; Juliana the merciful; Philip metropolitan of Moscow and martyr; Olga, grandmother of Vladimir; Theodosius, founder of the Caves monastery in Kiev; and Vladimir, apostle of Russia.

The vision of Fr. Bulgakov's theology was the inspiration for Sr. Joanna's work; the chapel thus contained the undivided Church across time and space and beyond these in the Kingdom. This was not only the Church about which Fr. Sergius wrote, lectured, and preached, but also the Church presumed in the eucharistic liturgy's prayers and in the scripture. It was also the dream of his work at the very start of the modern ecumenical movement, both in what would become the World Council of Churches and the Fellowship of St. Alban and St. Sergius.

Brother Christopher Mark, CSWG of the Monastery of Christ the Savior, Brighton/Hove provided the image from its current location at the monastery.

# TRADITION ALIVE

## On the Church and the Christian Life in Our Time / Readings from the Eastern Church

### Edited by
# MICHAEL PLEKON

A SHEED & WARD BOOK

ROWMAN & LITTLEFIELD PUBLISHERS, INC.
Lanham • Boulder • New York • Toronto • Oxford

A SHEED & WARD BOOK

ROWMAN & LITTLEFIELD PUBLISHERS, INC.

Published in the United States of America
by Rowman & Littlefield Publishers, Inc.

An imprint of the Rowman & Littlefield Publishing Group
4501 Forbes Boulevard, Suite 200, Lanham, Maryland 20706
www.rowmanlittlefield.com

PO Box 317
Oxford
OX2 9RU, UK

British Library Cataloguing in Publication Information Available

**Library of Congress Cataloging-in-Publication Data**

Tradition alive : on the church and the Christian life in our time :
readings from the Eastern Church / [edited by] Michael Plekon.
    p. cm.
  Includes bibliographical references and index.
  ISBN 0-7425-3162-7 (alk. paper)—ISBN 0-7425-3163-5 (pbk. : alk.
paper)
  1. Spiritual life—Orthodox Eastern Church. 2. Church—History of
doctrines—20th century. 3. Orthodox Eastern
Church—Doctrines—History—20th century. I. Plekon, Michael, 1948–
BX382.T73 2003
281.9—dc21

                        2003007576

Printed in the United States of America

∞™ The paper used in this publication meets the minimum requirements of
American National Standard for Information Sciences—Permanence of Paper
for Printed Library Materials, ANSI/NISO Z39.48-1992.

# CONTENTS

# FOREWORD

**A**mong Orthodox Christians in the twentieth century, few subjects provoked more reflection, discussion, and passionate debate than the subject of tradition. This is understandable. The subject of tradition was never absent in earlier presentations of Orthodox theology; typically it was coupled with the subject of Scripture in the course of discussions about authority. But tradition was largely taken for granted. In the twentieth century—a century of wars, revolutions, concentration camps, gulags, deportations, and exile—this became impossible. Traditional patterns of life and thought that earlier had seemed unshakeable were rudely swept away. The past—even the relatively recent past of prerevolutionary Russia—now seemed distant and alien. A wistful sadness attended virtually every memory. In the face of tragic new realities, the Gospel message of Christ's triumph over the powers of death and destruction seemed to have lost its power.

In this new situation, Orthodox Christians were forced to ask the question posed by Fr. John Meyendorff in one of the essays in this book: Does Christian tradition have a future? These Orthodox Christians had experienced firsthand the disorienting effects of historical discontinuity. They sensed the distance separating their own time from earlier, less problematic eras—from one or another now-vanished golden age. And quite understandably, they looked to the future with trepidation. Whether conservative or liberal, whether traditionalist or modernist, Orthodox Christians were unwilling to accept painful present realities as the way things always have been and therefore as the way they must always be. They looked at past and future from a new vantage point—and saw that neither past nor future looked as familiar and comfortable as once upon a time, back in the days before traditional patterns of life and thought had been swept away.

Although reflective Orthodox Christians in the twentieth century shared this new vantage point, they differed in their attempts to explain the meaning and shape of history. Some turned apocalyptic in their thinking: the Antichrist is clearly at work, the end is at hand. We therefore can expect nothing new or spiritually significant from history. In this situation, no real mission to society or culture is possible or even desirable. The only alternative to destruction is withdrawal from the world, preservation of a remnant church through strict adherence to norms and practices salvaged from a happier past—in other words, through strict adherence to what such people understood to be tradition. But others—no less affected by the tragedies of the century—nevertheless were more optimistic, or at least more willing to see God's Spirit still at work in human history, more willing to believe that in each new age and situation, men and women are capable of responding in faith to God's Word.

The selections in this book offer an introduction to the thought of the latter group of people. The essayists range from professional theologians to social activists; a few were, by almost any standard, eccentric. In their diversity, they suggest the wide range of charisms that can be found within the Orthodox Church in any age or place. But common to all of the essayists was an openness to history, an openness to new situations, an openness to other human beings created in the image and likeness of God. To understand the meaning of tradition, these people did not look to the past alone—an approach that so easily degenerates into archeology, antiquarianism, reaction, rejection of history, and escapism. They recognized that a living tradition does not make us prisoners of the past. Rather, it reveals the same spirit at work in both past and present, allowing us to face the future with hope. As we venture into a new century—a century that already has witnessed destruction and tragedy, giving rise to a host of new perplexities—the witness of these courageous men and women is especially valuable. They offer a message of hope to a bewildered world. We do not know what the future will bring, but we have faith that God is with us, for in the lives of these men and women we can see the power of the resurrection still at work in a world that is fallen yet loved by God.

—John H. Erickson, Dean
St. Vladimir's Orthodox Theological Seminary

# ACKNOWLEDGMENTS

I am grateful for PSC-CUNY faculty research awards 28, 29, 30, 31, 32, and 33 in the last several years, each of which helped me prepare this anthology as well as a number of other volumes and articles. The staff of the Research Foundation of CUNY were of great assistance. I also want to thank the dean and faculty research committee of the Weissman School of Arts and Sciences at Baruch College, CUNY, for reassigned time over the last several years for work in gathering texts, translation editing, and writing. Dean John Erickson and Professor Peter Bouteneff of St. Vladimir's Orthodox Theological Seminary graciously agreed to write the foreword and the concluding essays. Among the other translators I want to thank Professor Bouteneff, Frs. Alexis Vinogradov, and Alvian Smirensky for contributing their efforts. Anastassy Brandon Gallaher, an upcoming scholar of great promise, was especially helpful in providing texts, and Jonathan Spencer assisted in the scanning of essays. Father Stephen Janos' irreplaceable work in creating the Berdiaev website (www.berdyaev.com) must be mentioned. Permissions and material used in this anthology were gratefully received from Mrs. Juliana Schmemann, Fr. Stephen Platt of the Fellowship of Saints Alban and Sergius, Ted Bazil of St. Vladimir's Seminary Press, the Reverend Dr. John Behr of *Saint Vladimir's Theological Quarterly*, James McRay of St. Vladimir's Seminary, Father Viktor Sokolov, Didier Lefebvre, Professor Nikita Struve, Hèléne Arjakovsky-Klépinin, Brother Christopher Mark, CSWG and the monastery of Christ the Saviour, Brighton-Hove, among others. To all the rest who helped by listening, reading, and responding, especially editors Jeremy Langford, Terry Fischer, and Brigitte Scott—many thanks.

# Introduction
# LIVING THE TRADITION

There is a treasure yet to be discovered and assimilated by Western Christians, namely the contributions of thinkers of the Eastern Orthodox Church in our time. Even before the Russian revolution that banished many to the West, a number had already returned to the faith from ideological exile and political estrangement, such as the "philosopher of freedom," Nicolas Berdiaev, and the Marxist political-economist-become-priest-and-theologian, Sergius Bulgakov. While neither their personalities nor their perspectives always meshed well, these Eastern Church thinkers were already open to Western ideas and the modern world. Many studied in the West, and drank deep from the most formidable voices in modern thinking: Marx, Freud, Nietzsche, Weber, and before these Kant, Kierkegaard, and others. They went further, embracing the society and churches of the West, while remaining authentic Orthodox Christians. The result, which Paul Valliere characterizes as a dialogue with modernity is sampled in this anthology. And it is anything but an echoing of modern Western ideas. Rather what one hears is remarkable for its creativity and freedom. A number of the essays are from the important collection of 1937, aptly entitled *Living Tradition* (*Zhivoe predanie*), in which several thinkers articulated their vision of the Christian life in the twentieth century. For them and for all the authors sampled in this anthology, it was imperative to find ways to live out Christ's gospel in a world and time rapidly changing, torn apart by revolution, economic depression, and war. The authors represent the first generation of émigrés, from the second generation, their students, and finally, our contemporaries.

Taken as a whole, the contributions are diverse yet challenging reflections on the living out of the Christian tradition in our time. The essays range widely, dealing with the obstacles to faith in our era—from unbelief and to the institutionalizing of the Church—the Gospel, and the domestication of Christian faith. The criticism comes not from outside but from within. Not from atheistic or politically motivated critics but from monastics, priests, theologians, committed Christians all of them. But it is not just criticism that we read here. There is also the recovery of the all too often forgotten divine dimensions of the Church, the transforming presence of Christ and the Spirit at all times. One thinks of Dostoyevsky's insightful phrase, that "beauty will save the world."

Among other things, this anthology is a response to the postmodern abandonment of the Church as but a flawed human institution, incapable of change. These essays also profess the faith in the face of theological despair at the Church's failings, such as Ephraim Radner's controversial argument that the Spirit has abandoned the Church. These writers, themselves persons of faith, were well aware of the human sinfulness in the Church. Nevertheless they believed in and talked about the continuing power of love and freedom within the Church. Further, they saw the Christian mission as one of "churching" the world (*votserklovenie*), transforming it in light of God's kingdom. They excluded no one, saw the Holy Spirit alive in all of the world and the churches.

The collection assembles essays from journals and publications difficult if not impossible to access, some translated here for the first time. The collection has been planned with a wide reading audience in mind, not only Russian studies or Orthodox theological specialists but for those of many confessional backgrounds within the Christian spectrum who have yet to hear the voice of the East on the Church and on the challenge of living the life of the Gospel in our time.

While it is true that all of the essays come from writers within the Eastern church, and the majority of these from the Russian Orthodox portion, this is by no means a volume merely for specialists in Russian studies or Orthodox theology. The figures whose writings are gathered here, while sometimes at odds with each other, do share several qualities. All were open to the world and to the Christian churches beyond the borders of their own Orthodox communities. All were taken up with the unique challenge that the modern world brought to Christian existence. Thus each one dwells on the particular demands of being a follower of Christ in a secularized, diverse, and often tumultuous historical period. Since all were from the Eastern Orthodox churches, most from the Russian church—at home and in emigration—the essayists had a singular sense of the worth of tradition and at the same time, the need for true tradition to be dynamic, changing, alive. These writers respected the canonical legacy in the church, the witness of fathers and mothers as teachers and exemplars of faith. Yet all realized that the Gospel would continue to be enacted in different ways, in different lives and times.

In many ways, their Eastern awareness of the communal or ecclesial character of Christianity stands out. No one is saved alone, and the faith entails a community of brothers and sisters. Likewise, the intensely liturgical character of the Eastern Church also is to be found in the authors presented here. In Paul Evdokimov's words, one does not simply say prayers, one becomes prayer, prayer in flesh and blood.

Another shared feature of their thinking is what I would call its personalism. It is not sufficient to speak as we do so often today, of structures and institutions, nor even of classes of people, oppressed or oppressing. It is not humankind in general, or the political elites or economic sectors that are the concerns of these writers. Within each of these strata and categories, like Dostoyevsky, they perceive the concrete, unique person. Social, statistical, even ecclesiastical groups there may be, yet each is composed of individual men and women with their most particular and messy histories of experience, feeling, and action. In Fr. Alexander Schmemann's broadcast talks from Radio Liberty included here, the personal, the very human quality of Christian faith is emphasized. Christ experienced little success, wielded no power during his earthly ministry. Yet he overturned death. Our understanding of this, the heart of faith, remains difficult to express conceptually. Only in childlike simplicity and directness can the Gospel be expressed, shared, communicated. Christ, one might say, must be incarnated, must become flesh and blood in every disciple.

Despite legalism and political appearances to the contrary, again even in the Church, what matters most, because it matters most to God, is the good of this human being, the suffering sister or brother before me. In St. John Chrysostom's phrase, the "liturgy that follows the Liturgy" is nothing else than the "sacrament of the brother and sister," our neighbors. Of all those represented here, the gifted poet and artist who created her own urban monastic life of humanitarian serve—Mother Maria Skobtsova—was the most articulate spokesperson for this essential personalism. In her brief selection, the reader can glimpse the ever-present reality of God's kingdom to this artist, nun, and servant of the suffering.

Respect for every child of God was the foundation for the openness of the thinkers gathered here. As Fr. Lev Gillet said of Paul Evdokimov at the latter's funeral service, that Evdokimov regarded every person as a child of God and each Christian as if there were but one Church and no schism, the same could be said of the writers brought together in this collection. They spoke, thought, wrote, and acted as if there were but one church and no schism, as if all humanity was the family of God. They saw no threat in the rapid changes of the modern era, detected nothing sinister in technology, science, contemporary artistic expression or lifestyle. They were at home with jazz and nuclear physics, with Impressionism and the challenge of young people. Having themselves, most of them, passed through crises of faith, they appreciated the doubt and questions of atheists and critics of traditional religion. Rather than perceiving their enemies in the voices of secularists and agnostics, they recognized them as discerning critics of the abuse of faith, the distortion of the Gospel throughout centuries of state protection and support. As evil as the Bolshevik revolution actions may have been, the majority of those whose writing is sampled here came to see the revolution as also a gift from God, purging the Church and providing it a new opportunity to make a good witness and to follow Christ in freedom. Father Bulgakov explicitly argued that to keep the mind of the Fathers meant, as the Fathers themselves did, to move beyond their positions in the Spirit's lead. Father Sergius himself aimed at sketching out in the modern era not some heretical system, but rather, a positive, constructive expression of the Christology of Chalcedon, a vision of God's humanity and the consequences of God becoming part of creation, of matter and time.

With the exception of Fr. Alexander Men, who lived exclusively in pre- and post-glasnost Russia, all the rest spent the better part of their lives in the West, either in Paris or in the United States. Fathers Alexander Schmemann and John Meyendorff both became American citizens and achieved the granting of autocephaly—independent status—to the Orthodox Church in America (OCA) by the patriarchate of Moscow. They raised their families, reached the high point of their priestly callings and scholarly careers, and died in North America. Some of those who were their predecessors and even teachers in the earlier generation of the emigration, such as Frs. Sergius Bulgakov, Nicolas Afanasiev, Cyprian Kern, Nicolas Berdiaev, Anton Kartashev, Paul Evdokimov, and Lev Zander, did not just remain within the "Russian Paris," but rather became intensely active in the emerging ecumenical movement, in the liturgical revival, in the general "return to the sources" of the post–World War II years. In many ways, the enthusiasms of the earlier generation often inspired the next. In some cases, the visions of the earlier generation only took shape in the actions of their successors—a eucharistically centered church, a renewed liturgy, more frequent reception of Holy Communion, a deeper participation in the life of the church by the laity, a richer experience of Christian life as a whole.

In the essays that follow, there is a great deal that is constructive, optimistic, and visionary despite the horrors of the decades and events in which the writers lived. The first generation either had to flee the Russian Revolution or were expelled by it to new homes in the West. Many saw for themselves the brutality of the revolution, not just toward the church but toward any dissension. Thus, we will find a very strong case made throughout for freedom, both in the church and in society. Often known as a "philosopher of freedom," Nicolas Berdiaev here presents two still relevant and penetrating indictments: one of the bourgeois domestication of the faith, and the other—a perhaps even more basic reminder of the worth of Christianity and the all-too-evident unworthiness—the sinfulness of Christians. Among the thinkers selected here, there is very little pining for a "golden age" of either church or culture from the past. Rather, in order for there to be a hopeful, open encounter of the church with the modern world, first there must be a serious examination of what was wrong in the recent past. The provocative collection on which this one is based, *Living Tradition*, of 1937, took on precisely the aspects of worship, church structure, and life most in need of criticism and renewal. It is no surprise that Fr. Sergius Bulgakov and Anton Kartashev were participants in the Great Council of the Russian Church of 1917–1918, which sought to reform many areas of church life, among them the quality of liturgical worship, leadership of both the clergy and the laity, theological education, and the relationship of the church and the individual Christian to the political and cultural contexts of modernity. From them we hear about what still are the signs of unity among divided Christians, gifts of a forgiving God, and what the consequences of such unities are for the reunification of Christians. From their colleague, Lev Zander, comes a striking view of the Holy Spirit's action in the ecumenical movement. The words of the writers gathered in this book are especially needed today, when ecumenical breakthrough have faded and positions and feelings among Christians still divided by historical schism have hardened.

Another common characteristic of the writers and essays included here is their profound sense of the Church. This was not so much homage to the institutional structures, though they did not lose sight of the historical reality of the Church. To drift off, content only with an idealized, theological vision of the Church would be, in Nicolas Afanasiev's view, to reject what was human and historical, and thus would be a slip into Nestorianism, a denial of the full humanity of Christ and his Gospel. Father Afanasiev not only forces us to look at the historical changeability of the canons but also at the eucharistic nature of the Church as both unity in reality and as a promise. The monastic theologian and priest Fr. Cyprian Kern, participant in the liturgical movement in the post–World War II era, contributed a restrained yet provocative essay on the shape of pastoral ministry to the *Living Tradition* anthology. Its contrast of the levitical versus the prophetic emphasis remains pertinent today, as the identity of the ordained and their place in the church is constantly scrutinized. Likewise, Fr. Alexander Men, much closer to our own time, presents the fundamentals of the sacraments and the church to Russian adults, preparing people without any religious experience whatsoever for baptism. In the excerpts from Men's talks on the creed, we hear the living tradition proclaimed in a humane, this-worldly fashion; we hear the same qualities in the ninety-six-year-old French lay theologian Elisabeth Behr-Sigel's address to the World Council of Churches (WCC), an account of the force of a truly living tradition. Another lay theologian and remarkable witness to the faith, Paul Evdokimov, challenges us to recognize that the true heart of the Church, the ultimate living tradition, is Christ himself, the head and body. Theologians Alexander Schmemann and John Meyendorff, who spent most of their adult lives working in America, did much to open the treasures of Orthodox Christianity within the country. From them we hear of the future of the Christian tradition, how it figures practically in the lives of the churches here today.

Lastly, the essays offer us a view not so much of ecumenism but of the ecumenical nature of the Church, the unity and universality shattered by schism and heresy over the centuries. Though often viewed as resolute on the Orthodox Church as the one and only true Church, even Georges Florovsky, in a famous essay that we could not reprint here, had to admit that the limits or boundaries of the Church do not follow the lines of her existing institutional expressions. However, in today's somewhat less optimistic, even antagonistic positions, most of those whose speak here can see no other vision of the Church than one that is ecumenical. And this means searching in prayer, conversation, study, and common action for a restoration of the unity destroyed by schism, the great one between the East and the West and those of Reformation in the West. While it has become *de rigueur* to be more cautious, even confrontational in ecumenical circles, the reader will find here—in such figures as Bulgakov, Kartashev, and Berdiaev, among others—very challenging visions of the Church's inclusivity, of the unity which continues to exist despite separation. Lev Zander goes right to the heart of what the ecumenical movement is. If the face of Christ can be recognized in every other Christian, despite the schisms and divisions of the churches, then the searching for unity—for the ecumenical church—must be truly an epiphany of Christ, a "Christophany" in the "Christ-bearers" (*Christophores*). A true extension of the Incarnation, this is a manifestation of Christ's will and his gift to be one with us. Especially now, over a half a century after this essay was written, when so many doubts and frustrations have arisen about ecumenical relations, we need to hear such a word of hope, such a constructive reading, such good news in hope.

In sum, the essays presented in this collection are not exercises in historical preservation for specialists. These are far from museum pieces of interest to only conservators or scholars. To be sure, there are other perspectives than those presented here, and recently the most conservative of these has attracted much attention, namely, the ultra-traditionalist stance that one sees no other Christian confession or "Church" and the Orthodox church as absolutely the *only* church. The authors presented here saw it otherwise. The Christian tradition—the heritage of the scriptures, liturgy and sacraments, the lives and teachings of holy men and women—this belongs to all Christians. No one "school" or movement or perspective dares claim exclusive possession or expression of it. Paul Valliere, in his masterful study *Modern Russian Theology*, has quite rightly argued that in many ways those represented here have been pushed aside, ignored by their students and successors, even condemned as extreme or less than faithful to the church's tradition. Other perspectives and their proponents might be said to have "won," in terms of dominance in publishing and teaching. Yet, none of these thinkers were ever formally found guilty of heresy. All were authorized in one or another way, to teach or otherwise serve in their local churches. And, all of them were more than mere specialists in the areas of theology and the spiritual life. Rather, to the extent that these authors were convinced of the holiness of the church and the living character of the Christian tradition, what they lived, in first place, and what they reflected upon in their writings is still a gift to us. This is *lectio divina*, "holy reading," not just about the Christian faith and the church but more importantly nourishment for the living out of the Gospel in our time.

Michael Plekon, professor, Department of Sociology/Anthropology, Program in Religion and Culture, Baruch College of the City University of New York and a priest of the Orthodox Church in America, attached to St. Gregory Orthodox Church, Wappingers Fall, New York

## SELECTED BIBLIOGRAPHY

Arjakovsky, Antoine. *La Génération des penseurs religieux de l'émigration russe: La revue La Voie (Put'), 1925–1940*. Kiev-Paris, L'Esprit et la Lettre, 2002.

Evdokimov, Michel. *Le Christ dans la tradition et la littérature russes*. Paris: Cerf, 1996.

Evdokimov, Paul. *Le Christ dans le pensée russe*. Paris: Cerf, 1986.

Meerson, Michael. *The Trinity of Love in Modern Russian Theology*. Quincy Ill.: Franciscan Press, 1998.

Nichols, Aidan, O.P. *Theology in the Russian Diaspora*. Cambridge University Press, 1989.

———. *Light from the East*. London: Sheed & Ward, 1995.

Plekon, Michael. *Living Icons: Persons of Faith in the Eastern Church*. Notre Dame, Ind.: University of Notre Dame Press, 2002.

Raeff, Marc. *Russia Abroad: A Cultural History of the Russian Emigration, 1919–1939*. New York: Oxford University Press, 1990.

Schmemann, Alexander, ed. *Ultimate Questions: An Anthology of Modern Russian Religious Thought*. Crestwood, N.Y.: SVSP, 1977.

Struve, Nikita. *Soixante-dix ans d'émigration russe, 1919–1989*. Paris: Fayard, 1996.

Valliere, Paul. *Modern Russian Theology: Soloviev, Bukharev, Bulgakov*. Grand Rapids, Mich.: Eerdmans, 2000.

Williams, Rowan. *Sergii Bulgakov: Towards a Russian Political Theology*. Edinburgh: T&T Clark, 1999.

Zernov, Nicolas. *The Russian Religious Renaissance of the Twentieth Century*. New York: Macmillan, 1963.

———. *A Bulgakov Anthology*. Edited and translated by James Pain. Philadelphia: Westminster, 1976.

*Father Nicolas Afanasiev (1893–1966), like others in this collection, was a refugee from the Russian Revolution. After service in the "White Army" of General Wrangel, he studied first in Belgrade and then in Paris. He acquired a combination of skills rarely found in one person. He was trained as a historian and as a canon lawyer, specializing in Scripture and liturgical theology. A faculty member of St. Sergius Theological Institute in Paris, he was the teacher of Frs. Alexander Schmemann and John Meyendorff, and his rediscovery of the "eucharistic ecclesiology" (as opposed to the "universal ecclesiology" of Cyprian of Carthage) shaped the Vatican II constitution on the church and provoked debate on the nature and shape of the church for the rest of the twentieth century. In reading Fr. Alexander Schmemann's remarkable studies in liturgical theology, the concerns and aims of his teacher are very much in evidence. Father Afanasiev's short but powerful* The Lord's Supper *contains his thinking about the shape of the eucharistic liturgy in the past and how it might be both restored and renewed in our time. His posthumously published* The Church of the Holy Spirit *is but a part of (one volume) what would have been a massive work on the church—Fr. Afanasiev's restoration of the ancient ecclesiology—with a good deal of historical criticism on his part. The other volume,* The Limits of the Church, *was not completed, but the main chapters were finished and a translation is now in progress. Even as part of the larger effort,* The Church of the Holy Spirit *is astonishing in its affirmation of the priesthood of all the baptized, its critique of the rise of law and of clericalism in the church, and of the eclipse of the eucharistic character of the "local church," the primary church for all Christians. An English translation is in preparation, and a number of his important*

*essays are available either in English or French versions. One of the last essays completed before his death, published posthumously, is the following careful study of the division (schism) between the Catholic and Orthodox churches, and the understanding of their mutual status as authentic churches that might undo the division. The sinful division of the churches preoccupied Fr. Afanasiev for many years, and along with colleagues such as Fr. Sergius Bulgakov and Anton Kartashev, he saw in the Eucharist the source of the unity of the church and the key to its recovery. Father Afanasiev lived long enough to see the convocation of Vatican II, a council that took the unification of the church seriously and which he attended as an official observer. He was also present at the lifting of the anathemas (condemnations) from the eleventh century by Pope Paul VI and Ecumenical Patriarch Athenagoras I. The first selection here,* Una sancta, *was written in memory of the "Pope of Love," John XXIII, and is a bold historical examination of what constitutes the Church, what the Great Schism does and does not mean, and what the healing of the same must entail. Another of his essays here, "The Eucharist: The Principle Link between Catholics and the Orthodox," continues this idea by reflecting on the enduring link among divided Christians—the Eucharist. The last selection is Fr. Afanasiev's careful investigation of what is permanent and what is changeable in the church's canons, an issue that still remains controversial.*

## FOR FURTHER READING

Afanasiev, Nicolas. *Tserkov Dukha Sviatogo/L'Eglise du Saint-Esprit.* Translated by Marianne Drobot. Paris: Cerf, 1975. English translation by Vitaly Permiakov, edited by Michael Plekon, in preparation by St. Vladimir's Seminary Press.
———. *Trapeza Gospodnia.* Paris: Cerf, 1952. An English translation as *The Limits of the Church*, by Alvian Smirensky, to be published by St. Vladimir's Seminary Press, along with other essays, in preparation.
———. "The Church Which Presides in Love." In *The Primacy of Peter*, edited by John Meyendorff. Crestwood, N.Y.: SVSP, 1992.
Nichols, Aidan, O.P. *Theology in the Russian Diaspora: Church, Fathers, Eucharist in Nikolai Afanas'ev, 1893–1966.* Cambridge: Cambridge University Press, 1989.
Plekon, Michael. "Nicolas Afanasiev: Explorer of the Eucharist, the Church and Life in Them." In *Living Icons*, 149–77. Notre Dame, Ind.: University of Notre Dame Press, 2002.

# *UNA SANCTA*

*To the memory of John XXIII, the Pope of Love*

**I**

1. The decision of Pope John XXIII to convoke a new Vatican council immediately reawakened the old hopes for a reuniting of the Christian world, and now, the first session of the council having already completed its work, these hopes remain intact. After the Vatican Council of 1870, the problem of the unity of the churches had been completely removed from the program, so it seemed. The formulation of the dogma of the primacy of the Roman pontiff and the proclamation of the dogma of papal infallibility undid all the connections that until then had linked the catholic church to the rest of the Christian world.[1] Now the problem has been posed anew, even though strictly speaking, nothing new or concrete has been done to revive it. What could the new Vatican council do to truly contribute to the reunion of the churches? This council is a council of the catholic church and it can be nothing else but that. The catholic church has the right to expect many things from this council for herself, but to what extent are the decisions of the council concerning the internal life of the catholic church able to influence that of other churches? The declarations of the responsible representatives of the catholic church do not allow hope for

---

First published in *Irénikon* 36 (1963): 436–75. Translated by Michael Plekon.

change in the realm of dogma. It is not even possible to give an account of these confessions. Nevertheless these declarations do contain something new even in their tenor—at least in its form and tone—something that cannot be found anywhere else. But all of this is of little matter and cannot explain why, all at once, so many hopes for the reunion of the churches have emerged again. In order to understand this, it is necessary to give an account of the "ecumenical tension" within which the Christian world actually exists. Thirty or forty years ago, Christian consciousness had been indifferent to the ecumenical problem and only rare souls were interested in it. But now the problem has become an essential one for Christianity. Many things have been accomplished, yet we still await intensely the definitive solution to the ecumenical problem, a solution that would have a profound impact on the catholic world as well. Only this state of ecumenical tension can explain why the new Vatican council has illumined once again the hopes that were extinguished for such a long time. The future will show to what point these hopes will be capable of realization, or if they will only remain illusions.

2. The consciousness of the Russian orthodox was favorably disposed to the news of the convocation of the council. It was welcomed as a sign of the possibility of the solution of the problem of the reunion of the two churches— orthodox and catholic, a problem which, though it did not seem to be the order of the day, had never disappeared from orthodox consciousness. Orthodox theological writings had placed on the program for debate the conditions for the reunion of the churches. In the generally held view, dogmatic divergences had provoked the separation of the churches. It was therefore the norm then, that if the divergences were removed, reunion would be possible. If for some, the path toward reunion would be open if the doctrine of infallibility could be removed in one fashion or another, for others reunion would not seem to be possible unless all of the dogmatic differences were resolved. Here the renaissance of the polemic concerning the *Filioque* had been significant. When the council opened there arose the hope that it would find an exhaustive interpretation of infallibility and that of the primacy. Now it appears that we are able to hope that the council will truly give an explanation of the dogma of infallibility, this in order to respond to internal demands of the catholic church. But in any case this would not be an explanation that would do away with the dogma, and this is the only conclusion that would satisfy orthodox theologians. Whatever the action of the council in this matter, it is necessary to admit frankly that the hopes of which I spoke have no chance of becoming ecclesial reality.

3. If we admit that the suppression of dogmatic differences is a condition to the reunion of the catholic church and the orthodox church, the enduring question of knowing how to suppress them remains. When it comes to dogma, the possibility of compromise is excluded. One cannot come to an agreement about dogmatic truths. It may be necessary to accept them or reject them, or at least reject them as absolute and obligatory truths. If one cannot agree, nothing re-

mains except to affirm oneself in the ancient attitude of orthodox theology (otherwise absolutely identical, *mutatis mutandis*, to that of catholic theology) to know that the catholic church ought to reunite itself to the orthodox church, after having rejected the doctrines that the orthodox church maintains to be dogmatic errors. This point of view is somewhat attenuated in actuality, when one considers this reunion not as a reattachment to the historical orthodox church, but as an affirmation of "orthodoxy" and the authentic tradition of the church. This idea, advanced by Fr. Alexander Schmemann, witnesses to a certain mutation in the ancient attitude of orthodox theology.[2] Is the movement toward orthodoxy, as sketched out by Fr. Schmemann, unilateral or bilateral? In other words, is it addressed not only to the catholic church, but to the orthodox church as well? Father Schmemann indicates nothing about this. It seems as though the second possibility is excluded for him. It would hardly be acceptable for orthodox theology. Such a movement toward orthodoxy is again less possible for the catholic church, which believes itself to possess the fullness of the tradition of the church. Suppose that catholic theology examines the opinion of Fr. Schmemann, then naturally one would have to pose the question of knowing how historical orthodox theology differs in orthodox understanding from orthodoxy. The majority of orthodox theologians would probably respond that there is no difference.

Theology, catholic as well as orthodox, while studying the question of the reunion of the churches is interested only in the dogmatic differences between the two churches, and does not observe that there exist two preliminary questions—the solutions of which are indispensable not only to the reunion of the churches but even for engaging in useful dialogue between the two churches. If we speak of the separation and the reunion of churches divided by the rupture of the church's unity, it will first be necessary to elucidate the nature of the unity of the church.[3] Another question is closely connected to the first. It is necessary to begin by knowing exactly what is the nature of the separation of the churches. Put otherwise, what does the "separation" of the churches mean ecclesiologically?[4] The possibility of the reunion of the churches depends, to a great degree, upon the solution of this problem. In effect, if we affirm that we have before us a division of the church, the two parts of which remain nevertheless churches, the question poses itself in a very different way than if we concluded that after the division of the church, only one part remained the church and the other ceased to be this. It is necessary to say this frankly, for all the diplomacy possible doesn't change much of anything. In our everyday language we certainly do speak of the catholic church and the orthodox church, but in reality the use of these words demands an ecclesiological explication. How can we speak ecclesiologically of the division of the church? Is this not a negation of our faith in "one, holy, catholic, and apostolic church?" On the other hand, if one recognized the quality of church in the other part of the divided church, one would be minimizing the importance of dogmatic differences, leaving them integral as they are. If one or the other parts are both the church, then this means the sacraments are celebrated and salvation is possible in both, for this is the purpose of the church.

## II

1. The questions of the nature of the Church and of the nature of the division of the Church are purely ecclesiological problems. These must be posed and discussed from an ecclesiological perspective. The Church, as established by Christ, has remained integral throughout the course of history. She has not changed nor can she change. Nevertheless, in the same course of history our reflections upon the Church have not remained the same. Our doctrines of the Church have changed and these changes have made themselves felt in the ecclesial organization.

Actually, universal ecclesiology is the predominant system in ecclesiology. According to this system, the Church that exists empirically is considered as a unique, organic structure—the mystical body of Christ. In actuality the organic structure is divided into parts—the local churches, that is, the communities of the faithful having a bishop at their head. The sum of the local churches, in their concrete existence, shows the Church to be one and unique. The ecclesial nature of the local churches flows from their rooting in the universal Church. Cyprian of Carthage's ecclesiological doctrine formulated the principles of this vision for the first time. I will not dwell here on Cyprian's doctrine of the Church, which has been sufficiently examined elsewhere.[5] Yet I should first indicate how Cyprian poses the question of the unity of the Church and that of the nature of schism in order to approach my own conclusions here.

2. The unity of the Church was an indisputable truth not only for Cyprian, but also for all of his contemporaries, and even for the Christians of the eras both before and after him. The church "Catholic" was one and it followed for Cyprian that one could not be at the same time inside and outside the Church.[6] The fullness of interior unity excluded any existence outside this fullness. Speaking of the Church, Cyprian said, "She is a garden enclosed, my sister, my promised bride, a garden enclosed, a sealed fountain of living water (Sg 4:12). If the beloved, the spouse of Christ, is an enclosed garden, it cannot be open to strangers and to those outside. If it is a sealed fountain, those outside have no access.[7] All those outside the Church do not belong to her. Thus, the heretics and schismatics are outside the Church. Otherwise it would be necessary to admit that they are part of the true Church, which is unique. But then there would not be a Church among the right-believing, the orthodox, for there cannot be two Churches. Therefore, the Church might be found among the orthodox or among the heretics, but she cannot be among both of them at the same time. The heretics and schismatics are not inside the Church but outside, outside the enclosed garden, without access to the sealed fountain. Conse-

quently the church "catholic" has nothing in common with heretics and schismatics. The heretics do not believe in the same Father, Son, or Holy Spirit as do the orthodox. If their blood is shed in persecutions, they are not witnesses to Christ, martyrs. Their sacrifice is empty, sterile, as is everything about them.[8] There is but one bride of Christ, and the one who is not with her is against Christ. Christ himself has established for all ages the unity of the Church by saying: "There will be but one flock and one shepherd" (Jn 10:16). And this flock is the Church "catholic," and not the heretics and schismatics, for there is only one flock, and these are not part of it.[9] Only the children of the Church are in the flock and, having God as their father, must have the Church as their mother, and this is impossible for those who blaspheme the Father and Christ the Savior.[10]

3. Therefore, the Church cannot be divided. If one or another local church detaches herself from the Church, she is then outside. The local church then falls into an ecclesiological void. There was one deduction of Cyprian's that was to have immense practical importance. In the parts of the Church that were detached—that is to say, in the heretical and schismatic communities—there could be no sacraments. Cyprian himself was thinking primarily of the sacrament of baptism, but it goes without saying that what he said concerning baptism would include all the rest of the sacraments as well. Later on, theology and ecclesial practice came to recognize certain sacraments celebrated in heretical and schismatic communities, while rejecting others. For Cyprian, baptism, just as all the other sacraments, was established by the Church and accomplished in the Church. For him it was an indisputable fact that baptism could not be repeated. Cyprian could not foresee that later theology would make a separation between the sacraments and the Church. For Cyprian, baptism, and consequently all the other sacraments, could not be detached from the Spirit. Where the Spirit is, there is baptism, and where the Spirit was not, there could be no baptism. But the Spirit could not be separated from the Church and the Church could not be separated from the Spirit. If the heretics and schismatics could truly baptize, then one had to say that they possessed the same faith and truth as the Orthodox. This would mean that they possessed the same Spirit whose gifts were distributed by the Church Catholic and therefore one would have to say that they, the heretics and schismatics, were in the *catholica*. If this was the case then there was nothing for the orthodox to do except "put down their arms, make themselves slaves, hand over to the devil the Gospel, the law of Christ, the majesty of God. . . . Then the Church gives in to heresy, the light to the darkness, faith to infidelity, hope to despair, reason to error, immortality to death, love to hatred, truth to lies, Christ to the anti-Christ."[11] Clearly this would be completely absurd and even a sacrilege. If the heretics and schismatics could baptize, then the Church was among them and the orthodox would become the heretics, yielding to the former the first place they in fact possessed. But the Church was not among the heretics because she is one and cannot be divided

into parts and the Holy Spirit was not among the heretics, because the Spirit is one and could not be among the profane and those outside the Church.[12]

## III

1. Cyprian's teaching on the unity of the Church as a universal and organic reality was adopted by both catholic and orthodox theology. As paradoxical as this might seem, the tragedy of the actual ecclesial situation consists in that the one and the other both hold the same theological position.

Orthodox and catholic theology both believe that only one true Church can exist and that there cannot be two Churches. This thesis, which flows from a universal ecclesiology, is an absolute necessity for Cyprian and for contemporary theology. The negation of it would be equivalent to a negation of the universal ecclesiology. Two universal Churches cannot exist, otherwise we would have to recognize two Bodies of Christ. Nevertheless, Christian consciousness in our time is unable to merely resign itself to the grandiose tragedy of the division of the Christian world. This revolt of Christian consciousness is reflected in theological literature that attempts to provide correctives to the teaching of Cyprian on the Church. Beyond the limits of the Church, there does not exist an ecclesiological void, as Cyprian thought, but only a kind of diminished existence of the Church—certain "vestiges" of the Church remain so that the separated parts of the Church continue to live one ecclesial life and the sacraments continue to be authentically celebrated among them. This kind of corrective is able to give some satisfaction to Christian consciousness, but from the perspective of ecclesiology it is meaningless. The nature of the Church presupposes that either she exists in her fullness or she does not exist at all, but there can be no partial existence nor can there be vestiges existing here and there. The Church is one in all the fullness of her nature and she is the only true Church, and it is not possible to have the Church where there is error. Contemporary theology is ready to admit that such and such a heretical community holds on to a part of the true teaching and confesses the authentic apostolic tradition in part. Nevertheless this second corrective is also meaningless, for these communities cannot become the Church simply by the fact that they have partially kept the true teaching and apostolic tradition. True teaching can only be preserved by the Church, and outside the Church everything becomes distorted and falsified. Here is the thesis of Cyprian, which cannot be overcome by contemporary theology. If there were two churches, the dilemma posed already by Cyprian remains intact. Either the one or the other is the Church and in no case can both together be the true Church. As long as we remain within the domain of a universal ecclesiology we cannot resolve this dilemma.

2. Now I can return to the question already posed: How do the catholic church and the orthodox church mutually regard each other? From the point

of view of the universal ecclesiology, common for both, each regards the other as a schismatic and even heretical community, having lost completely or in part its ecclesial nature, the cause of this being separation from the true Church. The habitual use of the word "church," both for catholicism and for orthodoxy should not deceive us, for this is but a conventional linguistic usage not justified by contemporary theology. For the orthodox the only true Church is the orthodox church. For the catholics it is the catholic church. There can be no other point of view according to a universal ecclesiology. The solution of the problem of the reunion of the orthodox church and the catholic church must take as its point of departure this reality. This is the premise absolutely necessary not only for resolving the problem but already for even posing it. In taking account of this premise we ought to admit that in the domain of universal ecclesiology there is no problem of the reunion of the churches. This problem is born from the idea of the division of the Church. This idea did not exist either in orthodoxy or in catholicism until recently and, properly speaking, it does not really exist even now. If in our days we often speak of the division of the Church in order to characterize the actual state of the Christian world, this is a formula that is not justified either by the teaching of the catholic church or by that of the orthodox church. This formula witnesses simply to our desire to attenuate the situation of the Church and to surmount the difficulties of the present time in following the easier path. In her nature the Church cannot be divided. There is no division, but there is a detachment of the Church of diverse heretical and schismatic communities that find themselves outside the Church by this fact alone, that they are detached. Thus one cannot propose as a goal the reunion of the Church with a "non-Church." The problem of the reunion of churches— catholic and orthodox—is reduced to the return to the bosom of the true Church of the separated part that has ceased to be the Church. It is necessary to recognize frankly and honestly that this is how both the one and the other of these churches understand the problem of reunion. Actually, the ecumenical idea is possessed by Christian consciousness to such a point that the two churches avoid openly posing the question, in this manner endeavoring to give the problem a form as least painful as possible for the other side. The problem of reunion thus posed, the dogmatic differences lose their primordial importance. If one of the two churches should reunite itself to the other by the path of returning to the true Church, she would then have to adopt the dogmatic teaching of the latter. Certainly one is able to discuss dogmatic divergences, and this actually happens. But the goal of these discussions is not the search for a certain agreement on the basis of mutual concessions, which is impossible in the realm of dogma, but only the acceptance of dogmatic truths in light of their explication.

3. Union by the path of adherence presupposes the preliminary solution of knowing which of the two churches is the "one, holy, catholic, and apostolic." The tragedy of our ecclesial situation is that this question is resolved long since

by one or the other church. Each of the two churches considers herself to be the true Church, and consequently, in the system of a universal ecclesiology, the other (as I have previously indicated) is not the Church. Each of the two churches thinks that she possesses the true teaching and the authentic apostolic tradition, all the while admitting, in our day, that the other possesses them in part. Such is the profound and fundamental conviction of each of the churches. If there had existed in either of them the shadow of a doubt about this, then it is certain that the reunion would have occurred a long time ago.

Leaving aside internal conviction, is there any objective sign by which one would be able to discern which of these churches is the true Church? This question is truly without an object because in the matter of faith there are no objective signs by which one could discern which was the true Church—at least there are no signs that are exhaustive. It is useless to say that reunion would have long ago taken place if such signs had existed. However, since I am orthodox, I am convinced that the position of the orthodox church is more solid and stable in comparison to that of the catholic church. The dogmatic differences that exist between the two churches were not formed in their entirety except after the break. The orthodox church has always held the teaching that was the common heritage of the undivided church before the separation. In the eyes of the orthodox, this argument is of the greatest importance, but it is unable to furnish an indisputable sign by which one could judge the authenticity of the church. In effect, if we hold ourselves to this argument, we would recognize as true churches the Nestorian and Monophysite communities who could not recognize the dogma of Chalcedon. If we proceed further in this direction, we ought to recognize that the churches coming from the Reformation are true churches for they base themselves on Holy Scripture alone. By itself, the dogmatic development of that which is contained in Scripture cannot serve as an argument for authenticity or error. For in order to find an argument there, we would have to admit that dogmatic development has stopped since the Seventh Ecumenical Council. But this last thesis cannot be proven, and otherwise it cannot as such be admissible for all of orthodox theology. For example, in actuality a good number of orthodox theologians admit the teaching of Gregory Palamas, which has not been accepted by any ecumenical council. It follows then that what is important is not dogmatic development but the tenor of this development—in what measure is it based on Scripture, tradition, and the teaching of the Fathers of the Church? This leads us anew into an impasse, for both the one and the other church refer themselves to Scripture, tradition, and the teaching of the Fathers. The arguments that orthodox theology advances against the new catholic dogmas do not appear to be convincing to the catholic church, even as the arguments of catholic theology are not convincing to orthodox theology.

Without having the possibility of objectively deciding which of the two churches is the true Church, we are not able any longer to decide which of them ought to reunite to the other. For this it would be necessary that one of the churches give an account that in its faith she is in error; that is to say, in terms of a universal ecclesiology, that she recognizes herself as not being a church. In what manner could either of these two churches arrive at such a position? Despite all her desire of sincerely and ardently wanting to come to an ecclesial reunion, would this not terminate in the one or the other of the churches committing "ecclesiological suicide?" How could she, as Cyprian said in the text cited earlier, deny all that her historical existence and life consisted in previously? We admit that such a thing is possible for love of the truth, but each of the two churches believes that she possesses the truth. How could she feel herself to be in error, thus forgetting all her past life? If in universal ecclesiology the union of the churches appears to be impossible—for the problem of union does not exist in this view—again even less can one speak, in this domain, of the adherence of one church to the other. Whatever the action of the new Vatican council, it will not resolve the problem of the reunion of the catholic church and the orthodox church, for it would not be able to eliminate the thesis according to which it is not possible to have two true Churches. The position of the Roman church, which considers herself the true Church, is not only understandable but also legitimate from the point of view of catholic doctrine on the universal church. But the position of the Orthodox church—absolutely analogous—is also understandable and legitimate.

4. Thus can we say that the reunion of the churches, catholic and orthodox and others, is but a utopia? If this is so, then what can we say about the tendency of the contemporary Christian world toward reunion? Why should the unity of the Christian world, which, with certain reservations, was a fact until the eleventh century, be turned into a utopia? If this unity did exist, it should be able to exist now as well, otherwise we ought to admit that division is a normal state for the Christian world and that the unity of ancient times was but an error. If this is so, this is not our error but Christ's, who spoke of only one flock and one shepherd. Here is why the question is imposed on us—namely, of knowing if the obstacles that have been accumulated on the path of reunion are truly insurmountable. We have seen that these obstacles are in fact real, but is this reality not conditioned by the universal ecclesiology itself and by the understanding of the unity of the Church that flows from it? Certainly it would be an exaggeration to affirm that the doctrine of the universal church had been the cause of the division of the Christian world, but this doctrine, and above all the doctrine on the unity of the Church and on the principle of this unity, has greatly supported the division. I then will address the question of the principle of unity of the universal Church.

## IV

1. The doctrine of the universal church, insofar as being part of the ecclesiastical body (*compago corporis ecclesiastici*), demands a response to the question

of knowing how, in actual existence, the unity of this assemblage is safeguarded, and if there exists an empirical sign of the belonging of one church to this ensemble. For Cyprian this question was of exceptional importance, for it was crucial to know definitively whether the heretical and schismatic communities were part of the *catholica*, the Church Catholic. The local church, being only part of the universal church, did not possess in herself the principle of the unity of the Church. In order that the parts of the universal church would not be in disagreement in actual existence, the principle of their unity should not be found outside themselves nor within them, but in their ensemble—that is, in the universal church herself, which contained all the parts.

According to Cyprian, the principle of the unity of the episcopate is the principle of the unity of the universal church. The unity of the Church demands the unity of the bishops, and the unity of the bishops protects the unity of the Church.[13] The Church is one because God is one, Christ is one, and the faith is one. *Episcopatus unus est*: "The episcopate is one because the seat of Peter is one, in which unity was established."[14] "There is only one God, one Christ, one Church, one seat that the word of the Lord has established upon Peter as foundation. Another altar cannot be set up, another priesthood cannot be established other than this unique altar, this unique priesthood."[15] This seat is occupied by the entire episcopate together, so that each bishop is a successor of Peter but only as long as he is part of the episcopate. Because of this each bishop, as bishop of a local church, is also a bishop of the church Catholic, in which there is but one seat that belongs to the one and only episcopate of which each bishop is a member. Each bishop does not act in isolation, independently of the others, but all of them together form "a multiplicity united in peace" (*concors numerositas*). As all the local churches form a "body" (corpus) in which each church is united to the others by close bonds, the bishops also form a "body" in which each is united to all the others by the peace that rules in the episcopate as a whole. It is true that a portion of the flock of Christ is entrusted to each of them, but this does not evoke any division within the episcopate, which remains indivisible.[16] With respect to the whole—the episcopate—the multiplicity of bishops is a secondary phenomenon and we perceive that each of the bishops govern a portion of the flock just as in the *catholica* we note each of the local churches. The Church is not fragmented into particles, and the flock is not divided by the distinction between the parts and the whole.[17]

It is not so surprising that the role of peace plays so great a role in Cyprian's system. He attributes an extraordinary importance to this. It would not be correct to believe that he presents the concord of the bishops as the result of an agreement or treaty based upon their good will. The personal element is not of importance because the peace of the bishops flows from the very nature of the episcopate—from its ideal nature, not the actual circumstances of its activity or incumbents. According to its nature the episcopate is one and unique. In its ontological unity it is not at all possible for there to be discord because each of the members possesses the seat in common together with all the rest. This common possession (*in solidum*) excludes discord and also excludes the member who is in discord with the others. From the moment that the member is found to be in discord with the others he loses his place in the episcopate, the peace and unity of the episcopate remaining intact. The distancing of this or that bishop from the "multiplicity united in peace" of the bishops leads to the fall of his local church from the universal church, for the one is mutually (*invicem*) linked to the other.[18] Thus, for Cyprian, the universal church and the local church on the one hand and the episcopate and the bishop on the other are correlative ideas.

2. Cyprian's teaching on the episcopate, insofar as it is the principle of the unity of the universal church, gives us the distinctive, empirical sign of the latter. According to Cyprian, therefore, the bishop is the sign of the local church belonging to the *catholica*; not the bishop by himself, but rather, the bishop as part of the "multiplicity united by peace" of the bishops. It is through the mediation of the bishop that the local church confided to him finds herself in the *catholica*. The episcopate is for him the distinctive empirical sign of the *catholica*. Cyprian would say of the Church that she was a closed garden and a sealed fountain. The limits of this closed ensemble are traced by the episcopate, and outside of these limits there is no Church. On the other hand, the limits of the local church are defined by those under the power of the bishop. Only those who are with the bishop belong to the local church—that is, those who are beneath his power. Cyprian expressed this very clearly in his well-known formula: "The bishop is in the Church and the Church in the bishop, and if anyone is not with the bishop, he is not in the Church."[19]

3. Cyprian's thesis on the episcopate as a distinctive empirical sign of the belonging of one church to the universal church has kept its importance until the present. This or that church is part of the *catholica* if its bishop is in communion with the whole of the episcopate. The belonging assumes two forms: for the catholic church it is determined by communion with the bishop of Rome, transformed into a juridical submission to the latter, and for the orthodox church it is determined by communion with the head of the autocephalous church of which the local church is a part. This communion with the head of the autocephalous church has acquired as well the character of juridical submission. In their turn the autocephalous churches are in communion, the one with the other, without being juridically in submission to each other.

## V

1. In the order of ideas of universal ecclesiology, the Church of God on earth is a universal entity, embracing all the local churches there. All the attributes of the Church: holiness, unity, catholicity, and apostolicity are characteristic of this universal reality. The local churches as parts of the universal church do not

themselves possess these attributes. They only possess these attributes through the universal Church, insofar as they are part of her. Such is the basic thesis of Cyprian as well as that of contemporary universal ecclesiology. Nevertheless, there is another thesis opposed to that of Cyprian. All of the attributes of the Church that I indicated belong to the local church. This thesis is found in the primitive ecclesiology that I have called eucharistic.[20] The fundamental difference between universal ecclesiology and eucharistic ecclesiology consists precisely in the opposition between these theses in their understandings of the unity of the Church, and above all the principle on which this unity is based.

As the body of Christ, the Church manifests herself in all her fullness in the eucharistic assembly of the local church, because Christ is present in the Eucharist in the fullness of his body. This is why the local church possesses all the fullness of the Church. Put differently, she *is* the Church of God in Christ. The fullness of the nature of the Church determines her unity, which finds its expression in the eucharistic assembly of each local church. In the earliest days, there was one and only one eucharistic assembly in each local church. This is no historical accident nor is it the witness of an insufficient development of ecclesial organization. On the contrary, it was the expression of the fundamental understanding or thesis of eucharistic ecclesiology: the Church is where the eucharistic assembly is. It is also possible to formulate this in another way. Where the Eucharist is, there is the Church of God, and where the Church of God is, there is the Eucharist. It follows that the eucharistic assembly is the distinctive, empirical sign of the Church. Those who participate in the eucharistic assembly of a local church belong to this church. The actual limits of the Church are determined by the limits of the eucharistic assembly.

In affirming that the eucharistic assembly is the principle of the unity of the Church, the thesis that the bishop is the distinctive empirical sign of the local church is not excluded, because the bishop is included in the very concept of the Eucharist. According to its very nature, the eucharistic assembly could not exist without its president or, according to the terminology established by usage, without the bishop. The foundation of the ministry of the bishop is the eucharistic assembly; that is, the bishop is the one who presides at the eucharistic assembly. Consequently, when we speak of the eucharistic assembly, we are in fact speaking of the bishop. According to universal ecclesiology, the bishop, as the principle of the unity of the local church, is not included in the eucharistic assembly but is considered a separate part of this unity, because this ecclesiology detaches him from the assembly. This difference, at first view seemingly insignificant, has had enormous consequences for the entire ecclesial organization and above all, for the understanding of the unity of the Church. According to eucharistic ecclesiology, the unity of the Church is a true unity because it is the unity of the Body of Christ. Put otherwise, it is the unity of Christ himself, and it finds concrete expression in the eucharistic assembly. In universal ecclesiology, such a principle is not applicable, for in the Church, taken as a universal reality, there is no universal eucharistic assembly, nor can there be one.[21] Thus, in this ecclesiology the principle of the Church's unity does not reside in the Church herself, as we have seen, but only in one of her elements—namely, the episcopate. Let us observe that this element, though being most essential for the Church, does not manifest her entirely. Thus the limits of the universal church are defined by the limits of the bishops' power. Everything outside the episcopate's domain is outside the limits of the Church and this leads us inevitably to conclude that this or that heretical or schismatic group is outside the Church even if it is a eucharistic assembly. Therefore, in universal ecclesiology, the episcopate does not find itself within the eucharistic assembly, but above it.

2. Since the beginning of their existence each local church affirmed herself as autonomous and independent. This is an indisputable historical fact that no one contests even today. The autonomy and independence of local churches was not an accident of the historical process, but was an internal reality of ecclesial life, a reality that stemmed from the very nature of the Church. The many independent and autonomous churches were not scattered. On the contrary, they were in unity with one another. Here is another historical fact and it is hardly likely to be contested today. The union of local churches was not provoked by external events of the kind that later led to the formation of canonical-administrative regions, but rather the union came from internal reasons, centered in the actual character of the local churches themselves. Each local church would unite in herself just the local churches, for she possessed all the fullness of the Church of God and all the local churches together were united because the same Church of God dwelt in them all. Here is why this union of the local churches has a character all its own. This is not an association of parts of the Church or of diverse churches, but the union of different manifestations of the Church of God in actual human existence. It is the union of the Church of God with herself, through diverse representations. Within eucharistic ecclesiology the principle of the union of the local churches is that of the unity of the Church of God, which is found in the local church herself.

3. This union of local churches was not something abstract, but a real fact in the existence of the local churches. Because of this unity the isolation and introversion of a particular local church was excluded. She could not live in isolation from the others and could not remain a stranger to what happened in the other churches. She could not do this because all that took place in a church also affected the other churches. To put it another way, anything that happened in one church happened in the Church of God in Christ. In actual point of view, each local church would accept all that took place in another church and all the churches accepted that which occurred in another. The entire number of the churches, linked in Love, took as its own what occurred in each church that belonged to this union. This acceptance, or to employ a term used more regularly but with a slightly juridical nuance, this reception was not at all juridical nor social in general. It was the witness of a local church, in which dwelt the Church

of God, to that which was accomplished in other churches, in which the Church of God also resided—that is, it is the witness of the Church herself, or the witness of the Holy Spirit, to the Spirit dwelling in the Church. In accepting all that took place in another church, one or more local churches witnessed that what happened in her conformed to the will of God and thus also happened in the Church of God in Christ. Because of this, even a small local church in a tiny village would live in the fullness of ecclesial life. She would have the full consciousness that she was not merely a little particle of a great whole but a whole in which all was accomplished. Whatever happened in her happened in the union of all the churches. The fullness and unity of the Church was felt and experienced by each local church.

In principle, each ecclesial action of a church was submitted to the reception of the other churches, and this reception had a very easy, practical character (except if it concerned a particularly serious matter of discussion). In other cases the local church would know, due to a special wisdom, that everything done within her was accepted by the other churches. In possessing the witness of the Spirit to herself, she would know that this same Spirit witnessed to the same thing in each of the other churches. When there was need for reception, this was in practice made to the principal churches, and above all to the church that had priority in a union of local churches. The other churches would follow then the principal churches.[22]

4. The very idea of reception indicates that the local churches would not only be able to receive what was done in another church, but also refuse to do so. In refusing to accept this or that ecclesial action, the local churches would be witnessing that this action did not occur in the Church of God. Such a refusal was not a punishment but would express only the desire to help a weaker local church that had tolerated irregularities internally.[23] If this refusal of reception accomplished its purpose—that is, if the local church disavowed its irregular actions, peace would be reestablished in the union of the local churches, joined in Love. If on the contrary, the local church refused the assistance proposed to her, and despite the "non-reception" of her actions did not renounce her decisions, it could then be concluded that the communion between her and the other local churches had been broken. This church would find herself outside the union of local churches joined in Love. She would cease to live the common life with the other churches, and would be turned in upon herself, isolated from the others. This isolation of one or more churches would indicate that ecclesial life had been irregular because the isolation would witness to the weakening of Love and peace in this church. Since nearly the beginning of the existence of local churches there were cases of the break in communion. From the perspective of eucharistic ecclesiology these events can be explained. The eucharistic assembly of each local church is an ideal manifestation of the Church of God. In the other activities of her life, the local church approaches more or less a full and perfect manifestation of the Church. This is

the result of the eschatological tension in which the Church dwells in the world. The Church is already the beginning of the new age, while still dwelling in the old. This is the reason why we will always have in a local church certain irregularities of this or that sort, both temporary and permanent.

5. What exactly is this "exit" from the agreement in Love of the local churches, this nonparticipation in harmony, this distancing that results from the cessation of fraternal communion? For Cyprian, and for contemporary universal ecclesiology as well, such a split would signify that the church that was "distanced" had definitively been severed from the universal body of the Church. It seemed to Cyprian (and this point of view is always valid) that it was possible to separate a misguided church and her bishop from the Church universal because in his opinion there existed a supreme power of the Church that was able to accomplish such an act. From the perspective of eucharistic ecclesiology, such "excommunications" are impossible. There is no power superior to the union of churches above the local churches themselves as manifestations of the Church of God. A local church could not amputate another church from the Church because this would mean that the Church would be excommunicating herself. Even the whole of the union of local churches would not be able to do it, for this union is not above, not superior to, a single local church. The halting of fraternal communion between the union of local churches on the one hand and one or more churches on the other is nothing more than a matter of "cessation of relations," whatever these may be, with this or these churches. Above all there is the cessation of eucharistic communion, which means that the bishop of the local church with whom relations have been broken, and through him all the other members of this church, are deprived of the possibility of taking part in the eucharistic assemblies of other local churches, and vice–versa; that is, none of the members of the other local churches could participate in the eucharistic assemblies of the local church with whom relations had been broken. In the ancient church it is worth noting that the case of actual participation in the eucharistic assemblies of other churches was extremely rare and further depended on whether the removal of the church was temporary or permanent.[24]

As a result of the break in communion, the actions of the church "in broken communion" were not "received" by the other churches. We should note here that at this period no one raised the question of the validity of the sacraments celebrated in the church "broken from communion." Among the actions that came to be "received" were notably the establishment of bishops. In the case of the breaking of communion, the establishing of bishops was not "received" or "certified" by the other churches. This stemmed from the bishops of the other churches being unable to be in communion with a bishop consecrated in a church with which they had "broken communion." However, the validity of the sacramental consecration of such a bishop was never in doubt—only the reception of this consecration. All that could be said is that the other churches did not know if the election was valid or not. Cyprian first posed the question of the validity of sacraments celebrated in schismatic communities. It was inevitable that such a question arose for him since his judgment was from the perspective of universal ecclesiology. The position of Pope Stephen, interpreted later for us by Cyprian, had been conditioned by the premises of the more ancient ecclesiology for which such a question could not have existed.

The nature of the break in communion indicated that the local church deprived of communion with the other churches ceased to exist for the latter, for there were no longer links by which this communion could be realized. But such a church did not cease to remain in itself the Church of God despite its isolated situation. If we think that such a local church is no longer the Church, we reject the only distinctive sign by which we can judge the existence of a Church: where there is the eucharistic assembly, there is Christ, and there is the Church of God in Christ. This sign applies not only to churches that are part of the multitude-of-churches-linked-by-Love-and-peace but also to those that are separated. If this sign did not serve as an indicator except within the union-linked-in-Love, the eucharistic assembly would have lost its absolute value and would not be but a relative distinctive sign. In certain cases the eucharistic assembly would be a sign of the Church, and in others it would not be. As for the churches with which communion was broken, because eucharistic assembly, having changed its nature, had ceased to be that which it ought to be, the question of communion or non-communion with this church is lifted, because the very object of communion no longer exists. For every alliance of churches, such local churches cease to be churches because the Church of God cannot dwell there. We are not able to say anything more on this subject for it is only given to us to know that the Church is where the eucharistic assembly is.

The cessation of fraternal communion with one or many local churches, while very painful and witnessing to irregular conditions in the latter, is not however a complete break in the unity of the Church of God, because this unity is manifest, as noted before, in each local church. It is the unity of the church herself and not the unity of her manifestations in actual life.

6. A like thesis of eucharistic ecclesiology is not an element of theological speculation. It finds expression in the historical life not only before Cyprian, who promoted universal ecclesiology, but also after him, to the moment where universal ecclesiology is definitively affirmed and where the idea of the break in fraternal communion has been obscured by that of the separation of these or those churches from the universal structure. I will restrict myself to some historical facts. It is otherwise important to note that our knowledge of the practices of the pre-Nicene period is scarce and not always precise. First I should speak of the Paschal controversies in the era of Pope Victor. Despite much imprecision it is certain that the church of Rome, in the person of Pope Victor, had refused to accept the practice of the churches of Asia Minor concerning the celebration of Pascha/Easter; all the churches should follow Rome. Then the pope addressed a certain demand, or more exactly, a proposition, to the church

of Ephesus (then the leading church in Asia Minor) to renounce its practice. There had been nothing extraordinary in the actions of Victor. Clement of Rome had addressed a demand of the same kind to the church of Corinth concerning the dismissal of one or more presbyters. There is almost no doubt that the church of Corinth had followed the proposition of Clement and that therefore the question was resolved. As for Polycrates of Ephesus, he refused to accept Victor's proposition. As a result, there was a break in communion between the church of Rome and all the others on the one hand, and the churches of Asia Minor on the other. Eusebius, our only source though a historian from another period, said that the pope had cut off (ἀποτέμνειν), or had the intention of doing so, the churches of Asia Minor from the common unity (τῆς κοινῆς ἐνώσεως).[25] Modern historians speak of the excommunication of these churches. If we attribute to this term the modern meaning we use, then it is absolutely wrong in this earlier context.[26] The pope had not wished to excommunicate, and it appears, had not truly done but one thing. He had effectively broken communion with the churches of Asia Minor so that these churches found themselves outside the union of local churches. People of this era, and in particular Pope Victor himself, were far from thinking that the churches of Asia Minor had ceased to be the Church of God after this break in communion and consequently that the sacraments celebrated in them were no longer valid. The only result of the break was that the churches of Asia Minor were isolated from the other churches, which explains, most probably, why they appear to disappear from the stage of history for some time at this point. At least, we know nothing of these churches until the Council of Nicaea.

Afterward Eusebius tells us that many of the bishops were not in agreement with Victor. Eusebius lets us understand clearly that they did not agree with the break in communion, while having no problem with refusing to receive the practice of the churches of Asia Minor. Eusebius says that they counseled Victor "to show concern for peace, for unity with the neighbor, for love."[27] Among these bishops is Irenaeus of Lyons, and Eusebius cites passages of his letter. First, according to Eusebius, Irenaeus exhorts Victor not to completely cut off communion with the Churches of God. Eusebius even notes that Irenaeus backed the Roman practice with regard to the celebration of Easter. Irenaeus, then, writing in his own name to the church of Lyons, refused to receive (as Victor) the practice of the churches of Asia Minor, but he thought that this refusal should not lead to a break in communion. "The former presbyters from Soter," Irenaeus said, "notably those who had guided the church you rule today, that is, Anicetus, Pius, Hyginus, Telesphorus, Xystus had not themselves kept [the fourteenth day] and they had not imposed [their usage] on those who were with them. . . . No one however was ever rejected because of this conduct."[28] On this occasion, Irenaeus recounted in detail the history of the story of the visit that Polycarp made to Pope Anicetus. We do not know, it is true, what had been the subject of the "discussion" between them, but it is certain that it had to do with the celebration of Easter, for otherwise Irenaeus would not have spoken of it in his letter to Victor on the same matter.

> The blessed Polycarp visited at Rome under Anicetus. They were in disagreement with each other on a number of matters not of importance, but they were immediately at peace and they did not dispute with each other about this. Anicetus actually was not able to persuade Polycarp to stop observing that which . . . he had always observed. And Polycarp did not persuade Anicetus to keep his observance, for he said it was necessary to hold on to the custom of the presbyters who had preceded him. And things being like this, they were in communion the one with the other, and in the church Anicetus ceded the celebration of the Eucharist to Polycarp evidently out of deference. They left each other in peace. And in all of the Church there was peace whether one observed (the 14th day) or not.[29]

I allow myself to quote these passages from Irenaeus' letter, for it is of the greatest importance for me. Here is what I what to underscore in the narrative. The church of Rome, in the person of Pope Anicetus, had refused to adopt the practice of the church of Smyrna with regard to the celebration of Easter, just as the church of Smyrna had refused to adopt the practice of the church of Rome. We should not forget that in this era the church of Rome had already the priority among the churches. Thus her refusal ought to have had enormous significance. Nevertheless, this refusal did not lead to a cessation of communion between the two churches. To witness to this, Irenaeus cites the fact that Anicetus had authorized Polycarp to celebrate the Eucharist in the latter's own church. The refusal of reception by the entire union of local churches linked in Love of what was done in one or more churches could eventuate in the cessation of communion, if these churches did not wish to disavow that which had not been accepted by the rest of the churches. However, this break was not automatic. Communion was not able to be broken because such a rupture would be proof of an impoverishment of the "peace, of unity and of Love" among the churches. The example of what we call the Paschal controversies shows that what might cause a break at one time might not do so at another. Reception is a witness of the Church to what is taking place in the Church. The break in communion is a divisive action, an action that is not strongly linked to the refusal of reception, and which ought to be, in its turn, confirmed by the Church. This confirmation or reception is so much the more necessary action, but often, it is human will that leads to the break, provoked by purely human factors. Reception is a sort of assistance afforded by a strong church to one that is weaker. It therefore becomes an expression of Love between them. As to the break in communion, often it is not a help, but usually a means of attaining this or that goal of ecclesial politics.

Moving from the Paschal controversies to the baptismal ones in the time of Cyprian of Carthage, we find a situation analogous to that in the era of Pope Victor. In the person of Pope Stephen, the church of Rome had refused to receive the decision of the church of Carthage concerning the admission to the Church of heretics and schismatics. We do not know how these controversies were precisely resolved. In any case, to think that Stephen had excommunicated the African churches would be an inadmissible anachronism. All that he had been able to do (and which he most probably did) was to break communion with these churches. Evidently, the question of knowing if the African churches had ceased to be or were not churches did not even arise in his mind; the same with the question of the validity of the sacraments that were celebrated by these churches. In what concerned Cyprian himself, his situation was particularly difficult. From Cyprian's perspective on the Church, Stephen had departed from the majority consensus (*concors numerositas*) and, consequently, had removed himself from the Church. But Cyprian would not dare imagine the question from this perspective. How could the church which, according to Cyprian's own words, was the source and root of the church catholic (*ecclesiae catholicae matrix et radix*), find herself outside the universal structure of the Church?[30] In his discussion with Stephen, Cyprian then had to return to the positions of the ancient ecclesiology and consider the Roman Church as not being in communion with the African churches. The Great African Council of 256 resulted in a victory for Cyprian within that very council, but it was a defeat for his ecclesiological system.

It seems possible for me to end my brief look into history without speaking of the events that took place before and after the First Council of Nicaea in 381. It is actually very difficult to understand what took place in this period. There was a veritable cascade of excommunications of bishops, reciprocal most of the time, and one cannot really speak of the reception of these excommunications. Reception had been replaced by the law, which manifested itself with a particular distinctness in the decisions of numerous councils of this period. What is even more sad is that reception had been supplanted by completely arbitrary decision making.


## VI

1. The terrain seems to me to be sufficiently cleared so as to pass now to the essential question of this study. What are the relationships between the catholic church and the orthodox church from the perspective of eucharistic ecclesiology? It is clear, from the preceding pages, that the relations are defined by the absence of fraternal communion between the two churches. The lack of communion is an exceptional historical fact. In essence, what we have before us is not a break in communion of one or more churches with one or another local churches. On one hand, we see the catholic church which, because of her ecclesial organization, has become an immense canonical-administrative institution, and on the other hand, we have a series of autocephalous churches that do

not form an ensemble comparable to that of the Catholic church. The catholic church is not in communion with any of the orthodox churches, just as no orthodox church is in communion with the catholic church. Actually, the line of separation between the two churches coincides with the geographical and cultural borders dividing the East from the West. It is without doubt that these geographical factors have influenced the break in communion between the two groups of churches, but in our time these factors have, to a great degree, lost their primordial importance. Nevertheless, I find that it is erroneous to consider these factors, as we do sometimes, as so decisive so as to think that they have determined the inevitability of the process of separation between the church of the East and that of the West. Historically there had been no inescapable character and it was not possible that there should be. If the sense of the inevitability of the separation existed, it would have made itself felt from the very beginning and not after so many centuries. It is necessary to add that the break in communion took place not only between the East and the West but also, in a lesser measure, within the Western churches and within the Eastern churches.

2. The cessation of communion between the catholic church and the orthodox church is a historical fact. How we understand and judge it is more important than the fact itself. What does the break in communion between the two churches mean? From the perspective of eucharistic ecclesiology, the break is truly a break in communion between two *churches*, and not a break between churches and communities whose ecclesial nature is not recognized (or at least not entirely). For eucharistic ecclesiology, the orthodox church and the catholic church are both Churches, or to be more exact, each local church of both groups remains a Church—as it was before so it is after the "separation." I put "separation" in quotation marks for it did not take place and there is no separation. The Church of God is forever and remains one and unique. The break in communion was not able to produce the division of the Church which, by her very nature, cannot be divided into parts. We admit the habitual use of the term "separation" only to designate otherwise the break in communion that elicited the separation between the catholic church and the orthodox church. Each group has turned in on itself, lived its own life, and has not been interested in the other except to struggle against one another and to mutually accuse each other of heresy. Here there is a lack of the fullness of ecclesial life which, however, does not affect the nature of the Church of God. Even more, here is the proof of the state of sin of the local churches in actual reality, because we find divided that which God has united, put in unity joined by Love. This state of sin, though, does not affect at all the *una sancta*.

From the moment that the catholic church and the orthodox church both remain the Church of God, there can be no question of the validity of the sacraments in one or the other of the churches. The sacraments are valid within each church. For the other church they are not "witnessed" and "received" because of the absence of communion between both churches.

3. Why, when, and how did the break in communion between the two churches occur? There is not the possibility for me to examine these questions in detail here, for this would entail a special study in itself. I wish only to make two observations. First of all, with regard to the date of 1054 as the date of the "separation" of the churches, it is generally admitted that this date is merely a matter of convention because the "separation" may have taken place either before or even after 1054. This is not correct except partially. Every break in communion is always tied to a specific date. The year 1054 surely was the year in which the break in communion between Rome and Constantinople became an accomplished fact, and this communion has not been restored even in our time despite a number of actions taken in the direction of reestablishing it. The question appears differently when one asks if the "separation" had been unexpected or not. It is certain that the separation had been prepared by the history that preceded it. Even more, communion had already often been broken before 1054. It seems clear that the break in communion between Rome and Constantinople did not extend immediately to all of the Eastern and Western churches, and above all it is important to note that the break in communion between the two great churches was not completely grasped by the consciousness of the whole Church—so unaccustomed to this thinking—and only very slowly was this "separation" accepted.

The second observation deals with the question of knowing what actually took place in 1054, what were the facts that lead to the "separation." It would be more correct to put the question in this way: What new factors arose at the beginning of the eleventh century that became the cause of the separation in 1054? Let us lay aside the political questions concerning the Church and the state and observe that there was no new dogmatic divergence at this time, no new usage or liturgical practice in the life of the Church. The polemic engaged in after the "separation" turned on the divergences that had already existed. One could say that the point of this polemic was to legitimate the "separation," and not to explain it. Even a very superficial knowledge of the polemical works cannot but evoke a sad smile, beneath which is concealed the tragic feeling about the "separation"—that it was the result of sinful human will that consciously or unconsciously destroyed the unity of the churches.

4. Without judging from a confessional point of view (although this is possible for a theologian), we ought to admit that in the discussion between the catholic and orthodox churches, the position of the orthodox church is the more favorable than that of the Roman catholic. Both in theology and in the life of the orthodox church, there is nothing that the catholic church would not be able to accept, because really nothing new has been introduced into these and the content is essentially the same as at the beginning of the eleventh century. To justify the break in communion from the catholic side, the catholic church points to the fact that the orthodox church did not accept the doctrines that have received the character of dogma in the catholic church and were created

(with the exception of the *Filioque*) only after the "separation" of the churches. One cannot truly talk of "nonacceptance" of doctrines that divide the churches, for they were promulgated at a time when the churches were not in communion with each other. If we start to make suppositions about "what would have happened if," perhaps these very doctrines would not have become dogmas— that is, if communion had not been broken. It is not necessary to enumerate these doctrines here, even less to refute them. From my perspective, such polemical theology would be most sterile and detrimental to the peace of the church. Rather than helping us to overcome the division, such theology would only reinforce it. There is no doubt that among the dogmatic divergences, the doctrine of the primacy of the bishop of Rome and that of the infallibility that stems from this are by far the most important, and both catholic and orthodox theologians are in agreement on this. And nevertheless, it is conceivable that one would be able to see in these doctrines the essential cause of the division. I know that I risk raising many objections and even provoking irritation, but I must say that from my perspective this cause is not so much of an ecclesial but a juridical nature, and in the end, this is only an apparent reason since in the Church, there exists no power based on law.

5. Now I will address the last question I want to examine in this study. Is the break in communion between the catholic church and the group of orthodox churches capable of being overcome? I would once again here underscore that we are dealing with a break in communion between *churches*, and not relationships between one true Church and parts that have become detached from her while retaining certain "vestiges" of the Church and who, if one were to speak truthfully, could not be called "churches" in the proper sense of the word. The break in communion between the churches, due to the break in the unity based on the union of local churches, remains on an empirical, institutional level, and does not involve the deepest part of ecclesial life. According to eucharistic ecclesiology, when we participate in the eucharistic assembly, we are united with all those who at that moment also participate in eucharistic assemblies—not only those of the orthodox church but also those of the catholic church—for everywhere there is only the one and the same Eucharist being celebrated. There are not different Eucharists. We have completely forgotten this, because in our consciousness, the idea of eucharistic unity has been replaced by that of canonical unity. It is true that despite our division, we have not come to the point of denying the validity of the Eucharist celebrated by each other. And again, in the course of history there have been regrettable cases of this kind.

It could be said that restoring the relations between the catholic church and the orthodox church, which are currently defined as a cessation of the fraternal communion between them, would be the end of the great schism. Here is a proposition so indisputable that it would provoke no objection from either side. The point of the question is to know which condition would permit the restoration of communion between the churches. The response that is most natural would consist in saying that the restoration of communion would be possible when the causes that provoked the break in communion or that actually produced it had disappeared or lost their significance. At first, it would seem that the position of universal ecclesiology and that of eucharistic ecclesiology are identical in this regard, but in reality, there is a profound difference between them. The elimination of divergences, above all of the dogmatic kind, is the condition *sine qua non* for the return of the party detached from the one and only Catholic church, or more exactly, the condition by which the detached party would be able to become the Church once more. Such is the perspective of universal ecclesiology, just as for eucharistic ecclesiology there are two groups of churches that fully possess ecclesial character. The cessation of communion between them is a result, which is always there, of the nonacceptance of this or that doctrine. I said earlier that whatever binds the one to the other, these two actions are nevertheless different. In fact, one action has habitually followed the other. However, this is not absolutely necessary. The rejection of "reception" need not require the break in communion between the churches. As an ecclesial action, the break in communion ought to correspond to the will of God. In reality, in the course of history the break has been for most part the result of the sinful will of human beings, acting out of considerations of ecclesiastical politics. The "separation" of 1054 between Rome and Constantinople was not based on divergences of dogmatic nature because divergences of this sort had existed before this date and had not destroyed the communion between Rome and Constantinople then, however precarious this communion might have been. The separation was produced not only for reasons of ecclesiastical politics but also it had been provoked to a great degree by the mentality of the personalities who played roles in this drama. Let us admit that the break between Rome and Constantinople had been justifiable. Nevertheless, it did not attain the goal for which every break in communion was aimed and which consisted in continuing to remove dogmatic divergences. On the contrary, this break has resulted in a nearly complete isolation of the one church from the other and the impoverishment, and later the total end to the bonds of Love that ought to unite the churches.

To think that the annihilation of dogmatic divergences is the condition for the reunion of the churches would be to simply affirm their division. Modern ecclesial consciousness, orthodox as well as catholic, considers, with few and rare exceptions, the separation of the churches as a pathological state, as a sin against Love. Because of an effort in Love and despite the divergences, communion between the churches could be renewed and the reunion of the catholic church and the orthodox church would be possible. "If I have the gift of prophecy, understanding all the mysteries there are, and knowing everything, and if I have faith in all its fullness, to move mountains, but without love, then I am nothing at all" (1 Cor 13:2). By an effort in Love, the orthodox church *could* reestablish communion with the catholic church, the dogmatic divergences notwithstanding and without demanding that the catholic church renounce the doctrines that distinguish her from the orthodox church, because "[l]ove is always patient and kind; it is never jealous; love is never boastful or conceited; it is never rude or selfish; it does not take offense and is not resentful" (1 Cor 13:4). If the orthodox church had been in communion with the catholic church up to the time of the First Vatican Council, she would have been able, without accepting the decisions of the council, not to break communion and to cover by the truth of Love that which was the non-truth, in her estimation, of the dogma there promulgated. If for the catholic church the divine truth is greater than that of man, she *could* consent not to demand that the orthodox church accept these new dogmas. Within herself she would have remained what she is today, preserving the content and the doctrines that she actually possessed. Certainly, to attain this the effort in Love is necessary, a great sacrifice, an element of self-renunciation. To restrict the doctrine of the power of the pope within the limits of the catholic church would be, for the church of Rome, the result of a great sacrificial spirit toward the goal of reestablishing the union-of-the-churches-joined-in-Love. It has not at all to do with the Catholic church redefining her doctrine of the power of the pope as a *theologoumenon*, a theological opinion. The dogma would remain dogma but a dogma not recognized by other churches. If one were able to put to the side all that has accumulated around this doctrine and reject all the exaggerations, modern ecclesial consciousness would be ready to accept all that this dogma meant from the beginning in the ancient church.[31] For orthodox consciousness, the doctrine of the power of the pope, including the dogma of infallibility, is an erroneous dogmatic interpretation of the ancient doctrine of the Church and in particular that of reception. It was not the West but the East that in the primitive church contributed to the growth of the importance of the church of Rome. It was in the East that one of the great bishops had solemnly proclaimed, on the eve of his martyrdom, that the church of Rome was the one "who presided in Love."[32] It is not at all necessary, for the orthodox consciousness, to minimize the value of this witness. In Love, as the expression of the essence of the Church, and by the Love in which the Church lives, the church of Rome is surely the one that has priority. Her Love extends beyond her limits and spreads in a great wave over all the churches. It is from the East that Rome obtained the recognition of her priority at the moment when Rome would not ask it again. "Love . . .takes no pleasure in other people's sins but delights in the truth; it is always ready to excuse, to trust, to hope, and to endure whatever comes" (1 Cor 13:5–7). When Rome would demand that the East recognize her primacy, after having rejected Love—because she did not wish to believe that Love covers all and believes all, after having put law in the place of Love—the East refused to follow Rome's demands, not only because the New Rome desired to possess the primacy but also because of the fullness of Love. Ecclesial life, in its depths, could not reject Love, the very source of her life, in favor of law.

If, due to the sacrificial spirit of Love of the bishop of Rome, the union-of-the-churches-joined-by-Love were to be reestablished, the church of Rome would be able to occupy in this union of the multiplicity of churches the same place that she had in ancient time. From the perspective of actual ecclesiastical politics, Rome would have lost nothing and she would even have gained in this. For the Vatican "politicians of the church," it should be clear that after a series of less than fruitful attempts to bring back different confessions—orthodoxy above all—to the catholic church, such an objective is unattainable. Because of the reestablishment of the unity joined by Love and without imposing primacy by constraint, Rome would have certainly acquired it better by Love than by law. Just as in ancient times, the weight, the importance of the church of Rome's reception would be what it was before the "separation." The voice of Rome would be decisive in all perspectives. Nevertheless, these considerations of ecclesial politics—considerations which flow from human will, which ought not to play any role in the Church—should retreat before the necessity of following the will of God, which is active in the Church. Does not the will of God consist in the reestablishment of the fraternal communion between the churches, communion that was broken by human will? To oppose the will of God witnesses that the church, which despite this will affirms itself in the division, does not possess the truth. The truth, on the contrary, is on the side of the church that is conscious of her culpability because of the separation and seeks the restoration of the union of the churches in Love. We believe that the hour is near when the catholic church, after having transcended human passions, would extend a fraternal hand to the orthodox church, and that this hand would not remain suspended in the air. In the face of the intransigence in which we live, Love ought to be the strongest feeling, for only Love can conquer such hardness of heart.

6. In saying that the renewal of the communion between the catholic church and the orthodox church is possible—despite all the divergences that actually exist, however—I do not want to minimize the importance of dogmatic formulations, and even less to preach indifferentism or relativism when it comes to dogma. Dogmas cannot be dealt with in such ways. They remain what they are. If the orthodox church had renewed the communion with the catholic church, this would not have required the denial of her own doctrines, nor the obligation to accept those of the catholic church. If the catholic church had renewed communion with the orthodox church, she would not have been obliged to renounce her doctrines. The revival of communion between the churches would not have overcome the doctrinal divergences, but the broken state of communion in which the two churches find themselves could not and would never be able to overcome them. The objection that we often hear raised against the possibility of communion between the churches states that certain dogmas are true and others are false. This object lacks a purpose, for such a discussion is impossible. The true problem consists in knowing if the churches are able to be

in communion despite their dogmatic divergences. To be sure, ideally, the local churches ought to be in a state of absolute dogmatic harmony, but in the
course of history, this ideal has never been attained. History knows no period
in which there was absolute dogmatic harmony, neither before nor after
Nicaea. At that time there were no less divergences between the groups who
were in agreement than among those who disagreed. It should suffice to remember Marcellus of Ancyra, who defended Athanasius the Great and Rome
as well. The identity of dogmatic formulae is completely against what we are
able to aspire to with any guarantee that a veritable dogmatic concord would be
at the foundation of this identity. The history of dogmatic movements shows
that one and the same formula was able to unite several churches in which the
dogmatic thinking had nevertheless been different, and to disunite those with
which there had not been divergences about the content of the doctrine. On
certain cases it is easier to attain unanimity from the dogmatic perspective than
to establish the identity of dogmatic formulae, and in other cases it is the inverse that occurs. Certainly it is easier to find this unanimity concerning the
content of dogmatic formulae among churches who are in fraternal communion and who live the same ecclesial life than among those who have broken
communion with each other. Within the unity joined by the peace of the
churches, the refusal to receive this or that doctrine plays the role of a brake,
as in the church divided, reception automatically loses its importance. We always forget that the break in communion, provoked by whatever cause, if legitimate, in turn is an even greater disunion.

The reestablishment of fraternal communion between the orthodox church and
the catholic church in the actual state of things would not be the negation of the
division, which would in that instance be considered nonexistent, but would be a
victory over this division by the power of Love—that is, by the Church and because of the Church. Cannot the true cause of the separation of the churches, in
the final analysis, be reduced to some having lost the truth of doctrine and the others the truth of Love? Does not the loss of doctrinal truth by some witness to the
loss of the truth of Love by the others? Very often, the loss of dogmatic truth is the
result of Love growing cold. One cannot reestablish the truth of dogmatic doctrine
for the others without having reestablished in oneself the truth of Love in Christ.
When Love has once again become the foundation of life in all the churches, then
dogmatic divergences that seem insurmountable will be removed in the light of
this Love. Christian people have placed knowledge above Love because they have
forgotten that "our knowledge is imperfect and our prophesying is imperfect" (1
Cor 13:9). When Love is raised higher than knowledge, then knowledge itself will
be perfected. Knowledge is not opposed to Love and Love does not exclude
knowledge, and when each Christian and all Christians together have come to understand that Love is above the division and that the division is a sin before God,
then the truth of Love, trampled underfoot, will be reestablished, and through
Love and its power, the truth of dogma will be restored as well.

The blessed Polycarp visited at Rome under Anicetus. They were in disagreement with each other on a number of matters not of importance, but they were immediately at peace and they did not dispute with each other about this. Anicetus actually was not able to persuade Polycarp to stop observing that which, with John, the disciple of Our Lord and the other apostles he knew, he had always observed. And Polycarp did not persuade Anicetus to keep his observance, for he said it was necessary to hold on to the custom of the presbyters who had preceded him. And things being like this, they were in communion the one with the other, and in the church Anicetus ceded the celebration of the Eucharist to Polycarp evidently out of deference. They left each other in peace. And in all of the Church there was peace whether one observed [the fourteenth day] or not.[33]

## NOTES

1. We have intentionally left the word "church" as the author requested in the lower case, along with "orthodox" and "catholic," in most cases. The author reserves "Church," in upper case, to refer to the one, universal Church of God in Christ. In other cases, it seems as though he sees "churches" as local, though fully the "Church."

2. Alexander Schmemann, "Unité, séparation, réunion à la lumière de l'ecclésiologie orthodoxe," *Contacts* 26 (1959): 73–88.

3. It is to Fr. Schmemann's merit that he posed this question in the context of the reunion of the churches in the future. See his article cited in note 2.

4. This question has been posed by Fr. Georges Florovsky, "Le futur concile de l'Église romaine," *Le Messager orthodoxe* 6 (1959): 3–8.

5. I have dealt with Cyprian's thinking many times in my writings, most notably in my study, "The Church Which Presides in Love," in *The Primacy of Peter*, revised edition, edited by John Meyendorff (Crestwood N.Y.: SVS Press, 1992).

6. Epist. LXIX, III, 1. *The Letters of St. Cyprian of Carthage, Ancient Christian Writers*, volumes 43, 44, 36, 47, translated by G. W. Clarke (Mahwah, N.J.: Paulist Press, 1984, 1986, 1988).

7. Epist. LXIX, II, 1.

8. Epist. LXXIII, XXI, 1.

9. Epist. LXIX, V, 1.

10. Epist. LXXIV, VII, 2.

11. Epist. LXXIV, VIII, 3.

12. Epist. LXXXIV, IV, 2.

13. De unitate ecclesiae, V. *The Lapsed: The Unity of the Catholic Church, Ancient Christian Writers*, volume 25, translated by Maurice Bevenor (Mahwah, N.J.: Paulist Press, 1957).

14. Epist. LXXIII, VII, 1.

15. Epist. XLIII, V, 2.

16. Epist. LIX, XIV, 2; De unit., V, 3.

17. Epist., LXVIII, IV, 2.

18. Epist., LXVI, VIII, 3.

19. Epist., LXVI, VIII, 3.

20. On eucharistic ecclesiology see my studies: "Le Sacrement de l'Assemblie," *Internationale Kirchliche Zeitschrifte* 4 (1956); "L'apôtre Pierre et l'éveque de Rome," *Theologia* XXVI (1955); "La doctrine de la primauté á la lumière de l'ecclésiologie," *Istina* 4 (1957); "The Church Which Presides in Love," cited in note 5, and other studies in Russian.

21. See my article, "Statio orbis," *Irénikon*, volume 1 (1962).

22. On the role of the church that has the first place or priority, see my study "The Church Which Presides in Love."

23. The epistle of Clement of Rome is the most ancient work (and the best known) in which the desire is expressed to come to the aid of a church that has allowed in herself irregular actions not accepted by the church of Rome, insofar as this latter church possessed priority.

24. The ancient idea of eucharistic communion had nothing in common with the contemporary notion of "intercommunion," for the simple reason that this second notion did not exist. There was no organizing of special eucharistic assemblies for this or that group. The eucharistic assembly was arranged by the local church and not outside of her.

25. Eusebius, Hist. Eccl., V, XXIV, 9. *The Ecclesiastical History, Nicene and Post-Nicene Fathers*, series II, volume I (Grand Rapids, Mich.: Wm. B. Eerdmans Publishing, 1956).

26. For example, see Bardy in his translation of Eusebius' *Ecclesiastical History* and Lebreton in *Histoire de l'Église de Fliche*, edited by Martin.

27. Eusebius, V, XXIV, 10.

28. Eusebius, V, XXIV, 14–15.

29. Eusebius, V, XXIV, 16–17.

30. Epist., XLVIII, III, 1.

31. See H. Alivisatos, "Les conciles œcuméniques V, VI, VII et VIII," in *Le Concile et les Conciles*, p. 122 (Chevetogne, 1960).

32. Again, see my study already cited, "The Church Which Presides in Love."

33. Eusebius, *Hist. Eccl.* V, XXIV, 16.

# THE CHURCH'S CANONS: CHANGEABLE OR UNCHANGEABLE?

*Canon law—it would appear to be dry, highly specialized, very much a matter of particular historical situations and sensibilities. Yet, though trained as a canonist and historian, among other things, Fr. Afanasiev does not give us here an analysis only for specialists. Rather, the bedrock question is about how truth does not change, while much else in the life of any people, culture, or for that matter, the Church, must change if it is to be alive.*

## I

The Church is founded on a rock. "You are Peter and on this rock I will build my Church and the gates of hell shall not prevail against her" (Mt 16:18). These words could be inscribed on the front of the principal churches of all confessions, including Rome, but, of course, without the Roman Catholic interpretation. The belief that the Church of Christ is unshakeable and unconquerable comprises one of the most basic convictions of Christianity. In the age of profound world crisis and in the dusk of humanity's historical paths, this unshakeable quality of the Church is a haven for the Christian soul. The face of the earth is changing. Mankind is entering unknown and unexplored paths, and we ourselves, just like our children, do not know under what new conditions we will be living. When the soil on which we are accustomed to stand falters and

First published in Russian in *Zhivoe Predanie* (Paris: YMCA Press, 1937), 82–96. Translated by James LaBeau and published in *St. Vladimir's Theological Quarterly* 11: 2 (November 1969): 54–68.

sifts out from under our feet, the rock of the Church will remain. "Everyone
then who hears these words of mine and does them will be like a wise man who
built his house upon the rock; and the rain fell, and the floods came, and the
winds blew and beat upon that house, but it did not fall, because it had been
founded on the rock" (Mt 7:24–25). She will withstand the storms of man even
more: "Heaven and earth will pass away, but my words will not pass away" (Mk
13:31). In the midst of the changing and the ever new, she alone remains
changeless. In the midst of the temporal, she alone is eternal.

But how should we understand and to what should we attribute the unal-
terable in the Church? Is everything in the Church changeless? And in what
sense is the Church herself changeless? Such are the questions that, under
various aspects, stir modern Christian thought. These are not only academic
questions. They are questions vital to Christian life, since the solution of another question depends on them—that is, what should and must be the attitude of the Church towards modern life and its problems. If everything in the
Church is changeless and there is nothing temporal in her, then this means
that modern life concerns the Church only to the degree in which the Church
must keep and preserve her sanctity in the life of the world in order to bring
it to the time of fulfillment. This presupposes that the Church, to a certain degree, is withdrawn from the world: that there is one road from the world into
the Church, but there is no road from the Church into the world. This would
be correct only if the Church, together with its members, could leave the
world. But she does not lead them out of the world ("since then you would
need to go out of the world" [1 Cor 5:10]) and, accordingly, the Church cannot leave her members in the world alone. The Church faces the world, not
the desert. She abides in the world and builds in the world until "the fullness
of time" (Ep 1:10). In relation to the world, the Church—aside from a concern
for self-preservation—also has positive concerns. If this is so, then there must
be in the Church not only that which is unalterable, but also that which
changes—along with the eternal, that which is temporal. Where then is the
eternal and temporal in the Church, where is the dividing line between them,
and what are their interrelationships?


## II


Dogmatic decisions concern the inner truths of faith, which are unchanging
and mandatory for all. They are distinct from time and absolute. But are the regions of the eternal and immutable in the Church only limited to dogmas? Besides dogmas we also have canonical decisions regulating the Church's external
order and structure. How should these decisions be considered? Do they belong exclusively to the temporal realms, and in virtue of this are they changeable? Or are they, just as dogmas, included in the realm of the eternal, or at

least connected with that which is eternal and absolute in the Church? In answer to these questions, Protestantism says that canonical decisions are the product of *jus humanum* and are, consequently, mutable—either separately or jointly. Catholicism distinguishes between *jus divinum* and *jus humanum* (divine law and human law). Those canonical decrees that are based on divine law are unchangeable and absolute, and no church authority can revoke them. Dogmas are distinguished from canonical decrees only by their content. Decrees derived from *jus humanum*, which also comprise the *jus ecclesiasticum* (ecclesiastical law), are subject to change and even repeal by the corresponding ecclesiastical organs. Thus Protestantism and Catholicism, each in its own manner, establish a distinction between the changeless and changing, the realm of the eternal and the realm of the temporal in the Church. The realms of the eternal and temporal correspond to the regions of the divine and human, *jus divinum* and *jus humanum*: these two spheres are torn apart and acquire a nature of self-containment. But this answer is not adequate, since in spite of emphasizing the existence of two spheres in the Church, it does not establish any interrelation or connection between them.

What is the Orthodox Church's position? Aside from the recently accepted view—under the influence of Catholicism—in which canonical decrees are divided into decisions based upon *jus humanum* and *jus divinum*, the existence of *jus humanum* is unknown to Orthodoxy. In any case, it was unknown to both the ancient Church and the Church of the ecumenical councils. The Council *in Trullo*, in listing the decisions that are mandatory, added, "Let no one be permitted to change or revoke the above rules and to accept others in place of the rules presented" (Canon 2). The Seventh Ecumenical Council proclaimed even more decisively and energetically that

> We welcome and embrace the divine canons, and we corroborate the entire and rigid statement of them set forth by the renowned apostles, who were and are trumpets of the Spirit, and those both of the six holy ecumenical councils and of the ones assembled regionally for the purpose of setting forth such edicts, and of those of our holy fathers. For all those men, having been guided by the light dawning out of the same Spirit prescribed rules that are to our best interest . . . [since] if forever the prophetic voice commands us to keep the testimonies of God (*ta martyria tou Theou*) and to live in them, it is plain that they remain unwavering and rigid (Canon 1).

The existence of *jus humanum* was also unknown to the Byzantine commentators of the twelfth century. Nonetheless, in the age of the ecumenical councils, as it had been earlier and was later, canonical decrees were revoked and changed by the Church in both the fullness of her life and through her highest power, the councils—they themselves changed the decisions of previous councils. The Council *in Trullo*, after having announced the immutability of the canons, wrote in the famous twelfth canon that introduced celibacy for the episcopate:

> We have therefore made it a great concern to us to do everything possible for the
> benefit of the flocks under hand, and it has seemed best not to allow such a thing
> to occur hereafter at all. We assert this, however, not with any intention of setting
> aside or overthrowing any legislation laid down apostolically, but having due regard
> for the salvation and safety of peoples and for their advancement with a view to
> avoiding any likelihood of giving anyone cause to blame the priestly polity.

*Jus humanum* does not exist in the Church. All decisions are divinely inspired
("They are all enlightened by one and the same Spirit"), and they must remain
indestructible and unshakeable. Does this mean then that the Orthodox
Church by denying *jus humanum*, in contrast to Protestantism, which only recognizes *jus divinum*? But then how is it possible to account for the assertion
that the canons are indestructible and unshakeable when they are altered, albeit that these changes are not, at the same time, a corruption or revocation of
former decrees? The question approaches a somewhat obvious paradox. In fact,
how is it possible to understand the actions of the Council *in Trullo* in changing the Apostolic Canon on the permissibility of a married episcopate and in-
troducing celibacy, and at the same time affirming that this decision does not
revoke or corrupt the canon? An attempt to understand the affirmations of the
Council *in Trullo* must be, at the same time, an attempt to clarify the Orthodox
teaching about the temporal and eternal in canon law.

## III

Christian thought tends toward two poles, while remaining in the boundaries of
Christianity. One is called Monophysitism and the other is generally labeled
Nestorianism. In other words, the content of Christian thought is outlined by
the Chalcedonian doctrine. Aside from its direct relationship to questions about
the natures in Christ, the Chalcedonian dogma has a particular meaning in the
teachings of the Church. The New Testament Church is the chosen people of
God (1 Pet 2:9). The chosen people of the New Testament in their totality comprise the Body of Christ, whose head is Christ himself (1 Cor 12:22, 27). To
abide in the Church means to be included in the Body of Christ, to become its
member through partaking of the Body of Christ. "The cup of blessing which
we bless, is it not a participation in the blood of Christ? The bread which we
break, is it not a participation in the body of Christ? Because there is one bread,
we who are many are one body, for we all partake of the one bread" (1 Cor
10:16–17). The eucharistic gathering is the gathering of the chosen people of
God with Christ God, in his presence; it is the gathering of the Church, for
where two or three are gathered in his name, he is there also. It is the fullness

of the Church, since the whole Christ is present in the eucharistic sacrifice. Thus, the eucharistic gathering concretely and mystically embodies the Church. This embodiment occurs in empirical reality and has itself an empirical aspect.

Like the Eucharist, the Church has an empirical reality and an empirical nature. Her dual nature is the dual nature of being both a divine and human organism and is similar to the dual nature of Christ. The relationship of the empirical and spiritual natures is determined by the Chalcedonian formula: undivided, inseparable, unchanging, and unmingled. The invisible, spiritual being of the Church is manifested through her empirical nature. Therefore, the division of the Church into visible and invisible, such as is characteristic of Protestantism, is incorrect in that it destroys the Church's empirical reality. The Church is one, just as Christ is one, being visible and invisible at the same time. The fullness of the Church is contained in the invisible, which indissolubly includes in itself the visible Church; but it does not merge with the visible nor does it engulf the visible. In the same way, the visible Church contains the fullness of the Church, not just the self-contained visible part. To divide the Church into the visible and invisible is ecclesiastical Nestorianism, and hence a refutation of the Church's God-man nature, since the visible Church is inevitably related exclusively to empirical reality. Existing in an empirical reality, the Church, through its empirical nature, enters into history and herself is clothed in the fabric of history.

The organic structure of the Church as the Body of Christ presupposes a particular order, or *taxis*, deriving from the very essence of the Church. This order is the law of church life and of its organization, revealed as absolute truth, as a dogmatic teaching. This includes the teachings on the structure of the body of the Church, the composition of the ecclesiastical society, and the doctrines of the Church's hierarchy, of the sacraments, etc. This order not only concerns the spiritual essence of the Church, but also her empirical fabric, since the latter is inseparable from the former and is organically tied with it.

Contrary to Rudolf Sohm's opinion, the ecclesiastical structure did not develop in a historical process due to the penetration of law into the Church. The Church's structure is not connected to law, as such, but resulted from the very essence of the Church. From the very beginning the Church entered history as a society having a determined form of structure. In the so-called charismatic period, the Church already had the determined structure of her historical existence. True, the early Christian communities only began to be clothed in the fabric of history, but the fabric was transparent, and through it was seen clearly the Church's genuine essence.

The forms of the Church's historical existence are quite varied. For anyone acquainted with the history of the Church, this is so evident that it requires no proof. One historical form in the course of history was replaced by another. Nevertheless, despite all the various historical forms, we can find in them all a certain constant nucleus. The nucleus is the dogmatic teaching about the Church—in other words, the Church herself. The historical forms of church life are conditioned by the content of the dogmatic teaching. Church life can acquire only those forms that are consistent with the essence of the Church and that are capable of expressing this essence in given historical situations. From this it follows that a change in the content of the dogmatic teaching about the Church must give rise to a corruption in the doctrine about the order and structure of the Church's body, and the latter will find its expression in the forms of the historical existence of the Church. Even in antiquity—in the first age of Christianity—heretical societies had a structure different than that found in the Catholic Church. The more the doctrine about the Church was distorted, the less the structure of these societies resembled the Church's, and in extreme cases, in Gnostic societies, there was nothing in common with it. The varieties of ecclesiastical structures found today in Catholicism, Protestantism, and Orthodoxy to a great extent are also explained by the variety of dogmatic teachings about the Church. On the other hand, the unity of dogmatic teachings makes for a basic unit in the historical forms of church life. The communities of the Catholic Church in the first centuries of Christianity developed the same ecclesiastical structures, despite the complete lack of formal relations between them and the lack of a common canonical legislation.

The dogmatic teaching about the Church is embodied in the historical forms of ecclesiastical life. However, this embodiment is never complete, but remains relative. The historical life of the Church is not capable of embodying the essence of the Church to its fullest. It can only more or less approximate it. Therefore the possibility of some kind of ideal canonical form is excluded. The recognition of the existence of an ideal form would bring about an improper absolutizing of the relativity of the Church's historical fabric. The Church lives in the general historical life of her age. Her historical forms, unlike the dogmatic, are to a great extent conditioned by the general conditions of life in history. The dogmatic teachings are a constant factor and not dependent on a historical process. The teachings are embodied in the fabric of history, which is continuously subjected to various changes. The Church does not change her forms of historical life accidentally or arbitrarily, nor does the Church accommodate herself to contemporary life and passively follow the times.

Historical conditions do influence the forms of church life, but not in the sense that these conditions prescribe various changes in the Church's life, for the Church herself, from the depths of her essence, changes her forms of historical existence. The Church strives, under given historical conditions, to find a form that would more fully and completely express the Church's essence—the Church herself and her dogmatic teaching. Thus we come to a very important conclusion: the interrelationship between the Church's historical existence and her essence is such that the historical existence is that form in which the essence of the Church is embodied in history. By employing this formula it is easy to ex-

plain why the recognition of only one ideal form of the Church's historical existence would correspond to an improper absolutizing of that existence. If such a
form did exist, then it would be recognized that the temporal existence of the
Church ceased to be temporal and that the Church was divorced from a general
historical life. More essentially, this would bring into oblivion the Church's empirical aspect, which cannot be absolutized. Nor can it be engulfed by the
Church's spiritual nature. The oblivion of the empirical nature is the other pole
in the doctrine on the Church—ecclesiastical Monophysitism.

## IV

The interrelation between the forms of church life and the Church's essence is
established through canonical decrees. At the present time a solution has not
been obtained to the question of whether these norms have a legal character or
not, and also whether it is possible to admit the existence of ecclesiastical law
in the Church or, as Sohm thinks, whether this contradicts the essence of the
Church. Neither has the problem of the essence of law been solved, a cardinal
point in this question. Leaving this question aside, it is essential to emphasize
how the canons differ from ordinary legal norms. The latter establish and regulate order in social organisms belonging completely to an empirical existence.
Even if we admit that they bring the life of social organisms into accordance
with "legal sense" (Rechtsgefühl), this still does not remove us from the empirical realm, since this "legal sense" is in itself an empirical value.

On the other hand the Church is a divine-human organism, which is the essential characteristic separating it from all other social organisms. The canons
do not establish the basic order of this organism (presented in the dogmas
about the Church); they only regulate the canonical structure of the Church so
that it can more perfectly reveal the Church's essence. Therefore, in corre-
spondence to jurisprudence, there are no decrees in canonical literature that
we would be able to label "fundamental."[1]

Canons fashion dogma into a form of norms that must be followed in church
life in order to be consistent with the dogmatic teachings. Canons are a kind of
canonical interpretation of the dogmas for a particular moment of the Church's
historical existence. They are, in fact, a model, a rule, of form of life for the
Church's community. They express the truth about the order of church life, but
rather than expressing this truth in absolute forms, they conform to historical
existence.

Proceeding from this characteristic of the canons, the division of canons between those based upon divine law and those based upon human law should be
resolutely repudiated. That which in canonical decisions is referred to as divine
law does not apply to the canons, but to the dogmatic definitions. No matter
how we may define law, canons in no way belong to the field of law. Everything

in scripture refers to the areas of faith and morality, and Christ left no canonical definitions that could determine the structure of the Church in her historical existence.

Nevertheless, is it possible to conclude that all canons are based exclusively on human law just because of the lack of canons based upon divine law? We admit—and we must admit—that there are some canons that in reality refer to human law. These are mainly governmental decrees concerning the affairs of the Church. However, the Church never confused these decrees with canons and always distinguished between *kanones* (canons) and *nomoi* (rules). We can also ascribe to human law those Church decrees not having their foundation in dogmatic teachings, but in considerations of a nonecclesiastical nature; but we cannot, at the same time, declare that all the canons accepted by the Church are lacking in grace and are nonecclesiastical. *Jus humanum* only regulates empirical organisms. If human law existed alone in the Church, the Church would belong exclusively to the realm of empirical reality. The Protestant belief that canonical definitions are based solely on human law is an inevitable conclusion derived from the Protestant teaching about the Church. This interpretation sees the visible Church as solely an empirical entity, and as a consequence human law naturally operates in the Church. Ecclesiastical Nestorianism is thus reflected in the canonical realm by the recognition of *jus humanum* as its exclusive guiding principle.

If Protestantism recognizes the presence of only human law in the Church, then it is inwardly consistent and adheres to its dogmatic teaching. For the Orthodox Church, however, such recognition contradicts the doctrine of the Church. The Church as an organism is human and divine and full of grace. Everything in the Church is filled with grace: "Where the Church is, there is the Spirit of God, and where is the Spirit of God, there is the Church and all is grace."[2] Hence even the genuine Church decrees possess grace: They, just as dogmas, are revealed truths. The formula "It pleases the Holy Spirit and us," can be applied equally to both dogmatic and canonical decrees. According to the Seventh Ecumenical Council the latter are "divine" rules. The dual nature of the Church defined in Chalcedon is opposed to both ecclesiastical Nestorianism and Monophysitism. In accordance with this, the divine-human source of canonical decrees is affirmed by Tradition. If it is necessary to speak about law in the Church, then we should not speak of divine and human laws as separate entities divorced from one another, but we should speak of a single divine-human law. The will of the Church (her divine-human will) manifests itself through the canonical decrees in order that her historical forms of existence embody her essence.

Canonical decrees, just as dogmas, are divinely inspired, but from this it should not be concluded that they coincide with one another. The distinction between dogmas and canons does not lie in the source of their being, but in the fact that dogmas are absolute truths and canons are applications of these truths for the historical existence of the Church. Dogmas do not concern temporal existence, while canons are temporal. This temporal aspect does not, however, diminish their divinely inspired nature, since the temporal does not refer to that nature. They are temporal in the sense that they are applied to that which is temporal, the historical forms of the Church's existence. The truth that canons express is in itself absolute, yet the content of canons is not this truth itself, but the mode through which this truth must be expressed in a given historical form of the Church's life. Canons express the eternal in the temporal. The temporal is the "how"—the mode of application—while the eternal is that which is applied.

The problem of changes or immutability in the canons is solved by their eternal-temporal character. The historical forms of the Church are pliable and alterable since the essence of the Church is embodied in definite historical conditions. Canonical decrees follow historical forms since they direct these forms toward a more complete expression of the Church's essence. They are changed inasmuch as the Church's life undergoes changes under various historical conditions. If the historical conditions in which the Church lives always remained constant, then the canons would not experience any changes. As truths of divine revelation they are indisputable—"We uphold the all-encompassing and unshakeable enactment of these rules" (Canon 2 in Trullo)—but in a relative, not absolute, sense; they are relevant only for their own age. The underlying dogmatic truth of the canons cannot be changed; only their application and embodiment in a canon can be altered by the historical existence of the Church.

Just as in physics a force can act only if it has a point of application, so too canons are active only if they have a point of application in the conditions of the Church's life for which they were decreed. If this point of application no longer exists, then the canons become inactive. Either they altogether cease to be active or they undergo changes, or to be more exact, they are replaced by others. If we restrict the scope of our investigation to only the most narrow understanding of canons—that is, as decrees of the councils and the Holy Fathers—then we will find a series of canons completely inapplicable to our present church life, as, for example, all the decisions concerning the receiving of the lapsed into the Church or those relating to the penitential discipline and institutions that have disappeared or that have been replaced by others, such as the *chorepiscopoi*, the *oikonomoi*, the *ekdikoi*, etc. We even find decisions that church authorities do not presently require to be fulfilled any more. In the fourth century the church authorities required everyone present at the liturgy to participate in the Eucharist (Apostolic Canon 9 and Canon 2 of the Council of Antioch), but as a consequence of new conditions of life the Church abandoned these demands. To this category belong also the canons regulating the transfers of bishops and clerics from one region to another. The number of such examples could be significantly increased since in reality the majority of the canonical decisions contained in the Book of Rules can no longer be applied to modern church life in their literal sense. If they are applied, then it is not in the meaning in which they were published. New understandings are constantly being infused into the old canons, so that, in fact, a new decision is brought about, but expressed in the old form. Often, the old canonical decree is so much mingled with the new content, that the old content is completely blotted out of the Church's memory. Canon Twelve of Antioch directs a condemned bishop to appeal to a "larger council of bishops." In accordance with the later-created patriarchal regions as jurisdictional entities, the "larger council of bishops" was seen as a council of bishops of a patriarchal province. Thus Balsamon writes, commenting on this canon, "The canon says that a deposed (bishop) should appeal not to the Emperor, but to a larger council of bishops. For this reason a (bishop) deposed, for example, by the metropolitan of Ephesus or Thessalonica, should be justly prompted to appeal to the Ecumenical Patriarch." The "greater council of bishops of a diocese" mentioned in Canon Six of the First Ecumenical Council is understood in exactly the same way. Meanwhile, as is demonstrated by Canon Fourteen of Antioch, the councils of Antioch and Constantinople interpreted "greater council" as not a patriarchal council, but a provincial council enlarged with bishops from neighboring provinces. The correct meaning of the famous Canons Six and Seven of the First Nicene Council remain to the present unclear or, in any case, controversial.

In the age of creative conciliar activity the Church enlarged, replaced, and changed old canonical decrees. Along with this the "unshakeable content of the canons"—even those that were changed—was not violated. If the new decision genuinely reflected the Church, then the dogmatic teaching that served as the basis for both the new and the old canons remained unchanged. The old canon continued to reflect a truth, but only for a past epoch. This is exactly how the Council *in Trullo* acted when it considered it necessary and in keeping with its epoch to introduce celibacy for the episcopate, and directed that all previously ordained bishops should leave their wives. The council was correct to write that it published the new decree "not with any intention of setting aside or overthrowing any legislation laid down Apostolically, but having due regard for the salvation and safety of people and for their advancement." The Apostolic Canon was a canonical decree; it expressed the dogmatic teaching about the Church's hierarchy, but it expressed the hierarchy in conformity with its era. When the historical conditions of life changed, it was necessary to issue a new decree in order to express the same dogmatic teaching. Whether or not the canonical conscience of the Council *in Trullo* was correct is a question of a different order, but it is completely clear that the historical era of the Council *in Trullo* greatly differed from the times of the apostles. An indication of the changes that took place in the historical conditions is Justinian's demand that candidates for the episcopate be unmarried—that is, either single or widowers without children.

If the organs of the Church's authority, especially in periods of decline in creativity, inadequately follow the Church's reality, then the life of the Church itself will make up for this deficiency. Then arise the Church's customs, which

constantly acquire the norm of canons. The Church always gives great importance to custom, especially when it is based upon tradition. "An unwritten custom of the Church must be respected as a law." In such cases a custom serves
as an addition to and an interpretation of canonical decrees. But custom can
make up for deficiency in canonical creativity both in a positive and negative
fashion. It will suffice to cite a few more striking examples. Apostolic Canon 9
and Canon 2 of Antioch, mentioned above, prescribe that "all the faithful who
enter the church and hear the Scriptures should remain for prayer and Holy
Communion." According to the accepted customary interpretation, this canon
has come to be understood in the sense of requiring only presence at, not participation in, the Eucharist. In interpreting Canon Two of Antioch, Balsamon
writes:

> Read what is written in the Apostolic Canons (8 and 9) and in accordance with
> them understand the present canon, and say that those who refrain from Holy
> Communion (and are mentioned here) are not those who reject it or, as some have
> said, those who refrain out of reverence or humility (for the first should not only
> be separated, but excommunicated as heretics; the second type will be worthy of
> forgiveness for the sake of reverence and fear before the holy), but those who be-
> cause of their pride and contempt leave the Church before holy communion and
> do not wait to see the divine communion of the holy mysteries.

The interpretation does not end with this, for the same Balsamon a little further writes:

> And in as much as some say: why then doesn't the Ecumenical Patriarch, on the
> holy day of the Resurrection, wait to the end of the liturgy, but instead, rising
> from his seat, leaves, after the Gospel? Then we answer them: because the di-
> vine liturgy in its proper sense takes place after the reading of the Holy Gospel.
> . . . After the Gospel the celebration of the most pure bloodless sacrifice begins,
> and for this reason the Patriarch is correct when he leaves before this and after
> the Holy Gospel, and he does not transgress the canons. In such a manner no
> one transgresses if he leaves either before or after the Gospel, provided, of
> course that he does so out of necessity or because of a pious and unobjection-
> able reason.

In another example, Canon Nine of the Council *in Trullo* forbids a cleric to operate a tavern (*kapelikon*). After the Council *in Trullo* there arose a custom in
Byzantium of permitting a cleric to own a tavern under the condition he does
not personally operate it. In this connection Zonaras writes, "If a cleric owns
such an establishment (a tavern), and rents it out to another, then he will not be
subject to harm regarding his calling." Balsamon even more specifically writes,
"The present canon determines that a cleric should not have a tavern; i.e., he
should not be engaged in tavern trade; for if he has a tavern as a landlord and
rents it to others, there is nothing new in this, since this is done by monasteries

and various churches. Therefore read in the place of *energein* ("to act," "to work") the word *ekhein* ("to have").

In connection with such customs the words of Cyprian are brought to mind: *"non quia aliquando erratum est, ideo semper errandum est"*—"mistakes should not be committed under the pretext that they had been committed in the past" (Ep. 73, 22).[3] The true meaning of the Church's decrees is forgotten or distorted, and their place is taken by customs having no foundation in the Church's canons! The historical perspective is lost, and the appearance of a custom is associated with the ancient past, blessed by the works of the Fathers of the Church or the ecumenical councils. A false tradition is created that destroys the divine-human nature of the Church because the Church's life is led away from its dogmatic foundations. The inertia of this false tradition can be overcome only by a renewal of creative canonicity.

## VI

As we have seen, Orthodox teaching recognizes in principle the alterability of canonical decrees. It would be more exact to say that the Church demands a creative attitude toward contemporary life. The Church examines contemporary life as a theme and as material for its creativity. For this reason the doctrine of the immutability of the canons, which we often come across at the present time, represents a rejection of creative activity and creative attitude toward contemporary life. Nonetheless, it is impossible to avoid the historical situation in which one lives, since the modem life itself enters the Church, and if a creative attitude toward it is lacking, a passive acceptance of it is inevitable; there will simply be an adjustment to it, and passive adjustment is always detrimental to church life.

Moreover, the doctrine of the immutability of canons amounts to applying all existing decrees to any form of the Church's historical life. This inaccurate doctrine is usually derived from the premise of the "divine" character of the canons, an essentially correct premise. However, it heads in practice to an assertion of *human* will instead of the divine-human will in the Church. The divinely inspired character of the canonical decrees is defined by their being an expression of the Church's will, which is directed in such a way that the life of the Church under given conditions would correspond to its dogmatic teachings. The attempt to apply the Church's decrees when the conditions for which they were published no longer exist will bring about the opposite result, and for this reason such an effort will become an expression of the human will instead of the divine-human will. No one doubts the divinely inspired character of the canonical directions given by the apostle Paul in his first epistle to the Corinthians; nevertheless, if we tried to apply these directions and to resurrect artificially such institutions as the prophets, the apostles, the gift of languages, the gift of interpreting, etc., we would produce the greatest possible distortions in contemporary church life. To return to the first centuries of Christianity in the life of the Church is to reject history. The concern of the Church lies not behind her in the past centuries, but in the present and ahead in the future.

The true understanding of tradition consists not in a mechanical repetition of the past, but in the principle of the uninterrupted flow of life and creativity, in the undiminished grace that abides in the Church. In themselves, the spirit of canonical decrees lies in this true tradition. Decrees serve "for the salvation and the advancement of the people." Collections of canonical decrees have existed and will continue to exist, but the first canon, a most important and fundamental one, will always be lacking in them. It will be lacking because it is found in tradition, and in this canon is contained the understanding of canonical tradition. This canon tells us that canonical decrees are canonical only when they achieve that for which they were intended: to serve as a canonical expression of the dogmatic teachings in the historical forms of the Church's existence.

It is rare to find a moment in Church history that so persistently demands a creative attitude toward contemporary life as the present time. The familiar historical conditions of church life that were established and crystallized over the centuries are now being fundamentally changed. The new is in no way similar to the old. The conscience of the Church cannot accept the thought of a mechanical adaptation to modern life, since that would constitute a defeat by modern life. Out of her depths and her essence the Church is creatively searching to discover those forms of historical existence in which the dogmatic teachings could be most fully expressed. These new forms of historical life require creative canonical work. The Church cannot live only by the existing canon law, which is in reality the law of the Byzantine Church supplemented by the decrees of local churches. The Church has the right to accomplish creative canonical work at all times, not just in a restricted period of time.

No matter how open to criticism this activity may be, it is nevertheless impossible to avoid it. All creativity is threatened with the possibility of error. If in the past there were errors in the doctrinal rulings of some councils, they are all the more possible in the realm of canons. These errors occur when the decrees do not draw church life together with its doctrine, but rather separate doctrine from life. The sources of such errors lie in man's will, which often errs and accepts falsehoods for truths, and sometimes even contradicts the Church's will. *Jus humanum* infiltrates the Church as an interpretation of this historical existence. The wider the realm of *jus humanum* in the Church, the coarser the historical forms of the Church's existence become, and the more difficult it becomes for the essence of the Church to pierce through the historical fabric. The law of man, by penetrating into the Church, tends to transform the Church from a divine-human organism full of grace into a legal institution. A well-known stage of development, ecclesiastical institutionalism, threatens church life with obvious distortions, since it threatens to suppress the Church's life in grace.

The sins of the historical Church are found in this realm. It is enough to re-call the system of coercion that was borrowed from secular life by canon law: forced imprisonment in monasteries; prisons for the clergy in the residences of bishops; the system of ransom in the penitential discipline; the "founders' rights," both in their entirety and in their various distortions, which led to the transformation of churches and monasteries into objects of sale, exchange, in-heritance or gifts; the idiorhythmic monasteries with their brotherhoods, which transformed them into credit institutions. But there is no need to multiply such examples, for no matter how serious the distortions of the spirit of canonical de-crees, they were not capable, nor will they ever be capable, of suppressing the Church's life in grace. "The gates of hell shall not prevail against her" (Mt 16:18). Church life slowly and constantly sweeps away those decrees that are unnatural to it and corrects the distortions that they introduce into the reality of the Church.

However, errors in canon law are in the main—if not exclusively—a result not of creativity, but are on the contrary a decline of creativity, an extinguishing of the Spirit, the pale inactivity of death. During the creative epochs there was, as there always will be, enough strength in the Church to confront error with truth. Mistakes can be avoided only through a clear and correct canonical con-sciousness and under the condition that canonical creativity always remains full of grace in the Church. It is impossible to protect ourselves from error by re-fusing to be creative, since the very rejection is a yet greater error and a viola-tion of the divine-human will, and also because it opens up greater opportuni-ties for the operation of *jus humanum* in the Church. Only the Church and her blessed powers are capable of protecting herself from the errors of creativity—*ubi ecclesia, ibi et Spiritus Dei* ("Where the Church is, there is the Spirit of God"[4])—and the Comforter, the Holy Spirit "will teach you everything and re-mind you of all that He said" (Jn 14:26).

## VII

The temporal as an expression of the eternal, the alterable as an expression of the unalterable—of such an order are the interrelations of the temporal and eternal in canon law; such is it in the Church herself, in which the temporal and eternal are joined, so that if one absolutizes the temporal and alterable, the eternal and unal-terable themselves become relative. This joining springs from the very essence of the Church as a living divine-human organism. Life is in the Church herself, and she herself abides in life, in the "world," and she cannot go out of the world in so far as empirical nature is present in her. Thus the Church faces not the desert, but the world in which she has creative and constructive concerns. The Church cre-atively seeks, in the historical conditions of her existence, those forms of life in which she could more perfectly express her essence, and by this the Church acquires the ability to influence contemporary reality. A creative influence on life does not signify the acceptance of this life, for this life itself often rejects the Church. But whether she is rejected or accepted, the Church brings her light and judgment into the world by continuously changing the historical forms of her existence. Being in the world, she convinces the world "of sin and of righteousness and of judgment" (Jn 16:8).

The inalterability and indestructibility of the Church lies in the immutability of her *life* that cannot be overcome by the world. The more terrifying the present is and the more gloomy the future, the stronger the rock of the Church becomes and the more steadfastly we stand on it.

Through her historical forms of existence the Church not only exists in history, but history, too, abides in the Church. In the Church and through the Church the historical process acquires its purpose: it strives for the last extreme goal, to its concluding point. In paraphrase of the words of one German Protestant scholar, it must be said that "all Christian history to the present day, its internal real history, rests on the awaiting of the *Parousia*, Christ's second and glorious coming." The Church is striving forward and constantly awaiting this Coming, for which she unceasingly sighs, "Amen. Come, Lord Jesus!"

## NOTES

1. See the author's article "Canons and Canonical Consciousnes," *Put'* (1933), translated by Alvian Smirensky at www.holy-trinity.org (accessed May 2003).

2. St. Irenaeus of Lyons, *Against Heresies, Ancient Christian Writers*, volumes 43, 44, 46, 47, translated by G. W. Clark (Mahwah, N.J.: Paulist Press, 1984, 1986, 1988) 3:24:1.

3. *The Letter of St. Cyprian of Carthage, Ancient Christian Writers*, volumes 43, 44, 46, 47, translated by G. W. Clark (Mahwah, N.J.: Paulist Press, 1984, 1986, 1988).

4. St. Irenaeus, *Against Heresies*, 3: 24, 1.

# THE EUCHARIST: THE PRINCIPAL LINK BETWEEN THE CATHOLICS AND THE ORTHODOX

*In this very brief essay, Nicolas Afanasiev puts forward the simple and aston-ishing truth also realized by Sergius Bulgakov, Anton Kartashev, and others—that for all the division and antagonism, the Holy Spirit, in wisdom, has kept many authentic points of unity for Christians. Perhaps the central one is the continuing sacrament of both the Incarnation and Resurrection of Christ, the eucharistic presence of the Lord in the bread and cup.*

At this moment much is being written and said about the differences between the Catholic Church and the Orthodox Church. In general, this is being done not for polemical purposes but in order to prepare the stage for the future re-union of the churches. Perhaps in the very near future an official dialogue will be started between the Catholic Church and the Orthodox Church. In this con-text does it not seem strange that no one is discussing what will actually reunite the two Churches? This silence is not accidental, and reveals a certain ecclesi-ological attitude. We speak of the separation of the churches, but this expres-sion does not correspond to our ecclesiological conceptions. According to nearly general opinion, both from the catholic as well as the orthodox sides, it has nothing to do with a separation of the churches but a "detachment" of one part of the Church from the one, apostolic Church. The part that is "detached" in reality falls into an ecclesiological void. It is true that actually the rigor of such a point of view is, as far as one can see, lessened. In any case we see such

First published in *Irénikon* 3 (1965): 337–39. Translated by Michael Plekon.

a tendency to play down this rigor very much in evidence, a tendency that has received the approval of Vatican II.[1]

I propose in this brief article to show that the links between the catholic church and the orthodox church were never entirely broken and continue to exist until the present. The essential link between us is the Eucharist. Despite our division, despite the struggles that sometimes took on a very pointed character, we never denied among each other the validity of the Eucharist and consequently, the validity of the priesthood that is included in the Eucharist. This fact is extremely important in itself, but demands some explanation of its ecclesiological meaning.

The Eucharist was instituted by Christ during the Holy Supper. However, the Holy Supper itself was not yet the Eucharist, for Christ, who celebrated it in breaking the bread and blessing the cup, had not yet himself been "raised up" upon the cross, had not yet been glorified, and the Spirit had not yet descended upon the disciples. There would be a Eucharist after the passion, the sacrifice of Golgotha, the resurrection, the glorification of Christ when Christ's disciples came to celebrate this, according to his commandment, in the breaking of the bread and blessing of the cup.

Thus, the Holy Supper had not been the Eucharist, but the Eucharist is not a repetition of the Holy Supper that was accomplished "once and for all" (*ephapax*), and could not be accomplished anew. Nevertheless, then Eucharist is a prolongation of the Supper seen in a particular way: it is an ecclesiological Holy Supper accomplished by the Church. This is why the Eucharist implies not only the Holy Supper but also Golgotha, the resurrection, the glorification, and Pentecost. The first Eucharist, celebrated by the apostle Peter in Jerusalem, already was such an ecclesiological Holy Supper. The bread broken by the apostle Peter was the same bread that Christ had broken, and the cup blessed by him was the same that had been blessed by Christ. And this would be the same in all of the Eucharists that would be celebrated "until he comes." Just as during the Holy Supper he was present in the midst of his disciples, he is also present with us when we celebrate the Eucharist—but in a very particular way. He remains with us in the eucharistic gifts, which are the Body and the Blood of Christ through which we become his Body.[2]

From its very nature the Eucharist is one in time and space and cannot be divided because the Body of Christ is indivisible. The Eucharist, celebrated no matter where or when, always remain the same. The plurality of the celebrations of the Eucharist do not take away its unity even as the plurality of the local churches does not abolish the unity of the Church of God. In ecclesiology, unity and plurality are not mutually exclusive, but on the contrary, complement each other. When we take part in a eucharistic assembly we are united with all those who at that moment also participate in a eucharistic assembly—not only the assemblies of the orthodox church but also those of the catholic church as well, for always and everywhere one and the same Eucharist is celebrated:

Christ is "the same yesterday, today and forever."[3] This is why the Eucharist is not only a link between the catholic church and the orthodox church, but also the manifestation of the unity of the churches.

In our time the majority of Christians are deeply and painfully aware of the tragedy of the separation of the churches. Yes, it is our tragedy, a consequence of our sin. However, it is not necessary to exaggerate the importance of this tragedy, and above all, it is not necessary that this feeling become despair. It is necessary to recall that our separation, even if provoked by dogmatic differences, nevertheless has a canonical character. This separation always remains but on the surface of ecclesial life and never extends to its depths. Our canonical division (provoked by dogmatic differences), a division that in turn has given rise to even more profound dogmatic differences, has despite all of this never entirely broken our eucharistic unity. Although this unity does not find concrete expression for reasons of canonical order, we are not able to transform in reality our ecclesiological *koinonia*, our fellowship. It is even sadder still to have to say that because of our division, certain differences have appeared in the doctrine of the Eucharist and in liturgical practice. But again, these divergences do not impinge upon the very essence of the Eucharist, for we both celebrate the one and the same ecclesiological Holy Supper of Christ according to his command, "Do this in remembrance of me."

## NOTES

1. See my study, "Una sancta," *Irénikon* 4 (1963).
2. See my article, "Le Sacrement de l'Assemblée," *Internationale Kirchliche Zeitschrift* 4 (1956).
3. Again, see "Una sancta."

*Sergius Bulgakov (1871–1944), called by some the "Russian Origen," had a life and reputation not unlike the greatest theologian of the early church. The son of a priest, he attended seminary and, as he later put it, lost his faith in the rigid, lifeless theology taught there. A brilliant career in political economy brought him to professorships at the universities in Kiev and Moscow. His deepening criticism of Marxist theory, while nominally a Socialist, eventually led to his disillusionment with this secular form of salvation. He returned to the Christian faith after a series of realizations—conversion moments recorded in his memoirs. A delegate to the Great Council of Moscow in 1917–1918, he worked with Patriarch, now Saint, Tikhon (Bellavin) for renewal in many aspects of the Russian church's life. In the midst of the Revolution he was ordained a priest, began teaching theology, and in 1922, along with Berdiaev and many other intellectuals, was forced to leave the USSR. After a brief stint of teaching in Prague, he came to Paris, and from the founding of the St. Sergius Institute in 1925 until his own death in 1944, was its first dean and professor of dogmatics. He worked with the Russian Christian Students Association, with Orthodox Action, helped found the Fellowship of Sts. Alban and Sergius, and participated in several Faith and Order conferences at Lausanne, Oxford, and Edinburgh. It would not be inaccurate to identify him as one of the founders of the modern ecumenical movement. At the same time he produced an enormous authorship of amazing range and creativity. In the effort to speak positively of the Incarnation, the "humanity of God," rather than use the Council of Chalcedon's negative language, he sought to show how fidelity to the tradition of the Church meant not stale repetition of the Fathers' thinking but continuance of their*

*search for the truth as the world and culture around them developed. His ef-
forts to describe the relationship between God and creation in terms of the figure of divine wisdom, or Sophia, earned for him criticism by fellow theologian
Fr. Georges Florovsky and condemnation by younger theologian Vladimir
Lossky, who acted as prosecutor of his erroneous views in reporting Fr. Bulgakov to the Moscow Patriarchate. However he was never found guilty of
heresy, and was revered for his preaching, his pastoral care, and his moving celebration of the Liturgy. Along with Berdiaev, he contributed to the famous anthology of the intellectuals of 1909, Vehki (Signposts), and edited the journal
Put'. He was influenced by his close friend, the gifted polymath Fr. Paul Florensky, but his theological work was shaped by his devotion to the Liturgy, the
Eucharist, and the ongoing miracle of the Incarnation. Plunged into a coma by
a stroke in 1944, he lingered for several weeks, during which those caring for
him saw light radiating from his dying body. At his funeral Metropolitan Evlogy called him a sage and teacher of the church. His student, Fr. Schmemann,
despite criticism of his academic style, saw him as a prophet and guide to the
realm on high.*

*The two selections here reveal Fr. Bulgakov's passion for the Church's unity
and for her openness to the world. The first, "By Jacob's Well" was published in*
The Journal of the Fellowship of Sts. Alban and Sergius, *and expresses his conviction that despite the historical reality of division between East and West in
the churches, many real unities remain thanks to the goodness of God. His colleague, the historian Anton Kartashev, pursued the consequences of this in an
essay in the Fellowship journal, renamed* Sobornost, *included here. Later, Fr.
Nicolas Afanasiev would further develop the significance of the East and West
still being churches, both in his book* The Church of the Holy Spirit *and in the
essay included in this collection, "Una sancta." This understanding is rooted, as
Afanasiev points out, in the actions of church fathers such as Basil the Great toward groups that had been cut off from the greater church. The second selection is Fr. Bulgakov's contribution to the* Living Tradition *collection of 1937. In
the essay "Dogma and Dogmatics," he reflects upon what keeps the Church's
tradition alive—the work of God and the creative efforts of future generations
of believers. Fidelity to the "mind of the fathers" is to do what they did, to connect the truth of the faith with the reality of one's time.*

## FOR FURTHER READING

Arjakovsky, Antoine. *La Generation des Penseurs Religieux de l'emigration russe: La
    Voie (Put') 1925–1940.* Kiev/Paris: L'Esprit et la Lettre, 2002.
Bobrinskoy, Boris. "Le père Serge Boulgakov, visionnaire de la Sagesse," *Supplément au
    SOP* 196 (March 1995).
Bulgakov, Sergius. *Apocatastasis and Transfiguration.* Translated by Boris Jakim. New
    Haven, Conn.: The Variable Press, 1995.

———. *The Bride of the Lamb*. Translated by Boris Jakim. Grand Rapids, Mich.: Eerdmans, 2001.

———. *The Friend of the Bridegroom*. Translated by Boris Jakim. Grand Rapids, Mich.: Eerdmans, 2003.

———. *The Orthodox Church*. Revised edition. Translated by Lydia Kesich. Crestwood, N.Y.: SVSP, 1988.

———. *Social Teaching in Modern Russian Orthodox Theology*. Translated by Boris Jakim. New Haven, Conn.: The Variable Press, 1995.

———. *Sophia, the Wisdom of God*. Translated by Patrick Thompson, O. Fielding Clark, and Xenia Brakevich. Hudson, N.Y.: Lindisfarne Press, 1993.

———. *La lumière sans déclin*. Translated by Constantine Andronikov. Paris: L'Age d'Homme, 1990.

Gallaher, Anastassy Brandon, "Bulgakov's Ecumenical Thought, Part I." In "Bulgakov and Interocommunion, Part II," *Sobornost* 24: 1 (2002): 24–55; 24: 2 (2002): 9–28.

*Le messager orthodoxe* 57 (1971).

*Le messager orthodoxe* 98 (1985).

Plekon, Michael. "Sergius Bulgakov: Political Economist and Priest, Marxist and Mystic." In *Living Icons*, pp. 29–58. Notre Dame, Ind.: University of Notre Dame Press, 2002.

Schmemann, Alexander. "Trois Images," *Le messager orthodoxe* 1: 57 (1972).

Valliere, Paul. *Modern Russian Theology: Bulcharev, Solovieo, Bulgakov*. Grand Rapids, Mich.: William B. Eerdmans Publishing Company.

Williams, Rowan. *Sergii Bulgakov: Towards a Russian Political Theology*. Edinburgh: T&T Clark, 1999.

Zernov, Nicolas, and James Pain, eds. and trans.. *A Bulgakov Anthology*. Philadelphia: Westminster, 1976.

# BY JACOB'S WELL

An article on the actual unity of the apparently divided Church: in prayer, faith, and sacrament (John 4:23).

The language of the New Testament frequently contains the term "the Church" or "the Churches." On the one hand there is the mystical unity of the Church as the Body of Christ, on the other hand there are the specific communities in which such life was realized. We still use the same terms, not only in the above-mentioned sense but also in that of different Christian confessions. We must admit that such a use of the word "Churches" often shocks us, for in our own minds, for example, we often think that actually there exists only one Church, namely the Orthodox Church—whereas all that stands outside Orthodoxy is not the Church. But the evidence of the use of language cannot be explained away by mere civility or hypocrisy, for it contains a concept that a sort of these "non-Churches" belongs to "the Church." For actually these Churches are distinct to us from the non-Christian world. Already in the Gospel narrative we trace this relativeness in connection with the idea of the Church. Our Lord, who came not to destroy the law but to fulfill it, belonged himself to the Jewish Church. He was a faithful Israelite carrying out its precepts, and this in spite of all its exclusiveness. And yet we get a solemn witness about the Church universal in our Lord's conversation with the Samaritan woman by Jacob's well. We are equally struck here both by the very fact that this conversation (which so astonished the disciples) took place, and

First published in English in *The Journal of the Fellowship of St. Alban and St. Sergius*, no. 22 (1933), 7–17.

by the universal "good news" of Our Lord's message: "Believe Me, the hour is
coming when you will worship the Father neither on this mountain nor in
Jerusalem . . . but the hour is coming, indeed is already here, when true worship-
pers shall worship the Father in spirit and in truth: that is the kind of worshipper
the Father seeks" (Jn 4:21, 23). And he then reveals to her, a Samaritan, that he is
the Christ.

All the events in the life of Our Lord have not only a temporary but also an
eternal significance, and this is also true of this conversation with the Samaritan woman. For even at the present time we find that we stand by Jacob's well
and also ask Jesus Christ about where and how we must worship the Lord. And
even now we, who are the "Jews," know what we worship "for salvation is from
the Jews" (*Nulla salus extra ecclasiam*—"Outside the Church there is no salvation"). And in our day also our Lord reveals himself to the Samaritan woman
and calls on all to worship in spirit and in truth. The harsh, unbending, unre-
lenting institutionalism of the one saving Church conflicts here with a service
in the Spirit, which "blows where it pleases, and you can hear the sound, but
you cannot tell where it comes from or where it is going" (Jn 3:8). There exists
between the Church and the Churches not only a relationship of mutual expulsion but also one of concordance. This unity is simultaneously something already given and something we must attain to. No single historical church can
so confine its attention to itself alone as to ignore the Christian world beyond
its own limits. Even heresies and schisms are manifestations taking place only
within the life of the Church—for pagans and men of other faiths are not
heretics and schismatics to us. One can picture differently the ways to Church
unity, but its very existence already assumes the fact of actual unity. The Church
is one, as life in Christ by the Holy Spirit is one. Only, participation in this unity
can be of varying degrees and depths.

Therefore, quite naturally, there are two aspects in the relation of Orthodoxy
to non-Orthodoxy: a repulsion in the struggle of truth with an incomplete truth,
and a mutual attraction of Church love. History and a sad realism apprehend
more of the former aspect of this relationship, for the spirit of schism and division is not only a characteristic of "heretics" and "schismatics." The will for division is the evil genius that first split up the West and the East, and which ever
since pursues its devastating work further and further.

But can the realization of the truth of our Church be silenced even for a moment, or conversely, can we ever fail to be aware of the untruth of those who
think differently? Might not such an attitude result in the sin of lack of faith,
which seeks to avoid confessing its own truth and perhaps suffering for it? And
so in repulsion and attraction, unity and division, we see a peculiar dialectic of
church life, which comprises the thesis and the antithesis, and we observe that
the greater the exertion of the one, the acuter the other. The way of "ecumenical" church life, which strived for Church unity, is simultaneously associated both with a fuller realization of confessional differences and a growing

consciousness of unity. But although there seems to be no escape from this antinomy, the Spirit of God actually transcends it through a new kind of synthesis that is brought about, not by means of a new agreement or compromise, but
by a new inspiration. The distinction between various confessions lies first of
all in dogmatic differences, and then in the religious and practical discrepan-
cies that result from them. These are on the surface and are apparent to all.
But that which constitutes Church unity (that which is already given), and the
striving toward unity (which actually exists as the basis of unity)—this is hidden in the very depths. Meanwhile this task is a duty both of Church love and
of practical utility. One must realize and express the positive spiritual basis of
Christian "ecumenism" not only as an idea but also as an actuality existing by
grace. We experience it as a breathing of God's Spirit in grace, as a revelation
of Pentecost, when people begin to understand one another in spite of the diversity of tongues.

Let us try to express quite concisely this positive basis of unity, which actually exists even now in the Christian world.

## PRAYER

The division that occurred in the Church, whatever its origin, was associated
with a separation in prayer and remains as an unhealed wound in the Body of
the Church. Such is the logic of our frail nature, which cannot contain the entire truth, but only parts of it. Dissociation in prayer, having once arisen, strives
to become permanent, lasting, and constant. We are now faced by the strange
and provoking sight of Christians praying to God and their Savior, our Lord Jesus Christ, in separate communities. Moreover, this division is enforced in the
rules of the Church, which arose, it is true, in the fourth and fifth centuries, but
which retain even now the force of actual law. They have not been cancelled
formally, although life itself cancels them. The general purpose of these rules
in the first place was of course to banish "indifference" by applying protective
measures, which were then in accord with the acute struggle with heresy. But
measures of defense lose their significance when there is no attacking party—
and we see this state of affairs in a whole range of interconfessional relationships in our own time. We are bound to recognize not only that which separates
us, but also that which remains common to us all, notwithstanding all divisions.
The ability to distinguish in life all that constitutes the common heritage of the
whole Christian world is the great achievement (only possible through grace) of
contemporary "ecumenism," namely the movement striving for Church unity.
An encounter between Christians of different confessions, as Christians, is a
great joy that is bestowed on us in our time by the Holy Spirit and a new revelation of the universal Pentecost. Nothing is easier to criticize than this "pan-
Christianity" by pointing out that there can exist no "Christianity in general,"

but only one true Church in its indestructible concreteness and wholeness. This is true, no doubt, in the sense that the fullness of worship in an ordained and divinely inspired cult can only exist in unanimity. But even so there still remains Christianity as such—as faith in our Lord, love for him, and worship directed to him—and this Christianity endures not only in Orthodoxy but as something common to all confessions. We are particularly clear about this and aware of it in missionary work where Christians are compelled, when confronted by pagans, to get a fuller and deeper consciousness of their own Christianity.

The united prayer of Christians, belonging to different confessions, in Churches and outside them, is becoming a more and more usual occurrence at the present time. This new practice is not merely a liberty that is quite out of place where strict discipline is exercised, but a common Christian achievement, a capacity for uniting in that which is an actual reality. A time will dawn when the Orthodox Church will define certain rules for this practice and will give the required directions. Meanwhile all this is done in a groping manner, as circumstances demand. This united common prayer can be based dogmatically on the fact that the name of our Lord is hallowed and called on by all Christians. Christ is present in his name to each one who prays thus, "For where two or three meet in My Name, I am there among them" (Mt 18:20). In truth all Christians who call on Christ's name in prayer are already actually one with Christ; when we lift our eyes to heaven, earthly barriers cease to exist for us.

But is this actually so? Do these barriers remain even in our union in prayer? Yes, in a certain sense they remain. For we cannot unite in everything with our brethren in prayer. For example, we cannot pray together to the blessed Virgin and to the saints with Protestants. We can find differences in worship even with Roman Catholics, although these differences may not be so essential. But we are not compelled to be silent about these differences, and, if so, is this not treason to Orthodoxy? We must not close our eyes to the fact that such dangers, generally speaking, do exist. The position of Orthodoxy in its relation to the Protestant world is especially unfavorable in this case, precisely because Orthodoxy, for the sake of communion in prayer, is forced to adapt itself by, as it were, minimizing itself, and thereby losing some of its fullness. Of course, if this is done out of love for the sake of Church "economy" it is permissible, for it is then regarded as a sacrifice of love, in accordance with the apostle Paul's principle of being "all things to all men." Our brethren, however, should realize that this is only a sacrifice of love and a condescension to their weakness, not a denial of our own faith.

However, in communion in worship with the non-Orthodox we must "know our measure" so that no distortions or poverty may result in our prayer life. But there is also a positive side to this communion in prayer. We are wont to pride ourselves on our liturgical wealth, as compared to the severe and simple rites of the Protestants. And yet we must not close our eyes to the fact that, in actual practice, we are far from realizing to the full this wealth of ours, so that in some instances it lies upon us as a dead weight of custom. Protestantism, in spite of its apparent liturgical poverty, knows a living extempore prayer, in which the human soul in a childlike way turns directly to our Father in heaven. This is the wealth of Protestantism even though it is associated with liturgical poverty.

## THE WORD OF GOD

The Holy Gospels are the common property of the entire Christian world. Through the Gospels Christ himself speaks directly to the human soul. The soul listens to him and adores him in worship. Generally, in our attitude to the non-Orthodox, we underestimate the power of the Gospels. The four Gospels give us a marvelous icon of our Savior, drawn by the Holy Spirit of God—a veritable icon in words. When the Eternal Book is studied not only by the mind but also with the heart, when the soul "bows down over the Gospels," then the sacrament of the Word, born in that soul, is celebrated.

People incline to minimize this direct impact of the Word of God (*effiacitas verbi*—"efficaciousness of the Word"), addressed to every single soul, stressing in an exaggerated way the significance of holy tradition for its correct understanding. In practice the significance of holy tradition for a living response to the Word of God should not be exaggerated. It has bearing on theology and on certain disputed questions of a dogmatic nature. One might add here that the importance of tradition does not in any way exclude, but actually presupposes, a direct response to the Word of God, which has its life in the Church—both in its *soborny* (Catholic, communal) consciousness (tradition), and in personal interpretation. And what is especially important is the fact that nothing can replace our personal life with the Gospel (the same applies to the whole Bible). We should be ready to admit the fact that among Orthodox nations the personal reading of the Word of God is considerably less widespread than it is among Protestants, though this is partly replaced by its use in divine worship. The Bible and the Gospels are common Christian property, and the entire Christian world without distinction of confession bends in prayer over the Gospels. It may be urged that a true understanding of the Gospels is only given to the Church. This is, of course, the case in one sense, yet sincere and devout readers of the Gospels through this alone are already within the Church—that is, in the one and Evangelical Church.

## THE SPIRITUAL LIFE

A Christian who lives in the Church necessarily has also his personal life in Christ, which is simultaneously both personal and "of the Church." Dogma and dogmatic peculiarities cannot fail to be reflected in this personal experience. But in the absence of Christological differences there is a very wide field of common faith, even where dogmatic divergences actually do exist. For can one say that "Christ is divided" for a contemporary Orthodox, Roman Catholic, or believing Protestant? In their love of our Lord and their striving toward him, all Christians are one. This is why the language of the mystics and their experience is common to all. We find that spiritual life, in which the divine is really tasted, unites Christians to a far greater extent than does dogmatic perception. When we sense these tremulous contacts our souls respond to them independently of confessional relationships. It may be that this is the most important result of interrelations of various confessions, which though not reflected in formulae and resolutions, represent a spiritual reality. During the Lausanne Conference this feeling of a kind of common spiritual experience of unity in Christ was remarkably strong. It became clear to all that something had happened above and beyond anything written down in the reports and minutes. On the other hand, apart from this kind of experience as such, there cannot be any Christian unity; for this can only be realized through Christian inspiration in a new vision of Pentecost, for which we aspire and which, in part, we already obtain. This unity in Christ, established by the similarity of Christian experience, is a kind of spiritual communion of all in the one Christ, established long before Communion from the same chalice can take place. This de facto similarity in the experience of the Christian world, in spite of all its multiplicity, is insufficiently realized. Unfortunately, we tend to stress our dogmatic disagreements much more than our common Christian heritage. A mystical intercommunion has always existed among Christians, and in our days more so than previously. Mutual fellowship among the representatives of theological thought, an interchange of ideas, scientific and theological research, a kind of life in common "over the Gospel"— all this tends to make the existing division between Christian confessions already to a certain extent unreal. Symbolic theology is also tending more and more to become "comparative" instead of being "denunciatory." This is even more evident when we come to mystical, pastoral, and ascetic works, and especially to the lives of the saints. With what attention and devotion the Western world (for example Anglicanism) gazes at the images of the Russian saints, or conversely, with what interest we ourselves regard the images of the Western saints, such as St. Genevieve, St. Francis of Assisi, and others. And we ought to cultivate deliberately this spiritual interpenetration, which is naturally increasing more and more. In this way we shall appropriate to ourselves the gifts that have been bestowed on others, and through comparison we shall come to know our own nature more fully and deeply.

Thus there exists even now a certain spiritual unity within the Christian world, although this is not expressed in any formulae. But we should add to this mystical, adogmatic unity of the Christian world the reality of its dogmatic oneness. Owing to certain one-sidedness, Christians of various confessions are acutely sensitive to their dogmatic differences, while they do not feel their mutual agreement in the same way. The definition "heretic," which is really only applicable to certain features of a world outlook, is extended to the entire man, who is completely anathematized for a particular heresy. This was so throughout the course of Christian history. But it would be absolutely inconsistent for us to adopt such language today. For it is time at last to say openly that there exist no heretics in the general sense of the term, but only in a special and particular sense. Such an interpretation, among many others, can be given to the words of the apostle Paul: "It is no bad thing either that there should be differing groups among you" (1 Cor 11:19). Of course, in itself, a special heresy stands also for a common affliction, which is detrimental to the spiritual life without, however, destroying it. And it is perhaps difficult and impossible for us really to define the extent of this damage during the epoch when the particular dogmatic division arose. We must not also lose sight of the fact that in addition to heresies of the mind there exist heresies of life, or one-sidedness. One can, while remaining an Orthodox, actually tend toward Monophysitism in practice, by leaning either toward Docetic spiritualism or Manicheism, or toward Nestorianism by separating the two natures in Christ, which leads in practice to the "secularization" of culture. And perhaps in this sense it will be found that we all are heretics in various ways. Yet it by no means follows from this that Orthodoxy and the Orthodox do not exist. It only shows that heresy, as such, impairs (though it does not destroy) life in Christ and in his Church. The notion of a heresy, as of a division, only exists within the limits of the Church and not outside it, and it implies a defectiveness in church life. It is therefore a mistake to interpret dogmatic anathematizing as a spiritual death warrant or a complete severing from the Church. As a measure of discipline, an anathema is a spiritual death warrant for a particular Church community, for it represents a separation from the fellowship of the Church. But this disciplinary measure cannot and must not be extended to the whole life of the Church, for even the heretics remain in the Church, and it is not given to us to know to what degree they are condemned because of their heresy.

From this it follows that if heresy is only partial damage, we must take into account in dealing with heretics not only that which is heretical but also that which is Orthodox in them. For example, through having an incorrect doctrine on the *Filioque*, do Roman Catholics cease to believe in the redemptive work of our Lord, or in the sacraments of the Church? And although this seems obvious, all Christians must yet realize not only their divisions but also their agreement. Our Creed, the Nicene Creed (it is true, in its defective form owing to the *Filioque*), together with the ancient Apostolic and Athanasian Creeds, constitute the general confession of Orthodoxy, Roman Catholicism, and Protestantism, and we must never lose sight of this basis of our dogmatic unity.

## THE SACRAMENTS

At the present time it is in the sacraments that the Christian confessions are most effectively separated from one another. Sacramental fellowship is still only a remote aim, which still remains unaccomplished in the relationships between Orthodoxy, Roman Catholicism, and Protestantism. In the relationship between Orthodoxy and Roman Catholicism on the one hand, and Protestantism on the other, the main barrier is the absence of valid orders and apostolic succession. This barrier does not arise between the first two confessions. Now, in the vast majority of Christian confessions, sacraments are recognized, in spite of all the diversity of theological teaching associated with them. What attitude ought we to adopt toward the efficacy of these sacraments, and in what measure can this or that theological interpretation associated with them be considered decisive? Although the latter can effect the efficacy of sacraments (only, however, from the side of *ex opere operantis*, and not of *ex opere operato*), nevertheless, given the existence of a common faith (say in the Eucharist), the significance of doctrinal diversity in the realm of eucharistic theology may be greatly exaggerated.

We ought to insist first of all, as a general principle, on the efficacy of the sacraments in various Church communities. But can we adopt such a principle as our guiding line? Or are sacraments, generally speaking, ineffective beyond the canonical limits of a Church organization, to be regarded only as devout customs, or according to the blasphemous opinion of some as "sacraments of the demons?" The latter opinion is the child of confessional fanaticism that can never be confirmed by theological arguments, and is on the contrary in direct contradiction to the true mind of the Church. One might also add that a mere recognition of the power of the sacraments outside Orthodoxy is sufficient, for such a reduction of the question merely to that of their subjective effectiveness (*ex opere operantis*) evades a direct answer to the question as to their objective value (*ex opere operato*). It undoubtedly holds that, in the absence of canonical Church fellowship, the sacraments celebrated outside the canonical limits of a given church organization—canonically and practically, as it were—cease to exist. But does this canonical ineffectiveness (*nonefficitas*) imply their mystical invalidity (*nonvaliditas*)? Does it mean that on being separated canonically, and in a certain measure dogmatically also, we find that we are separated from our mysterious unity and fellowship in Christ and in the gifts of the Holy Spirit? Has Christ been really divided in us, or are the non-Orthodox thereby no longer "in Christ," being estranged from his Body? One ought to think deeply before answering this question, which is perhaps the most essential for us in our relations with the non-Orthodox. This question falls into two parts: the significance of canonical divisions and that of dogmatic divisions, in relation to effectiveness of sacraments.

The first question is answered by stating that canonical divisions (*raskol*) only prevent the possibility of a direct and unmediated communion in the sacraments and do not destroy their efficacy. The invisible fellowship therefore of those who have been separated is not broken. This constitutes great joy and consolation when we are faced with the sad and sinful fact of canonical divisions in the Church. We ought to consider that although we are canonically divided from the Roman Catholic Church, we never ceased to remain with it in an invisible sacramental communion (*ex opere operato*, so to speak). Generally speaking, if one wanted to be consistent in denying the efficacy of the sacraments on a canonical basis, one could only do it by accepting the Roman Catholic teaching on the supremacy of the Pope and obedience to his jurisdiction as an essential condition of belonging to the Church. However such a deduction is not made even by the Roman Catholic Church, which admits the effectiveness of sacraments in Orthodoxy. The Romanizing tendency in Orthodoxy sometimes goes further than Rome in this direction, conditioning the effectiveness of the sacrament by canonical stipulations, though theologically such a point of view cannot be supported. Conversely, one could say that the divided parts of the Church, at least where apostolic succession exists, are in an invisible, mysterious communion with one another through visible sacraments, although these are mutually inaccessible.

Now let us consider to what extent a digression from dogmatic teaching can destroy the efficacy of the sacrament. We ought to mention here, first of all, the cases where the damage affects not separate sacraments but their celebrants. We speak here of Protestantism, where, through the destruction of a rightly ordained priesthood through grace, the question of the actual efficacy of the sacrament is raised in spite of its full recognition in principle. Can one speak of "sacraments" in Protestantism? Fortunately there are grounds for answering this question not only in the negative. The basis of the answer lies in the fact that the Orthodox Church recognizes the efficacy of Protestant baptism, which is evident from the fact that it does not re-baptize Protestants who join it. This admission is of extraordinary significance. It testifies to the fact that, at least in regard to the sacrament of spiritual birth in the Church, we abide in fellowship with Protestants as Christians and members of the one Body of Christ. Baptism also contains within itself the general possibility of a mysterious life in the Church; in this sense it is the potential of all future sacraments. In Protestantism there is only a partial existence, both because of the diminution of the number of sacraments, and especially, through the absence of priesthood. But even so, does this allow us to draw any conclusion as to the complete inefficacy of sacramental life in Protestantism, in particular, for example, regarding Holy Communion? Strictly speaking we have no right to come to such a conclusion, and not only because of the subjective basis pointed out by Bishop Theophanes, but also because of the objective principle of a sacrament, according to which the sacrament belongs to the entire Church—although it is realized through the priesthood by virtue of its inevitable participation. There is no such priesthood in Protestantism, but the people of the Church—the "royal priesthood"— remain there, and the potential power of Holy Baptism is fulfilled and revealed there in other ways, in certain devout rites and prayers instead of in effective sacraments. But if these are ineffective, can we say that they are nothing? One cannot say this, for the priesthood is not a magical apparatus for the celebration of sacraments, but a ministration of the Church that exists in the Church and for the Church. Therefore we ought to interpret Theophanes' expression "according to their faith it shall be given them" in the sense that our Lord does not deprive this flock of his grace, although it has been separated from the fullness of Church life. Nevertheless we can speak of communion in sacraments (apart from baptism) in relation to Protestants only in the general and indefinite sense of their participation in the life of the Church through grace, but of nothing beyond this. A more direct and true communion in sacraments with the Protestant world is hindered by the absence of a rightly ordained priesthood: this is the threshold over which Protestantism must pass, the reestablishment of an apostolically ordained hierarchy.

These barriers do not exist, however, for those sections of the divided Church that have retained this succession and have therefore a correctly ordained priesthood. Orthodoxy and Roman Catholicism belong to this category, together with the ancient Eastern Churches (as well as the Episcopal Church in Protestantism and Anglicanism, particularly in the case of a positive solution of the question of Anglican ordination). The priesthoods of Roman Catholicism and Orthodoxy are mutually uncanonical owing to the existing schism, but this does not prevent their mutual recognition of each other. The following conclusion, of the utmost importance, follows from this: Churches that have preserved their priesthood, although they happen to be separated, are not actually divided in their sacramental life. Strictly speaking, a reunion of the Church is not even necessary here, although generally this is hardly realized. The Churches that have preserved such a unity in sacraments are now divided canonically in the sense of jurisdiction, and dogmatically, through a whole range of differences; but these are powerless to destroy the efficacy of the sacraments.

What is required for a complete reunion, and where do we start? The predominant formula runs: sacramental fellowship must be preceded by a preliminary dogmatic agreement. But is this axiom so indisputable as it appears? Here on one scale of the balance we have a difference in certain Christian dogmas and theological opinions, and an estrangement that has been formed through centuries; on the other we have the unity of sacramental life. May it not be that a unity in the sacrament will be the only way toward overcoming this difference? Why should we not seek to surmount a heresy in teaching through superseding a heresy of life, such as division? May it not be that Christians sin now by not heeding the common eucharistic call? And, if this is so, then for Orthodoxy and Rome there still remains a way to their reunion on the basis of a fellowship in sacraments.

Of course, the Holy Spirit alone can make it clear that reunion is not far away. but already exists as a fact that only needs to be realized. But it must be realized sincerely and honestly for the sole purpose of expressing our brotherhood in the Lord. And the way toward the reunion of East and West does not lie through tournaments between the theologians of the East and West, but through a reunion before the altar. The priesthood of the East and the West must realize itself as one priesthood, celebrating the one Eucharist; if the minds of the priests could become aflame with this idea, all barriers would fall. For in response to this, dogmatic unity will be achieved, or rather, a mutual understanding of one another in our distinctive features. *In necessariis unitas, in dubiis libertas, in omnibus caritas*—"In what is necessary unity, in what is of lesser importance freedom, in all things, love."

A realization of our unity as something given, and at the same time, of our disunity as a fact that we cannot ignore is present, is a vital antithesis in the soul of the modern Christian. This antinomy cannot leave him in peace. He cannot remain indifferent to it, for he must seek its resolution. The ecumenical movement of today is the expression of this search.

# DOGMA AND DOGMATIC THEOLOGY

> Therefore every scribe who has been trained for the kingdom of heaven is like a householder who brings out of his treasure what is new and what is old.
>
> —(Mt 13:52)

## I

**D**ogmatic theology is the systematic setting out of dogmas which, taken together, express the fullness of Orthodox teaching. Yet it must be asked whether such a dogmatic inventory can lay claim to comprehensiveness. Do all dogmatic questions have answers in the form of dogmas formulated and voiced by the Church? No. The number of dogmas is limited and, in the case of many, if not the majority, of questions, we are presented only with theological doctrines. Popular opinions in any case are not dogmas but *theologoumena*. Dogmatics is similar to a map of a continent not yet fully explored, where charted regions coexist with the uncharted, and the borderlines are interrupted by pale and uncertain dotted lines. In fact, undisputed dogmas of the Church concern only a very limited number of definitions: the teaching on the Holy Trinity (as found in the Nicene-Constantinopolitan Creed), and mainly those about the God–man (as found in the definitions of the seven ecumenical councils). Even

---

First published in *Zhivoe predanie/Living Tradition*. Paris: YMCA Press, 1937. Translated by Peter Bouteneff.

in the subject of pneumatology we enter the territory of theologoumena (as Bolotov has noted).

In the great majority of areas dealt with in dogmatic theology, we remain on the shaky ground of theological doctrine. These include areas of primary importance, such as the teaching about the world and the human person, about God's will and predestination, about the Church, about grace and the sacraments—notably all the questions concerning eucharistic theology—as well as about history and eschatology. This whole area is left to the discretion of theological doctrine: although presented as Church dogma it cannot pretend to infallibility, precision, or universally binding authority, and in any case allows for different theological opinions. (The boundary of accepted differences in each case is a *questio facti.*)[1]

Dogmatic theology does not stop at the specific dogmas; it is much broader and therefore must inevitably be supplemented from sources other than the clear and obligatory dogmatic definitions. This "supplementing" happens on the basis of the living tradition of the Church, the analysis of dogmas, and the study of doctrines.

In this, therefore, we are dealing with the immediate life of the Church, which includes dogmatic facts of the first importance. These need to be elucidated in all their meaning and opened up in their dogmatic content with the assistance of doctrinal theological explication. In this way they become dogmatic definitions. Here dogma is not so much a given as it is an object of pursuit for the dogmatic theologian. The very foundation of dogma assumes a combination of effort, creative intuition, factual research, and dogmatic construction (i.e., religious philosophy or, more precisely, metaphysics). Dogmatic construction is unavoidable when defining dogmas, as it was a part of the various theological schools and conflicting doctrines and opinions that existed in the era of the ecumenical councils, and continues to exist to this day. For at the heart of dogmatic theology lies dogmatic quest, and therefore the possibility not only of finding but also of not finding.

Yet rivalry and conflicting opinion in dogmatic teaching are balanced in the life of the Church, because preceding these differences, and over and above them, exists the one life of the Church as its prevailing strength: the *lex orandi* in the largest sense is the *lex credendi*. The inexhaustible font of tradition irrigates dogmatic thought and doctrine. Unity in this life of the Church also predetermines unity in theological thought, although the latter always requires a dialectical freedom.

Of course, questions within dogmatic theology can be simplified and practically replaced by schematic formulation of quasi dogmas, which might formally satisfy a scholastic. This is what happens when one sets out broad, catechistic, scientific expositions. In such cases dogmatic theology is often taken for an inventory of dogmas, undistinguished from theological opinions—which are proved by citing church tradition and scripture. In such cases dogmatic theology is understood as something utterly complete and unchanging. It is given a face that is not its own, a scholastic mask, to the fright and revulsion of many. On the other hand, such pragmatic-pedagogical approaches can merit study, and it is appropriate to appreciate with all due respect the positive aspects of such teaching, as did Metropolitan Makarios and his Catholic predecessors. One must always stay mindful that what one is reading is simply a schematic description of something that in truth has yet to be dogmatically crystallized.

In dogmatic theology, therefore, we find dogmas as well as dogmatic facts that have been expressed in previous dogmatic definitions; we also have theological propositions[2] and theologoumena, which have not themselves received definite dogmatic definition. With regard to dogmas proper, the process of determining their ecclesiastically infallible expression is complete. On the other hand, theological propositions or theological opinions are at the stage that corresponds to the time before the ecumenical councils, when there were only theological schools with differing opinions. The challenge of dogmatic theology here consists above all in defining and explicating as precisely as possible these dogmatic facts in the life of the Church. (One example is the veneration of the Mother of God among the Orthodox, for whom the fullness in the practice of Mariology coincides with an absence of dogmatic formulation. The same is the case with the theology of the sacraments.)

It is likewise important to establish that the dogmatic facts of the life of the Church—its *lex orandi*—and the practical *credendi* have not only a significance but a commanding authoritative significance for the theologian. For the theologian they take the place of dogmas, and theological propositions are to be built based on these facts. At the same time, the theologian must inevitably construct them him- or herself, theologizing as responsibly as creatively, for these two are synonymous. Liturgical theology (including iconography, church architecture, liturgical rites, etc.), the living breath of the Church—its prayerful inspiration and revelation—is therefore immensely important for dogmatic theology. This is why the altar and the theologian's cell—his workspace—must be conjoined. The deepest origins of the theologian's inspiration must be nourished from the altar. Yet it is clear that liturgical sources must be subject to comparative-historical study to prevent them from becoming "dead-letter," or equal to the Word of God, which remains unique and incomparable in its authoritative significance.

It is important to show the primary significance that the Word of God has for dogmatic theology. It does not aspire merely to *human* wisdom or "philosophy," but receives its existence from revelation; in this sense the Word of God is the philosophy of revelation. The Word of God is the absolute criterion of theology. Theology cannot include ideas that could not be directly or indirectly confirmed by the Word of God, or contrary to it. The Word of God has an unplumbable depth and an absolute character for us. It is the true revelation of God, which has been understood by human beings in all eras of our existence, through all the history of ideas. This does not mean that the Word of God is some kind of *summa theologiae*, but that it potentially includes a *summa* in itself, as subjects for theology and dogmas, unfolding in human creation. The Word of God in this sense reveals its divine-human character. It does not bind creativity in its free inspiration, but defines it as a given (although a concealed) truth. Of course, the Word of God also exists as such for the Church, and only in the Church's life and its spirit does the Word of God open itself to human beings. The Holy Scriptures must be understood in the light of tradition. The Word of God contains in itself the pure gold of revelation.

## II

Dogmatic theology, if it is to exist in accordance with Church tradition, must take into consideration other landmarks of church history—patristics, historical scholarship, etc.—and do so with constantly broadening horizons. When it comes to the written tradition, the place of primacy is held by the authoritative writers known as the Fathers of the Church. It is universally understood that dogmatic theology has to be "according to the Fathers" and to agree with patristic tradition. But what does this mean?

Before all, we must uphold wholeheartedly the spiritual and theological authoritativeness of the Fathers' writings as monuments of Church tradition. The Fathers are, in a sense, the Church's witness to itself. This leads to a practical challenge for the theologian—to analyze as deeply as possible the contents of the tradition of the Fathers. For this it is necessary to bring in all possible elements of church history and critical textual analysis, which is so richly facilitated by contemporary resources and methodology. On the basis of such research we must firstly establish the actual views of the Church writers, and secondly, understand them in their historical context, their concrete circumstances and historical relativity.

Here it becomes clear to anyone who happens upon patristic writing that even in the realm of one and the same question, there is rarely a single patristic tradition. These often-contradictory (or at least different) opinions therefore force us to make a choice, to give preference to one or the other patristic tradition, as is in fact done. This means that the Holy Fathers' writings in themselves cannot be considered dogmatically infallible. They are authoritative witnesses but they cannot by any means be transformed into unerring texts. In some circles one finds a rabbinic approach to the writings of the Fathers as "tradition." But if in the interpretation of the Talmud it was possible to smooth out and harmonize the sayings of different rabbis, such a methodology is more difficult to apply to patristics, for here several different schools of opinion at times were in contradiction with each other, at times even anathematizing each other (cf., e.g., the Antiochene and Alexandrian Christologies).

At points the Church would make a de facto selection and put its accent on certain ideas of certain writers.

But in general to proclaim the inerrancy of the writings of the Holy Fathers as such is impossible, again, because of the existence of disagreements and even contradictions in their writings. Furthermore, such an approach toward their writings absolutely does not correspond to the specific weight that in reality is attributed to them by the Church itself. Indeed, to claim inerrancy in the works of each Church writer on any topic would truly be a patrological heresy. This heresy did in fact exist in the Middle Ages, and was frequent throughout the twelfth to fifteenth centuries in the East, as well as in the Roman Catholic West. (At the Council of Florence, patristic writings were placed on a par with Scripture by Cardinal Bessarion—and were therefore declared God-inspired.)

Such an approach could be consigned to quaint historic rarity if it were not sometimes evident even today as a leading force in theology. Yet Orthodox theology is not the Talmud, and a real veneration of the Fathers must reverence not the letter but the spirit. The writings of the Holy Fathers must have a guiding authority, yet be applied with discernment. Therefore, firstly, for all of their authoritative character, the writings of the Holy Fathers need to be treated as a criterion of historical relativity, one that has unavoidable limitations. Who in his right mind would take as the teaching of the Church St. John of Damascus on the zodiac, although it is included in his *Exact Exposition of the Orthodox Faith*,[3] or his *Dialectica*, where he simply repeats the teaching of Aristotle? This limitation of the Fathers' writings is much more greatly felt, of course, when it comes to their scriptural exegesis, which was utterly bereft of the modern hermeneutics of textual and historical scholarship. In this area, the Fathers' writings often appear to us simply antiquated, although they retain authoritative meaning in the dogmatic and pedagogical study of the Word of God.

The writings of the Holy Fathers in their dogmatic proclamations must also be understood within their historical context. One must not apply to them a meaning that is not inherent in the nature of the problems they were actually concerned with. One cannot seek in the writings of one period answers to the questions inherent in another. In any case the writings do not possess a universality applicable to all periods in history. The writings of the Fathers are historically conditioned and therefore limited in their meaning. This does not prevent them from having an eternal value insofar as they are woven into the dogmatic conscience of the Church, but it is important to establish that the writings of the Fathers are not the Word of God and cannot be compared to it or made equal to it. In principle, nobody is making such an equation nowadays, as was done before, but in *fact* it does happen, and this approach is harmful when put to ill use. We say this not to diminish the authority of the Fathers of the Church but so that this authority may be taken for what it is. (In fact, one of the dangers of theologizing "according to the Fathers" is a tendency toward patristic exegesis in support of *one's own* particular doctrine, prooftexting from statements put forward—sometimes tendentiously—in the patristic texts.)

The practical conclusion of all this is that the Fathers' writings cannot be accepted blindly as bearing dogmatic authority; they must be analyzed comparatively and critically. We must also add that the authoritative patristic tradition does not have exact boundaries in time and space. The principle that is generally applied is that this authority grows along with the antiquity of the writings—that is, in reverse proportion to their newness. Of course this principle also cannot be applied universally, as in all periods of Church history one meets with writers who sin against the truth, starting with apostolic and post-apostolic times. It is also impossible to delineate the precise era during which the Fathers' writings were the most applicable. We can say rather that in the history of Church writings, different periods emerge during which specific issues are treated (Logos theology, Christology, Trinitarian dogma, etc.), and that then, most importantly, the tradition of authoritative (and in this sense patristic) writing continues and is never-ending.

In other words, each historical period, not excluding our own, participates in the theological inspiration by which the authority of the Fathers' writing is established. We can observe this also in our day when this inspiration is received by churchmen such as Fr. John of Kronstadt, Bishop Theophan [the Recluse], St. Tikhon [of Zadonsk], St. Dimitri of Rostov, as well as by other writers and hierarchs. In other words, patristic writings do not and cannot form a completed canon. The patristic tradition is not locked into some historical frame. It is not only the past but also the present and the future. And if different periods in history have their own problematics and challenges, no one is forgotten by God. The legacy of the Holy Fathers, in spite of its holiness, as well as the necessity of detailed study, cannot be for us a finished task—done before us, completed for us, or achieved in our stead—to be accepted with a passive obedience. To the contrary, it is necessarily a part of *our* task: having this talent, we must not bury it in the earth but multiply it by our own creative efforts. We are convinced of this not of our own whim, but by an absolute necessity, although it is difficult to show this.

The point is that the Fathers' legacy of the past is a mosaic of different parts of history, produced by different historical circumstances. In no way is it comprehensive. On the contrary, it is limited in content and therefore cannot meet the demand for a satisfactory and comprehensive solution to problems that arise in dogmatic thought. It does not even pose a comprehensive list of questions. It is necessary to say clearly that for a whole array of problems that face us powerfully and distressingly nowadays, there is either no patristic tradition or there is an insufficient one. The reason is not that these problems are foreign to the Church, and nonecclesial as such, but simply that the classical patristic era never grappled with these problems. More exactly, it was occupied with other problems that were inherent to it. That is why we must accept that there is no sufficient or clear patristic teaching on many questions (such as pneumatology, sacramentology, and particularly eucharistic theology—the consecration of the holy gifts, the eucharistic offering, grace, and freedom, God's foreknowledge versus predestination and, to a significant degree, history, eschatology, and Christian sociology).

Of course, even on these questions there are definite opinions that possess authority, and which must be taken into consideration and studied. Yet the fact remains that in the classical patristic period, the modern problems that have arisen since the period of the Reformation simply did not exist. And where there is no question there can be no answer.

An honest appraisal of history forces us to admit that up to now Western Reformation and Counter-Reformation theology has been extremely authoritative for Orthodox theology. Alas, the identity of Orthodox theology appears here to a great degree more polemical, more reactive, than positive. Faced by the need to defend itself, patristic tradition occupied itself with heterodox opinions, of which some were accepted and others rejected. This amalgam is characteristic of the main Orthodox faith-teachings of this period (e.g., the "Orthodox Confessions" and the "Encyclical of the Eastern Patriarchs").

This fact once again testifies to the limitation of historic patristic tradition, and therefore the need for its creative continuation. Of course this concerns only theology. The fullness of the Church, its charismatic life, exists forever. But this fullness is sometimes more and sometimes less fulfilled in the history of the Church.

From this it follows that dogmatic theology is broader than patristic tradition. History has seen a misguided naïveté, which demands that all problems be reckoned "according to the Fathers," refusing or being suspicious of any problem that is not present in their writings. If we look at the most creative periods in the history of dogma we will see that each century bears its own problems— new problems compared to those of the past. While one must treat them in such a way that does not break with tradition, one should not cower from their "newness." To be suspicious of new problems and their consequent doctrines, or to forbid them somehow, would mean falling into antihistorical Talmudism and into a kind of patristic heresy.

## III

The absence of some problem or teaching in patristic writings does not make it nonexistent or irrelevant to the Church, as some have thought. This would be the case only if patristic writings were the sole and comprehensive source of Church tradition. But reality has it otherwise. Only the Word of God is such a source, and it itself is revealed in its true meaning in the Church—most importantly in the Church's prayerful and sacramental mystical life. The Church

holds within itself dogmatic revelation, but it requires faithfulness in this revelation. New theological propositions or theologoumena do not appear as mere
human intellectual constructions, but as *witnesses* to the life of the Church.
They are revelation expressed in theology (in the same way as it is expressed in
icons, hymns, rites, and sacraments) from the fullness of Christ. "See to it that
no one makes a prey of you by philosophy and empty deceit, according to human tradition, according to the elemental spirits of the universe, and not according to Christ. For in him the whole fullness of deity dwells bodily" (Col
2:8–9).

Such theologizing "according to human tradition" begins, in fact, around the
period of the Reformation and Counter-Reformation in Orthodox dogmatic theology, when it falls under Western influence. Here it theologizes less according
to the Fathers than according to Tridentine and generally Western theologians;
it maintains the appearance of patristic tradition but is deprived of its real power.
The entire teaching of the Church on grace and on sacraments is camouflaged.
It is not positive but polemical theology, dependent on Western tradition, and
especially on Western problematics. This polemical character of more recent
theology, which is accepted by many (and which only pretends to be patristic),
must be overcome. Within this approach, dogmatic definitions are polemical
both in their origin and content; Orthodoxy is defined as non-Catholic or anti-
Catholic, non-Protestant or anti-Protestant, or finally (even more tempting), as
a Catholicizing anti-Protestantism, or a Protestantizing anti-Catholicism.

We must not reject or diminish the riches of Christian achievements in
Catholic and Protestant theology, which contain real Christian truths. Even less
should we believe that the Orthodox theologian should distance himself from
Western theology. Indeed, it is already a long time since theology has moved
beyond intentional confessionalism, and in some of its aspects theology belongs
to the whole Christian world. This pertains to such disciplines as biblical studies, patristics, church history, archaeology, etc., and only an ignoramus would
shun the contribution of these fields. Still, finding itself in fraternal cooperation
with that of all other Christians, Orthodox theology must remain itself, nourished by the wellspring of truth entrusted to it. This requires renewed theological creativity—we may recall, for example, that the writers of the first millennium appear to be unable to orient us in some areas in the problematics and
life of the second millennium.

It is specifically in polemical ("accusatory") theology that there arises a great
many illusory dogmas or quasi dogmas whose provisional and relative character
is often insufficiently recognized. This false impression is created when dogmatic theology is deliberately given a complete and categorical character, resulting in pseudo-dogmas on every question. In reality a major portion of Orthodox dogmatics needs responsible and serious work. We need the genuine
and living tradition of the Church, untainted by confessional/scholastic preconceptions and subjected to objective study and evaluation. This is the theology

that must find expression and ultimately pave the way for an authoritative ecclesial discernment of dogma.

Unfortunately, we have a whole series of dogmatic preconceptions that are
mistaken for ready dogmas, the main one being that theological opinions expressed in dogmatic language are finalized dogmas of the Church. Here, the
principle of *in necessariis unitas, in dubiis libertas* is negated. Gone is the healthy
mutual tolerance of dogmatic opinions (a tolerance which of course would be absolutely out of place in the case of actual dogmas). In one dogmatic manual, you
have creationism expressed as an Orthodox dogma; in another, traditionism expressed the same way. In one case the Catholic doctrine of transubstantiation is
refuted; in another it is accepted as a sign of true Orthodoxy, and so forth. Such
simplification becomes particularly unbearable in eschatology, where the absence
of genuine dogmatic definitions gives full license to theological prejudices and
fosters the tendency to reject or even fight against research about it.

We still have not attained such dogmatic maturity that we can discern the difference between those fundamental dogmas, which have already been accepted as obligatory and authoritative, and dogmatic doctrine, with all its
changeability and instability. This inability to distinguish prevents the normal
development of theological thought and dogmatic research, which is indispensable to it as to any area of thought. Dogmatic research was a characteristic of
the patristic period: even the Fathers of the Church, before they became such,
were simply theologians seeking the truth.

Thus in dogmatic theology, room must be granted for research and analysis;
that is to say, research into what is truly included in the tradition concerning
this or that question, and the dogmatic working-through of this material into
theological propositions or hypotheses. In the process of such research, there
will inevitably arise new dogmatic problems dictated by a genuinely dialectical
ecclesial consciousness. It is therefore necessary to cast aside the preconcep-
tion that whatever is new is not of the Church. Obviously not everything new
in dogmatic theology is truly of the Church, but simultaneously it is all the more
*not* of the Church, or even anti-Church, to bind and fetter ideas by merely du-
plicating the old. This idea constitutes a rabbinical legalism, an unchanging
preservationism that is in fact actively reactionary and, in this sense, ironically,
is in itself an innovation. Immutability is impossible, being only a disguise for
regression. Such preservationism is basically un-Orthodox—Orthodoxy is alive
and, therefore, a growing and developing tradition, just as it was during the
flourishing period of the history of dogma.

## IV

This leads us to Orthodoxy's fundamental question of dogmatic development.
Is it possible? Is it permissible? And if so, in what sense? If asked in relation

to the fullness of the divine life which is inherent to the Church, there can be only one answer: this fullness is *given* in the incarnation of the Lord Jesus, in whom the whole fullness of God dwells bodily, and in the descent of the Holy Spirit at Pentecost, when the Spirit comes to the world hypostatically in the tongues of fire. And as Christ is "the same yesterday and today and forever" (Heb 13:8), and as "there are varieties of gifts, but the same Spirit" (1 Cor 12:4), so the fullness of revelation and the fullness of life in the divine foundation of the Church is *divinely* laid. But in the divine–human conscience of the Church, insofar as it includes temporality and relativity, this fullness enters only successively and partially—which is why the history of dogma, as we observe it in reality, exists. New dogmas arise, and it is only in this sense that one can speak of the existence of dogmatic development. How else can we understand the work of the ecumenical councils in relation to the previous era? We cannot think that this work is unique in the history of the Church and cannot continue; to the contrary, it does and it must. One of the gloomiest preconceptions in dogmatic theology is the idea that the seven ecumenical councils exhaust their own fullness, and that dogmatic thought cannot move ahead. This does not correspond to fact, inasmuch as life itself has brought dogmatic theology far beyond these delimitations (it is enough to observe the factual content of Christology today to be convinced that the seven ecumenical councils constitute only one chapter in Christology).

But most importantly, the limitation of dogmas to a particular period would mitigate against the very existence of dogmas, since it would apply human limitations to divine fullness. Dogma is not only static in its given character, but is dynamic in its role, or its development. And this dynamic character is expressed in dogmas' unfolding in history, and also in our understanding and explication of them in dogmatic theology. While they are given in the lived experience of the Church they are realized and crystallized in dogmatic thought and dogmatic creation, outside of which there is no dogmatic theology. Outside this context they are transformed into a dry and dead inventory. The creative task of dogmatic theology today is often replaced by the quasi-apologetic task of confessionalism—the defense and explanation of Orthodox dogmas in distinction or opposition to the non-Orthodox. In spite of this, theology must address itself to the positive and active unfolding of Church teaching; it must be included in Church life; in other words, it must become mystical, liturgical, and vitally historical. This teaching must not be afraid of new dogmatic problems, but rather address them with full attention and with the full strength of creative daring.

Of course, theology is only theologizing about dogmas; it is not the dogmas themselves, which are revealed to the Church. Theology describes a certain process—theological opinions are set aside, and from such opinions, theologoumena are crystallized, themselves sometimes long-considered quasi dogmas, but not dogmas in the strict sense of the word. Theologoumena then, which up to a point satisfy the needs of dogmatic instruction, by the will of God may (or may not) blossom into dogmas in the strict sense. Nowadays, everything spoken in dogmatic theology is called "dogma." In fact, dogmatic consciousness is satisfied with theological doctrines accepted as dogmas. There is nothing abnormal in this; on the contrary, it is perhaps in the order of things. But we must not overdo the meaning of dogmatic doctrine in its un-touchability and inerrancy. Doctrine should be looked over with a precision to which dogmas are not subjected. This study—the precise, creatively pedagog-ical (and not destructive) criticism of dogmatic doctrine—is one of the tasks of dogmatic study.

Dogmatics is theological science, a testimony to the content of religious life, its internal facts, and its self-determination. As such as it must accompany the development of life and its needs. It cannot be unreactive to life's creativity and its *newness*. History is self-repetitive—the present becomes the past, but enters into the future—and therefore its novelty is programmed from its past. An in-timate mystical life nourishes theology with themes that theology must hear, in-ternalize, and respond to. In this way, new dogmatic themes arise, new prob-lems and theological propositions—"new" not in the sense that they replace or negate the old ones, but express them in a new way. And if we live in a tragic and stormy period, a period that is also great and daring in its strivings, a great effort of theology is required if it is to respond to people's real questions. The-ology must not remain in paralyzed dread, or a pharisaic pride.

Our present time, with its particular problems, has the potential to be a great period in theology, but theology must rise to be worthy of its calling. After a centuries-long silence, Christian thought has once again come to concern itself with the problems of life. And in the teaching of the Church, Christian thought and the problems of life coincide dogmatically. When this happens it leads to the unfolding of dogmas about God-manhood. God-manhood pertains to all the contemporary issues of history and eschatology: Christian culture, social Chris-tianity, church and state, the unification of Christian traditions in one Church. And all these questions must take on a dogmatic meaning in order to be able to overcome that amoral pragmatism with which they are currently being ap-proached. They knock at the Christian heart, and request a dogmatic conscious-ness, but do not find an answer in the catalog of dogmatic laws that replace the living dynamic of dogmatic theology. Dogmatic theology is, or at least must be, a vital and ever-moving thought. Even more, it is the most alive of all aspects of human thought inasmuch as it deals with the questions closest to our life and the fullness of human personhood—questions of faith, or questions of how we view the world. The fact that people who have lost their faith and are now satisfied with some pitiful surrogate dogmas testifies not only to the utter importance of these needs, but also to the fact that these needs are not being met. Dogmatic theology is called to lead thought and life, to be a beacon and inspiration, con-templating the world, yet *conquering* the world. But for this, dogmatics must be dogmatics—that is, living and contemporary thought, full of Christian inspiration, the most creative work in the creation of true (Christian) culture.

Theology needs to be contemporary, or more precisely, to express religious thought about eternity in time, the supratemporal in the temporal. It follows unavoidably that relative to the development of religious thought and the expression of dogmatic opinions (and further, theologoumena), there also exists the need to review and to test already-existing revelatory dogmas—not, of course, with the purpose of "checking" them, but in order to perceive and receive them more completely. In this is fulfilled the dynamic quality of dogma: it is not only given in a precrystallized formula, but it is also a task for infinitely vital and intellectual exploration. We must also remember that dogmas possess a mutual transparence. They are given not as an external listing, as in a catalog or inventory, but are internally organically tied, so that in the light of one dogma the content and strength of the other is revealed.

This is why dogmatic theology constantly renews itself, since it should not be reckoned only as part of the record of Church tradition, where it must be accounted for in the light of historical research which studies and explains it. For example, the understanding of the concept of God-manhood, which is integral to the theological reflection of our time, opens up anew for us the meaning of Chalcedonian dogma, as well as the Sixth Ecumenical Council. The questions of social and cultural creativity are opened for us anew in the teaching about the Church. Dogmatics, as the sum total of dogmas, is not like a philosophical system that aims to unify its constituent parts. Rather, it is an organic whole in which each part lives through the life of the whole. Dogmas are explained in dogmatic theology, and dogmatic theology is explained by dogmas. In the history of philosophy, one system supplants the other, even though each has its own problematics. In dogmatic theology, each piece is taken as part of the whole, something which is foreign to an evolutionary dialectic, yet which can participate in antinomy.


## V

Nevertheless, a systematic approach to dogmas is inherent to dogmatic theology; dogmatic theology, as a science, is described in textbooks as "a system of dogmas." In other words, it is a kind of philosophy or, more exactly, a philosophy of revelation as a system of religious metaphysics, presupposing in turn a certain gnoseology. It is absolutely unnecessary to recoil from this connection with philosophy on the grounds that philosophy is a purely human quest for truth. Philosophy is a natural theology where falsehood and delusion are mixed in with truth, and which allows even the possibility of godlessness, where everything is a problematic or a quest, a hypothesis or a human conjecture. Theology on the other hand, as the philosophy of revelation, is infallible in its content while belonging to the realm of human creation as a philosophy. This is why philosophy and theology are tightly bound up with each other. Dogmas are truths of religious revelation that have a metaphysical content and therefore are expressed in the language of philosophy, as is only natural for this purpose. Dogmatic theology, therefore, is religious philosophy.

Philosophy, of course, is not without precedent; it draws its content from the self-revelation of life: *primum vivere, deinde philosophare*[4] (even if this is limited by a certain circular reasoning). For theology, the principle is *primum vivere, deinde theologizari*,[5] and therefore there is no formal difference between philosophy and theology. They differ in the character of the life experience from which they originate: in the case of one, it is something human—all too human—(although it harbors a "natural revelation"); in the case of the other, it is the theanthropic, the voice of God in the human mind, the "mind of Christ."

We know that the patristic period theologized with the language of ancient philosophy, which for us, even though we respect its unique and unsurpassed value, is no longer *our* philosophical language; in any case, the form it had for the Holy Fathers is foreign to us. It is not by accident but by a purposeful selection that Christological and Trinitarian dogmas are expressed in the language of Plato and Aristotle. This ought not mean that we must think the way Aristotle did, or express our contemporary philosophical constructs in his language (as is done until now in Roman Catholic dogmatic theology, owing to the powerful but enriching inheritance of Thomism and Aristotelianism). There is thus a voluntary (or involuntary) inevitability of the influence of contemporary philosophical thought. Dogmatists cannot avoid it. It is a kind of translation into modern language of the lexicon of the early church. The result is not a new dogmatic definition, which in its essence remains unchanged, but its philosophical interpretation, which is indispensable for a sincere philosophical internalization of dogma in our time. Without this process, a dogma will sound foreign to our thought, a formula worthy only of being learned by rote but not a living interpretation. This means that the theologian in point of fact is also a philosopher who must have a corresponding armor against philosophy.

The life of the Church is a continuous revelation of the full truth that the Church bears in itself. This revelation, which expresses the human-historical side of the divine-human process, is understood not through a passive mechanical action, but through the creative unfolding of the truth, in response to the calls of life and the quests of thought. The very possibility of continuing revelation presupposes the incompleteness of revelation in history and, therefore, a corresponding incompleteness of dogmatic theology as a system of dogmas. Therefore, theological opinions remain an important part of dogmatic theology or, at most, they are theological propositions and theologoumena bearing varying degrees of authority. Dogmatic thought—with full faithfulness to Church tradition, but also with the total sincerity of a free quest—is called on critically to discern, to establish and internalize different aspects of already-existing dogmatic teachings, as well as to respond to contemporary problems. By this is achieved the indispensable balance between the static and dynamic quality of dogma.

## NOTES

1. Even the Roman Catholic Church, with its tendency to give authoritative dogmatic statements, if possible, in all questions of the teachings of faith, is apparently unable to fulfill this task and even accepts the reality of theological disagreement—such as, for example, the difference between the Thomists and the Molinists concerning the question of freedom and grace. [Molinism refers to the teachings of the sixteenth-century Spanish Jesuit Luis de Molina, which emphasized the importance of human cooperation with divine grace. (Translator's note)]

2. Bulgakov frequently uses the term *theologem* (here translated as "theological proposition"), always pairing it with the more familiar term *theologoumenon*, which is commonly translated as "private theological opinion." (Translator's note)

3. John of Damascus, "Exposition of the Orthodox Faith." Post-Nicene Fathers, volume IX, series II, translated by S. D. F. Salmond (Edinburgh: T & T Clark, 1898).

4. "First to live, and then to philosophize."

5. "First to live, and then to theologize."

*Nicolas Berdiaev (1874–1948) is perhaps the best known and most unusual of the Russian intellectuals of the twentieth century. Never completing his studies at the University of Kiev, he nevertheless became an independent scholar and is probably best known for his emphasis on freedom in his philosophical writings. Forced out of Russia in 1922, he spent the rest of his life in the "Russian Paris," associated with various groups such as the Russian Christian Students Movement and Orthodox Action, and continuing to lecture and write independently. He edited numerous publications, perhaps the most important being the journal* Put' *(The Way). While originally at some distance from the church and the practice of Christianity, he, like Bulgakov, returned to the Liturgy and sacraments, although maintaining the Gospel freedom of Christians was often threatened by the institutional church. In both of the selections, here Berdiaev's fundamental vision of Christian freedom is in evidence, as well as his contention that there is much about the human enactment and expression of the faith that must be criticized.*

## FOR FURTHER READING

Berdiaev, Nicolas. *The Beginning and the End: Essay on Eschatological Metaphysics.* Translated by R. M. French. New York: Harper, 1952.

———. *The Destiny of Man.* Translated by N. Duddington. New York: Scribner's, 1937.

———. *Dream and Reality: An Essay in Autobiography.* Translated by Katherine Lampert. New York: MacMillan, 1950.

————. *Freedom and the Spirit.* Translated by O. Fielding Clarke. New York: Scribner's, 1935.

————. *The Meaning of the Creative Act.* Translated by Donald A. Lowrie. New York: Scibner's, 1955.

————. *The Meaning of History.* Translated by George Reavey. New York: Scribner's, 1936.

————. *The Realm of God and the Realm of Caesar.* Translated by Donald A. Lowrie. New York: Harper, 1953.

————. *The Russian Idea.* Translated by R. M. French. New York: MacMillan, 1947.

————. *Spirit and Reality.* Translated by George Reavey. London: G. Bles, 1946.

————. *Slavery and Freedom.* Translated by R. M. French. New York: Scribner's, 1939.

————. *Truth and Revelation.* Translated by R. M. French. New York: Harper and Bros., 1953.

Also, see Fr. Stephen Janos' excellent website devoted to Berdiaev, with extensive bibliographies and links to Berdiaev texts online, at http://www.berdyaev.com/ (accessed May 2003).

# THE BOURGEOIS MIND

**W**hat does the word *bourgeois* actually mean? It has remained unexplained, though it has been so much used and so often misapplied. Even when superficially used it is a word with a magic power of its own, and its depth has to be fathomed. The word designates a spiritual state, a direction of the soul, a peculiar consciousness of being. It is neither a social nor an economic condition, yet it is something more than a psychological and ethical one—it is spiritual, ontological. In the very depths of his being, or nonbeing, the bourgeois is distinguishable from the nonbourgeois; he is a man of a particular spirit, or particular spiritlessness, a lack of soul. The state of being bourgeois has always existed in the world, and its immortal image is forever fixed in the Gospels with its equally immortal antithesis, but in the nineteenth century it attained its climax and ruled supreme. Though the middle-class society of the last century is so spoken of in the superficial socioeconomic significance of the term, it is bourgeois in a deeper and more spiritual sense. This middle-class mentality ripened and enslaved human society and culture at the summit of their civilization. Its concupiscence is no longer restricted by man's supernatural beliefs as it was in past epochs, it is no longer kept in bounds by the sacred symbolism of a nobler traditional culture; the bourgeois spirit emancipated itself, expanded, and was at last able to express its own type of life. But even when the triumph of mediocrity was complete a few deep thinkers denounced it with uncompromising

Originally published in *Put'* 3 (March/April 1926): 3–13. The English version appeared most recently in *The Bourgeois Mind and Other Essays*, reprint edition. Translated by Countess Olga Bennigsen. Salem, N.H.: Ayre Publishers, 1992.

power: Carlyle, Nietzsche, Ibsen, Bloy, Dostoyevsky, Leontiev—all foresaw the victory of the bourgeois spirit over a truly great culture, on the ruins of which it would establish its own hideous kingdom. With prophetic force and fire these men denounced the spiritual sources and foundations of middle-class existence and, repelled by its ugliness, thirsting for a nobler culture, a different life, looked back upon Greece or the Middle Ages, the Renaissance or Byzantium. Leontiev has stated the problem strikingly:

> Is it not dreadful and humiliating to think that Moses went up upon Sinai, the Greeks built their lovely temples, the Romans waged their Punic wars, Alexander, that handsome genius in a plumed helmet, fought his battles, apostles preached, martyrs suffered, poets sang, artists painted, knights shone at tournaments—only that some French, German, Russian bourgeois garbed in unsightly and absurd clothes should enjoy life "individually" or "collectively" on the ruins of all this vanished splendor?

History has failed, there is no such thing as historical progress, and the present is in no wise an improvement upon the past: there was more beauty in the past. A period of high cultural development is succeeded by another, in which culture deteriorates qualitatively. The will to power, to well-being, to wealth, triumphs over the will to holiness and to genius. The highest spiritual achievements belong to the past, spirituality is on the wane, and a time of spiritual decline is a time of bourgeois ascendancy. The knight and the monk, the philosopher and the poet, have been superseded by a new type—the greedy bourgeois conqueror, organizer, and trader. The center of life is displaced and transferred to its periphery, the organic hierarchical order of life is being destroyed. In the new machine-made industrial-capitalist civilization of Europe and America, the spiritual culture of the old West, based on a sacred symbolism and sacred tradition, is being irrevocably annihilated.

One of those whose rebellion against the bourgeois spirit was most uncompromising and bitter was Léon Bloy, the remarkable and little known French Catholic writer. (I wrote an article about him, "The Knight of Poverty," in *Sophia*, June 1914.) Bloy, who lived all his life unrecognized and in poverty, has written an extraordinary book, *L'Exégèse des Lieux Communs*, which is a searching examination of the commonplaces of bourgeois wisdom. He gives a wonderfully witty metaphysical interpretation of the pronouncements that are the bourgeois's rule of life. Thus in the phrase *Dieu ne demande pas tant*— "God doesn't ask so much"—he endeavors to penetrate the secret movements of the heart, mind, and will of a bourgeois, to expose his peculiar metaphysics and mysticism. The bourgeois, even when he is a "good Catholic," believes only in this world, in the expedient and the useful. He is incapable of living by faith in another world and refuses to base his life on the mystery of Golgotha. "The magnificent superiority of the bourgeois is grounded on unbelief, even *after* he has seen and touched. No! Upon the utter impossibility of seeing and touching, due to unbelief." The bourgeois is an idolater, enslaved by the visible. "Idolatry is the preference of the visible to the invisible." "Business" is the bourgeois's god, his absolute. It was the bourgeois who crucified Christ: on Golgotha he cut the world off from Christ, "money" from the poor. The poor and money are great symbols for Bloy. There is a mystery of money, its mysterious separation from the spirit; and the middle-class world is governed by this money bereft of the spirit. Middle-class existence is opposed to the absolute, it is destructive of eternity. A bourgeois may be religious, and this middle-class religiosity is more hateful in Bloy's eyes than atheism. How many such bourgeois idolaters did he discover amongst "good Catholics"—the Lord Christ is very decorative in shops! Bloy studies the average bourgeois, but the problem can be deepened, for the bourgeois may manifest himself on a superior and more brilliant plane, even in the higher degrees of a spiritual life, where he paralyses all spiritual movement and extinguishes the fire that is the very essence of the spirit.

The bourgeois may be pious, he may even be just, but it was said, "Unless your justice is greater than that of the Scribes and Pharisees, you shall not enter into the kingdom of Heaven." The bourgeois's justice never exceeds that of the Scribes and Pharisees. He loves to give alms "in synagogues and in the streets" so as to be "honored by people," to "stand and pray in the synagogues and corners of the streets," to be "seen by all." He loves to judge, and is the first to cast a stone at the sinner. When the disciples plucked ears of wheat on a Sabbath, it was the bourgeois who taunted Jesus: "Behold, why do they on the Sabbath-day that which is not lawful?" And the answer he was given was one to upset all middle-class notions: "I tell you that there is something here greater than the temple. And if you knew what this means, *I want mercy and not sacrifice*, you would never have condemned the innocent. For the Son of Man is Lord even of the Sabbath. . . . The Sabbath was made for man, not man for the Sabbath." It was again the bourgeois who said, "The Son of Man comes eating and drinking . . . behold a man who is a glutton and a drinker of wine, a friend of tax collectors and sinners." For he has no love for tax collectors and sinners, his affections lie with the righteous Pharisees. The bourgeois is convinced that man is defiled by what enters his lips, though it has been said to him, "The things which come out from a man, they defile a man." And, addressing the bourgeois, Christ said, "Amen, I say to you that the tax collectors and prostitutes shall go into the kingdom of God before you. . . . Whoever exalts himself shall be humbled, and he that humbles himself shall be exalted." But, "Woe to you, Scribes and Pharisees, you hypocrites! You shut up the kingdom of Heaven in people's faces, neither going in yourselves nor allowing others to go in who want to." And, "For which is of greater value, the gold or the Temple that makes the gold holy?" When the bourgeois remarked that "He eats and drinks with tax collectors and sinners," Jesus replied, "The healthy do not need a physician, but those who are ill. . . . I have come not to call the just but the sinners." These words of Christ, too, are aimed directly at the bourgeois: "He that wants to save his life shall lose it: and he that loses his life for my sake shall find it. For what does it profit a man if he gain the whole world and suffer the loss of his own soul?" The bourgeois is out for the conquest of the whole world, and Jesus says to him, "Woe to you . . . because you love the best seats in the synagogues and salutations in the market-place." And his interests in this world are repudiated by Jesus in the words: "Seek not what you shall eat, or what you shall drink . . . for all these things do the nations of the world seek. But your Father knows that you have need of these things. But seek first the kingdom of God and his righteousness, and all these things shall be given to you." A bourgeois heart is condemned: "You . . . outwardly appear to men just, but inwardly are full of hypocrisy and iniquity." Christ said to those whom he chose, "If you had been of the world, the world would love its own; but because you are not of the world but I have chosen you out of the world, therefore the world hates you." "The world" is the bourgeois spirit. It is not God's creation, the cosmos that the Son of God could not deny, but the enslavement and the overburdening of God's creation by passions and concupiscence. A bourgeois is one who loves "the world." The eternal repudiation of the very foundations of his spirit is expressed in the words, "Do not love the world or the things which are in the world." To be bourgeois is bondage, a tie with "the world," an enslavement by it; it involves the rejection of the freedom of the spirit that follows upon liberation from the power of "the world"; it does not accept the mystery of Golgotha, it denies the cross. Bourgeois consciousness of life is in opposition to the tragic consciousness of life: the man who lives through a tragedy is free from the taint, and in the truly dramatic moments of life a bourgeois ceases to be one.

Where shall we find the spiritual roots of this sickness? In too strong a faith in this visible world and lack of belief in another, invisible world. The bourgeois is impressed with this world of material things, stirred, tempted by it; he does not believe seriously in another existence, in a spiritual being, he feels no confidence in his neighbor's faith. He always thinks, "I know you, you are all just the same as myself, only you refuse to admit it; you pretend and deceive yourselves." All live by the goods of this world, all are crushed by the outward actuality, and so, because he is conscious of this fact and acknowledges it, the bourgeois deems himself superior to his neighbors. He is no symbolist: the viewpoint according to which the entire visible and transitory world is but the symbol of another invisible reality is quite alien to him. He is a naïve realist, and only such a childishly realistic outlook is taken seriously by him. When he is a believer, belonging to some religious denomination, he is again the same artless realist. He may even be an Orthodox Christian, but he does not connect this "faith" of his with his outlook upon life and the world, which is marked by subservience to "the world," an oversimplified realistic acceptance of it. Whether nominally Catholic, Orthodox, or Protestant, the bourgeois would deny Christ, if he appeared to him, as the Scribes and Pharisees rejected him. The bourgeois never acknowledges any saint during his lifetime, but only long after canonization and universal acceptance. Middle-class existence is enslavement of the spirit, its being crushed by the external hard world. It is dependence upon the temporary and corruptible. It is being incapable of breaking through to eternity. The bourgeois is oppressed by the tangible, by what enters into him from outside. He cannot exist without some outward sanction, and authority has primarily been created on his behalf. Whenever he overthrows one authority he immediately sets up another, and submits to it. He is bereft of any spiritual fire, of any spiritual creativeness, but has his own "faith" and superstitions. He cannot believe, because faith is an act of freedom, a creative act of the spirit; denying the eternal, he trusts in the temporal; having no faith in the power of God, he believes in the power of things of this world with a reverence verging on idolatry.

The bourgeois does not always appear to us under the guise of a materialist enthralled by the earthly joys of life: this type is elementary and the least interesting of all. There is a superior type that strives to be the guardian of the spiritual foundations of life, aspires to be the benefactor of mankind, to ensure its happiness, to organize the world for it. There exists conservative bourgeois as well as their revolutionary counterpart. Often the bourgeois is a devotee, with the name of God ever on his lips. It is possible to profess materialism openly, and yet not be a bourgeois in the depth of the heart. When he is a "believer" the bourgeois really believes only in the power of this world of visible things and awaits the good of life only from them; such a one in our days confirms the truth of that saying of middle-class wisdom (analyzed by Léon Bloy), "God works no more miracles." He readily admits that God *did* work miracles, but this is only a way of saying that miracles are as impossible as they are absurd. He dislikes miracles, nay, fears them: they might upset all his prospects of an organized life. He lives upon the ready-made and he acquires nothing through a creative spiritual power. His faith calls forth no higher spiritual energy but is expedient for promoting worldly success: the very spirit of eternity is converted into a means for the conquest of the goods of life. From its beginning the priestly caste had a leaning toward the bourgeois: often the leaders' own spirit burnt low, and they dreaded every spiritual movement. Thus they betrayed their eternal vocation and paved the way to rebellion against the hierarchical principle itself.

When the bourgeois has stuck to his place too long, impeding the movement of everyone and everything till his power threatens life with inertia, there appears another type, with a greed for power and for the best in life, who says, "Clear out! I want your place." This parvenu bourgeois is no improvement upon his predecessor; he is even worse, but during the heyday of his conquest he seems a daredevil and quite unlike the pompous and steadfast bourgeois of old. The new bourgeois has a still greater greed for power and might, is still more ruthless toward the weak, is more intoxicated by his greatness, importance, and sudden predominance. The feeling of sin that weakened and limited the old type disappears completely with the new. In these last years the Russian communist has expressed this type of bourgeois conqueror, a type sinister in its godlessness. In him the middle-class spirit has shown itself in a purer, stronger, unlimited form; its devotees definitely profess the religion of earthly might, earthly power, earthly happiness. The bourgeois always hungers after the first places, loves "position," and when he secures it his self-satisfaction is boundless. This self-satisfaction is one of his characteristic traits. A weakening of the consciousness of the tragedy of life invariably accompanies his worldly successes. Delighted with himself and his "position," he is unable to attain to the wisdom of Ecclesiastes, "I have seen all the works that are done under the sun; and behold, all is vanity and vexation of spirit." He idolizes vanity and thinks his own works divine: "business" obliterates the object and meaning of life; "business" prevents the bourgeois from seeing the person, nature, the starlit skies. Instead, he is entirely taken up with his "business," his own magnificence. All his willpower is turned exclusively to the organization of existence and he loses the capacity of rejoicing in life. He is an organizer and businessman, and organization kills organic life in him. The new bourgeois expels the old. It is the perennial comedy of history. The new man who has entered on to the scene begins by pretending that he repudiates all middle-class values and ways, that his kingdom will not be a middle-class one. He is a socialist and revolutionary. But soon, very soon, the everlasting bourgeois features—the same in all times and with all peoples—reappear.

The bourgeois spirit is an eternal principle, one of the world—principles that manifest themselves ever under new forms. It does not decrease but increases, and on the summits of European and universal civilization it is at its mightiest. The rich person, spiritually enslaved by wealth and by enslaving others, is a prisoner of "the world," and it is more difficult for such a one to enter God's kingdom than for a camel to pass through the eye of a needle. But the poor person, envying the rich and spiritually enslaved by the desire of usurping his place and his wealth, is the same bourgeois and his entry into God's kingdom is in no way easier. Herein is enacted the eternal tragicomedy of history. The middle-class spirit takes possession of every social group, either in the shape of satisfaction with one's own "position" and desire to safeguard it at any cost, or in the shape of envy of one's neighbor, desire of a good position, and the will to attain it at any cost. And the historical scene presents the tragicomical picture of two bourgeois seizing each other by the throat, each imagining that he is defending some particular world opposed to the world of his enemy. In reality it is the same world, the same undying principle. Middle-class existence is not determined by a person's economic situation but by his spiritual attitude toward this position. Therefore in each class it may be spiritually conquered. The historical process of the creation of a nation—its legislation, economics, customs, idolatry of science—is ruled by middle-class standards, and this explains the fact that in the movement of history there is a certain hopelessness, that all these achievements are unsuccessful.

The bourgeois may exist in every sphere of spiritual life. One can be a bourgeois in religion, science, morals, art. We have spoken of the religious bourgeois whose image is depicted in the sacred books. In every sphere he wants to *appear* and is powerless to *be*. He lives by the seeming and evanescent force of that inert spiritual environment in which he occupies (or wishes to occupy) a "position," and not by the living ontological power of his own personality. When he appears as a scientist or academician he is self-satisfied, pompous, and limited; he adapts science to his own level, dreading the free play of thought and the liberty of the questioning spirit, ignoring intuition. The bourgeois moralist judges severely. His virtue weighs heavily upon everyone. He hates the sinners and publicans, and is the guardian of his neighbors' morals. But the average bourgeois is always somewhat of a moralist. This middle-class moralism may manifest itself under various shapes, from the most conservative to the most destructive and revolutionary; it may suddenly demand the crystallization of life and the cessation of all free movement, or the destruction of the entire world with its whole historical heritage. The bourgeois may be an extreme conservative or an extreme revolutionary, but in both cases he is chained to the visible world and knows no spiritual freedom. There is no grace in moralism, it proceeds from an outward source and is deaf to the music of Heaven. While he makes hell on earth, the bourgeois pretends to be preparing a future earthly paradise. The very idea of rationalization of life, of an absolute social harmony, is a middle-class idea that has to be opposed by the "man from the underworld," the "gentleman with a mocking reactionary face." The tower of Babel was built by the bourgeois. The spirit of Socialism is middle-class. An excessive desire of life causes enslavement to the goods of the earth. The overcoming of middle-classdom means a victory over the intensified will directed to "the world." Everything the bourgeois touches—the family, the state, morality, religion, science—all is deadened. Contemplation, which could set him free, is unknown to him. The paradox of his life consists in his repudiation of tragedy; he is weighed down and darkened by his nonacceptance of the internal tragedy of life, of Golgotha; there is a relief and freedom in the acceptance of the cross and the pain and suffering this entails. Because the bourgeois's consciousness of guilt and sin has become so weak he is the slave of "the world," and his ideal is that of worldly power and wealth, the mystery of Golgotha is unacceptable to him. The bourgeois spirit is nothing but the rejection of Christ; even those whose lips confess him may be the first to crucify him anew.

When the tragic consciousness of guilt, of the tension between the temporal and the eternal, is defeated by the concupiscence of life, power, and enjoyment, this spirit reigns supreme. This concupiscence was the moving principle of the civilization of the nineteenth and early twentieth centuries and, however radically it may have reformed itself, this civilization remains as it was, a middle-class civilization. The ancient symbolical cultures, founded upon sacred myths, had never been so bourgeois in spirit as the pragmatic civilization of modern times, whose might is growing and spreading. Formerly the bourgeois was a psychological type, now he is the socially predominant type. But even in ancient times a middle-class civilization, striving to displace a sacred culture, was fighting its way to the surface. The prophets branded its spirit with words of fire:

> Their land also is filled with silver and gold, and there is no end of their treasures and their land is filled with horses, neither is there any end of their chariots . . . [but] the lofty looks of man shall be humbled and the haughtiness of men shall be bowed down, and the Lord alone shall be exalted in that day. For the day of the Lord of Hosts shall be upon every one that is proud and lofty, and upon every one that is lifted up; and he shall be brought low. . . . And the loftiness of man shall be bowed down and the haughtiness of men shall be made low and the Lord alone shall be exalted in that day.

Jeremiah speaks of a bourgeois civilization: "Run to and fro through the streets of Jerusalem, and see now and know and seek in the broad places thereof if you can find a man, if there be any that does judgment, that seeks the truth, and I will pardon it." The worship of Baal marked the beginning and was a figure of all bourgeois civilizations, which invariably destroy a sacred culture: "Thus says the Lord: Cursed be the man that trusts in man and makes flesh his arm and whose heart departs from the Lord"; and its victory is thus spoken of: "Babylon has been a golden cup in the Lord's hand that made all the earth drunken; the nations have drunk of her wine, therefore the nations are mad." It was there in Babylon that appeared the first middle-class civilization recorded by history, and it dominated the whole East. Its spirit was vigorously denounced by Ezekiel: "Her princes . . . are like wolves ravening the prey, to shed blood and to destroy souls, to get dishonest gain . . . the people of the land have used oppression and exercised robbery, and have vexed the poor and needy: yea, they have oppressed the stranger wrongfully." And, "Woe be to the shepherds of Israel that do feed themselves! . . . The diseased you have not strengthened, neither have you healed the sick, neither have you bound up the broken, neither have you brought again that which was driven away, neither have you sought that which was lost; but with force and with cruelty have ye ruled them." To the vision of the ancient prophets were revealed the catastrophes that would inevitably follow upon the triumph of the bourgeois spirit. Such a civilization is conceived within the womb of a developing culture; the bourgeois type begins to predominate, and its spirit contaminates rulers, guides, and priests. It is then that the nations and their cultures are threatened by disaster—the wrath of God falls upon them.

But antiquity knew only a tendency toward the bourgeois spirit; it never saw its final triumph. It was left to our European culture to accomplish its victory and give the world's destinies into the hands of the bourgeois. The increase of populations and their unlimited needs, the will to life, to power, to domination, have brought about this triumph; but our civilization cannot endure; the bourgeois is destructive of eternity, and therefore he is not its inheritor. Men have long anticipated the doom of European civilization. In the impending cataclysms the new revolutionary bourgeois will attempt to spread his domination the world over, to make his spirit universal, to exalt it as the pearl of creation. But eternity does not belong to it. The hour will come when the Lord will say, "Behold, I, even I, will both search my sheep and seek them out!"

Spirit alone can defeat the bourgeois condition; no material means will succeed. It is not a material or economic phenomenon—industrial development as such is not bourgeois. This does not mean that the material structure of society is indifferent and cannot assume a bourgeois character, but that the bourgeois structure of a society is merely the expression of a bourgeois spirit, of a false direction of the will. It is a wrong conception of life, the concupiscence of the temporal, which transforms life into an inferno. In its finite and vivid type the bourgeois is an apocalyptic image, a figure of the coming kingdom of which the Sacred Scripture has spoken. The middle-class spirit is contrasted with the pilgrim spirit: in this world Christians are but wayfarers, and the inner feeling of this pilgrimage is inherent to the Christian in every walk of life. A Christian has no city—he is in quest of the City of God, which can never be the city of "this world"; whenever an earthly city is mistaken for the New Jerusalem, Christians cease to be pilgrims and the bourgeois spirit reigns supreme.

# THE WORTH OF CHRISTIANITY AND
# THE UNWORTHINESS OF CHRISTIANS

## I

**B**occaccio tells the story of a Jew whose Christian friend was trying to convert him. The Jew was on the point of agreeing, but before committing himself definitely he decided to go to Rome and see for himself in what manner the Pope and his cardinals lived, since they were the men at the head of the Church. This frightened the Christian, who thought that all his efforts would go for nothing and his friend certainly would refuse baptism when he had seen the scandals of Rome. The Jew duly went there and observed the hypocrisy, depravity, corruption, and greed that were rife among the Roman clergy and in the papal court at that time, and on his return his Christian friend asked anxiously what impression had been made on him. The reply was as deeply understanding as it was unexpected: "Since all the wickedness and abominations that I have seen in Rome have been unable to overturn the Christian religion, since in spite of them all it continues to grow stronger, it must be the true faith." And the Jew became a Christian.

Whatever Boccaccio's idea may have been, this tale shows us the only way of vindicating Christianity. Christians themselves are the greatest objection to their religion; they are a scandal to those who are favorably disposed toward it. This argument has been grievously abused in our day. The present weakness of

Originally published in *Christianity, Atheism and Modernity*. Translated by Donald Attwater. Warsaw and Paris: Dobro and YMCA Press, 1928. Online at www.chebucto.ns.ca/Philosphy/Sui-Generis/Berdyaev/essays/worth.htm (accessed May 2003).

faith and spread of complete unbelief lead people to judge Christianity by Christians; formerly it was judged, in the first place, by its eternal truth, its doctrinal and moral teaching. Our age is too preoccupied with man and what is human, so that Christianity is not seen behind its mask of bad Christians; notice is taken of their wrongdoing and their deformations of the faith rather than of the religion itself; their excesses are more easily seen than the great Christian truth. Very many today assess the Christian religion by those whose profession of it is exterior and degenerate: Christianity is the religion of love and of freedom, but it is judged according to the hostility and hate and acts of violence of so many Christians, people who compromise their faith and are a stumbling block to the weak.

We are often told that the representatives of other religions—Buddhists, Muslims, Jews—are better than Christians in that they are more faithful to their religious precepts; unbelievers, atheists, and materialists are pointed out who are more worthy of respect, more unworldly in their lives, more capable of sacrifice than are many Christians. But the whole of the unworthiness of these numerous Christians resides exactly in that they do not fulfill their religion, but rather alter and pervert it. They are judged by their inability to raise themselves to the heights of that which they profess. But how then can the shortcomings of Christians be imputed to Christianity when the reproach leveled at them is precisely that they are out of accord with the grandeur of their faith? These charges are clearly contradictory. If the followers of other religions are often more observant of them than Christians are of theirs, it is because these religions are more within the reach of man than are the heights of Christianity. It is indeed much easier to be a good Muslim than a good Christian. The religion of love is not less exalted or less true because its realization in life is an exceedingly difficult task. It is not Christ's fault that his truth is not fulfilled and that his commandments are spurned.

Believing and practicing Jews are always ready to tell us that the law of their religion has the great advantage of being practicable. Judaism is more adapted to human nature and to the ends of human life and calls for less renunciation. Christianity, on the other hand, is the most difficult religion to put into practice, the most trying to human nature, requiring painful self-sacrifice at every turn; Jews look on it as an idealistic dream, useless in practical life and for that reason harmful. We too often measure the moral value of people by their religion and ideals. If a materialist is good according to this light, devoted to his idea and ready to make certain sacrifices for it, then we are impressed by his greatness of soul and cite him as an example. But it is infinitely harder for a Christian to keep abreast of his ideal, for it means that he has got to love his enemies, carry his cross bravely, and resist the temptations of the world unflinchingly—things that neither the Jew nor the Muslim nor the materialist

is called on to do. Christianity takes us along the line of greatest resistance—
the Christian life is a crucifixion of self.

## II

It is often claimed that Christianity has failed, that it has not been historically
realized, and thence another argument is drawn: not only Christians but the
very history of their Church testifies against it. It must be recognized that the
reading of ecclesiastical history can be an occasion of scandal to those whose
faith is unsteady. These books tell us of the conflict within the Christian world,
of human passions and temporal interests, of the corruption and disfigurement
of truth in the consciousness of sinful mankind; very often they show periods of
church history that remarkably resemble those of civil governments, with their
diplomatic relations, wars, and so on.

The outward history of the Church is visible and can be set out so that it is
accessible to all. But her inward and spiritual history, the turning of humanity
to God, the development of holiness, cannot be seen so easily; it is more difficult to write about them because they are in a way obscured and sometimes
even overwhelmed by exterior history. We detect evil more easily than good, we
are more conscious of the outer than of the inner aspect of life; we have no difficulty in learning about the externals of our neighbors, their commercial un-
dertakings, their politics, their domestic and social institutions. But do we think
much about the way in which people pray to God, how they relate their inner
life to the divine world, in what manner they war spiritually with temptation?

Very often we know nothing, do not even suspect the existence, of a spiritual
side to those whom we meet—at the most we are conscious of it only in those
whom we know particularly well. We are quick to note the exterior manifestations of evil passions that anyone can see, but as for what lies behind them, the
spiritual struggles, the reaching out to God, the demanding efforts to live the
truth of Christ—we do not know them, we may even not want to know them.
We are told not to judge our neighbor, but we judge him continually, by his outward actions, by the expression of his face, without ever looking within.

It is just the same with the history of Christianity. It cannot be judged by external facts, by the human passions and human sins that disfigure its image. We
must recall what Christian people have had to contend with in the course of
ages, and their bitter struggles to get the better of "the old man"—of their an-
cestral heathenism, of their agelong barbarity, of their grosser instincts; Christianity has had to work its way through the matter that put up such a solid resistance to the spirit of Christ, it has had to raise up to a religion of love those
whose appetites were all for violence and cruelty. Christianity is here to heal the
sick, not the whole; to call sinners, not the righteous; and mankind, converted

to Christianity, is sick and sinful. It is not the business of the Church of Christ to organize the external part of life, to overcome evil by material force; she looks for an inner and spiritual rebirth from the reciprocal action of human freedom and divine grace. It is an essential quality of Christianity that it cannot get rid of self-will—the evil in human nature—for it recognizes and respects the freedom of man.

Materialistic socialists are given to proclaiming that Christianity is not a success, that it has not made the Kingdom of God real. It is nearly two thousand years since the Redeemer of the world appeared on earth and evil still exists, it has even increased. The world is saturated with suffering and the burdens of life are no less for all that our salvation has accomplished. These socialists promise to do, without God and without Christ, what Christ himself could not bring about: the brotherhood of man, justice in social life, peace, the Kingdom of God on earth—these unbelievers willingly use that expression, "the Kingdom of God on earth"!

The only experience that we have of materialistic Socialism in practice is the Russian experiment, and that has not given the expected results. But there is no solution of the question in it. Socialism's promise to make justice rule on earth and to get rid of evil and suffering does not rest on human freedom but on the violation of it; its ends are to be realized by an enforced social organization that shall make external evil impossible by compelling men to virtue, righteousness, and justice—and it is this constraint that constitutes the great difference between Socialism and Christianity. The so-called "failure of Christianity in history" is a failure dependent upon human freedom, upon resistance springing from our Christ-given freedom, upon opposition by the ill will which religion will not *compel* to be good. Christian truth supposes freedom, and looks to an interior and spiritual victory over evil. Exteriorly the state can set a limit to the manifestations of wickedness and it is its duty to do so, but evil and sin will not be overcome in that way. There is no such dilemma for the socialist, because he knows no problem of sin or of the spiritual life; the only question facing him is that of suffering and social injustice and their elimination by means of an organization of life from without. God does not use force, for he desires man's freedom and not merely an exterior triumph of righteousness. In that sense it may be said that he maintains evil and uses it for good ends. In particular, the righteousness of Christ cannot be actualized by force. But the justice of Communism is to be attained by compulsion, and this can be done the more easily because any freedom of spirit is denied.

The argument based on a historical defeat of Christianity cannot be sustained. The Kingdom of God cannot be imposed; if it is to be brought about we must be born again, and that supposes complete freedom of spirit. Christianity is the religion of the cross, and it sees meaning in suffering. Christ asks us to take up our own cross and carry it, to shoulder the load of a sinful world. In Christian consciousness, the notion of attaining happiness, justice, and the

Kingdom of God on earth without cross or suffering is a huge lie. It is the temptation that Christ rejected in the wilderness when he was shown the kingdoms of the world and invited to fall down and worship. Christianity does not promise its own necessary realization and victory here below. Christ even questioned whether he would find any faith on earth when he came again at the end of time, and foretold that love itself would have grown cold.

Tolstoy believed that Christ's commands could be easily fulfilled simply by recognizing their truth. But that was a mistake of his overrationalizing consciousness. The mysteries of freedom and of grace were beyond him, his optimism contradicted the tragic depths of life. "The good which I will I do not," says the apostle Paul, "but the evil which I will not, that I do. Now if I do that which I will not it is no more I that do it, but sin that dwells in me." This testimony of one of the greatest of all Christians unveils the innermost part of the human heart, and it teaches us that the "failure of Christianity" is a human failure and not a divine defeat.

## III

In the course of history there has been a triple betrayal of Christianity by Christendom. Christians first of all deformed their religion, then separated themselves from it, and finally—and this was the worst wrong of all—began to blame it for the evils which they had themselves created. When Christianity is adversely criticized it is the sins and vices of Christian men and women that are criticized, their nonapplication and perversion of Christ's truth, and it is to a great extent because of these human perversions, sins, and wickedness that the world abandons the faith.

Human beings pervert Christianity and then turn upon both the perversion and the real thing. The matters of which the detractors of Christianity complain cannot be found in the words of Christ, in his precepts, in the Holy Scriptures, in sacred tradition, in the Church's teaching, or in the lives of the saints. An ideal principle must be opposed by another, an actual fact must be met with another actual fact. It is possible to defend the cause of Communism by showing that it has been perverted and never properly applied, just as can be done for Christianity. Communists shed blood and denaturalize truth to gain their ends just as Christians have done, but to assimilate the two systems one to the other in consequence of this would be an obvious fallacy.

In the Gospels, in the words of Christ, in the teaching of the Church, in the example of the saints, and in other perfect manifestations of Christianity, there can be found the good news of the coming of God's kingdom, calls to love of one's neighbor, to gentleness, to self-denial, to purity of heart. But nothing can be found there in favor of violence, hostility, revenge, hate, or greed. On the other hand, in the ideology of Marx, which is the breath of Communism, you can find appeals to revenge, to the malicious animosity of one class for another, to the war for personal interests, but nothing at all about love, sacrifice, forbearance, or spiritual purity. Christians have often committed these crimes and professedly under the banner of Christ, but in so doing they have never been fulfilling his commandments. Our adversaries delight in saying that Christians have often resorted to force for the defense or spreading of their religion. The fact is incontestable. But it only shows that these Christians were blinded by passion, that they were still unenlightened, that their sinfulness perverted the most righteous and sacred cause, that they did not understand of what spirit they were. When Peter drew his sword in defense of Jesus and cut off the ear of the high priest's servant, Jesus said to him: "Put your sword back into its sheath, for all that take up the sword shall perish by the sword."

The Christian revelation and religious life, like all revelation and all religious life, presuppose the existence of man as well as the existence of God. And man, although enlightened by the light of grace which comes from God, accommodates this divine light to the eye of his own spirit and imposes on revelation the limitations of his own nature and consciousness.

We know from the Bible that God revealed himself to the Jews. But he was more than the wrathful, jealous, and avenging God reflected sometimes in the consciousness of the Jewish people. Men limited Christian truth too, and deformed it as well. Thus God was often represented as some Eastern potentate, an arbitrary monarch, and the dogma of the Redemption was interpreted as the cessation of his judicial proceedings begun because he was aggrieved against mankind, the transgressor of his will. It was this perverted understanding and human limiting of its doctrines that led people to give up Christianity. Even the idea of the Church was spoiled. It was made solely an external thing, solely identified with a hierarchy, with ceremonial observances, with the transgressions of parishioners; and it was looked on first, foremost, and above all as an institution. The deeper and more inward understanding of the Church as a spiritual organism, the mystical body of Christ (as St. Paul defines it), was forced almost out of sight and became accessible only to the few. The liturgy and the sacraments were treated only as external rites, for their profound and hidden meaning completely escaped these pseudo-Christians. And so people left the Church, shocked by the vices of the clergy, by the mistakes of ecclesiastical organizations, by a too-close likeness to a government department, by the hypocritical sham piety or the too ostentatious devoutness of the rank-and-file.

It must always be remembered that the life of the Church is theandric— namely, there is a divine element and a human element, and these elements interact. Her foundation is eternal and infallible, sacred and sinless; it cannot be altered, and the gates of hell shall not prevail against it. The divine elements in the Church are Christ, her head; the fundamental structure of our religion; the dogmas of divine revelation; the moral teaching of the Gospel; the sacraments; the action of the Holy Spirit's grace. But on the human side, the Church is fal-

THE UNWORTHINESS OF CHRISTIANS

lible and subject to change. There can be deformation, disease, failure, alteration, just as there can be creative activity, development, enrichment, rebirth. The sins neither of mankind in general nor of the ecclesiastical hierarchy in particular are the sins of the Church, taken in her divine essence, and they do not lessen her holiness. Christianity requires that human nature be enlightened and transfigured. Human nature resists and tends to pervert its religion. In the continuous tension between the two elements sometimes the one is in the ascendant, sometimes the other.

Christianity raises us and sets us at the center of the universe. The Son of God took on our flesh and by so doing sanctified our nature. The Christian religion points out to us the highest aim in life and appeals to our exalted origin and great mission. But, unlike other religions, it does not flatter human nature. It calls on us heroically to overcome our fallen and sinful state.

Human nature, undermined by original sin, is not very receptive. It cannot contain the divine truth of Christianity and has difficulty in grasping the divine-human notion involved in the coming of Christ, God-man. He teaches us to love God and to love the neighbor, and the love of the one and the other are indissolubly bound together. We love our brethren through God, through the Father, and by our love for them we evince our love for God. "If we love one another God abides in us and his love is perfected in us." Christ was both Son of God and Son of man and he revealed to us the perfect union of God and man—the humanity of God and the divinity of man. But the natural man finds this fullness of a divine and human love difficult in practice. Sometimes we veer toward God and away from humanity, ready for divine love but indifferent and cruel to our neighbors. It was thus in the Middle Ages. At other times we are excited about loving and serving humanity but without reference to God, even opposing the very idea of him as mischievous and contrary to the good of mankind. It is thus in our time, with its humanism and humanitarian Socialism. Then, when they have rejected the divine-human truth and disassociated love of man from love of God, people proceed to attack Christianity and arraign it for their own misdeeds.


## IV

The intolerance, fanaticism, and cruelty that Christians have so often displayed are products of the difficulty (to which I have referred) that human nature finds in containing the fullness of Christian truth, its love and freedom. We assimilate only a part of the truth and are content with that. The full light reaches only a few. We have a capacity for perverting anything, even absolute truth, and turning it into an instrument to serve our own passions. The apostles themselves—the companions of Christ in the flesh, enlightened directly by him—understood his truth only in part and in too human a way, adapting it to their limited Judaic ideas.

To reproach the Christian religion for the fires of the Inquisition and the fanaticism, intolerance, and cruelty of the Middle Ages is to tackle the problem the wrong way around. An attack on medieval religion, founded on a statement of indisputable (but sometimes exaggerated) facts, is not an attack upon Christianity but upon people. It is man attacking man. The theocratic principle was proper to medieval Catholicism. In virtue of it the church was considered too much as a state, and some even conferred on the Pope sovereignty over the whole world. But it was the barbarous nature of humanity, not the Catholic Church, that was responsible for the accompanying cruelty and intolerance. The world at that era was shot through with violent and bloody instincts, and the Church set herself to organize, tame, and Christianize this anarchic world. The resistance of unenlightened human nature was so strong that she did not always succeed. The medieval world may be regarded as formally Christian, but it was in essence half-Christian, half-pagan, and the ecclesiastical hierarchy itself was often enough sinful, bringing ambition and other human passions into the life of the church, and so, disfiguring the truth of Christ. But the divine element continued intact and enlightening; the evangelical voice of our Lord was always there to be heard in its purity. Had it not been for the Christian Church the world of the Middle Ages would have been drowned in blood, and spiritual culture would have perished altogether in Europe, for the best achievements of the culture of Greco-Roman antiquity were conserved by her and handed on to succeeding ages. The scholars, philosophers, and "intellectuals" of those days were all monastics, and it is Christianity we have to thank for the type of chivalric knight who made crude force gentle and its rough strength noble. And anyway, the natural ferocity of medieval man was sometimes better than the mechanization of his contemporary descendant.

Fanaticism did not so much characterize the Eastern Orthodox Church, which knew no Inquisition or similar violence in questions of religion and conscience. Her historical faults were due to a too great submission to the civil power. There were human perversion and sin both in the Catholic Church and in the Orthodox Church, but the errors of Christianity as practiced in the world were always the errors of individual Christians, arising from their natural weakness. If we do not live according to unsullied truth, it is we who are to blame, not truth. We require freedom and are not willing to be constrained to goodness. Nevertheless, we charge God with the consequences of the unlimited freedom that he has given us.

Is either Christ or Christianity responsible for the fact that human life is full of evil? Christ never taught the things that people criticize and repudiate in Christianity. If we had followed his precepts there would have been no reason for revolt against his religion.

In one of H. G. Wells's books there is a dialogue between people and God. They complain that life is full of wickedness and suffering, wars, excesses of all sorts, so that it becomes unbearable, and God replies: "If you don't like these things, don't do them." This remarkably simple passage is very instructive. Christianity on earth has to operate in a land of darkness, surrounded by the forces of wickedness, both natural and supernatural. The might of hell is arrayed against Christ and his Church. These evil powers are at work inside as well as outside the Church and Christianity, seeking to corrupt the one and change the other. But though the "abomination of desolation is set up in the holy place," (Mt. 24: 15) this nonetheless remains holy, and even shines more brilliantly. Those who have spiritual sight see perfectly clearly that to pervert Christianity and then blame it for that which it is not responsible for is to crucify Christ anew. He gives his blood eternally for the sins of the world, for those who deny and crucify him.

Truth cannot be gauged by human behavior, especially that of the worst of us. Truth must be looked in the face and seen by its own light, and among the human reflections of that truth judgment must be made according to the best of them. The Christian faith must be judged by its apostles and martyrs, by its heroes and saints, and not by the mass of half-Christian-half-pagans who do all they can to deform the image of their faith.

Two great tests were given to Christian people: persecution and victory. The first was surmounted, and by its martyrs and confessors under the Romans, Christianity triumphed in its beginnings as it does under communist persecution in Russia today [1928]. But the test of victory is harder, and when the Emperor Constantine bowed down before the cross and Christianity became the official religion of the empire a very long test of that kind began. And it was surmounted less successfully than the other. Christians often changed from persecuted into persecutor, they let themselves succumb to the temptations of the kingdoms of this world and their power. Then there crept into Christianity those perversions of its truth that have been made the source of accusations against it. Christianity is not responsible for that which its critics do not understand, the joy of earthly victory. Christ was crucified once more, for those who looked on themselves as his servants while they did not know of what spirit they were.


## V


Those people of today who are distant from Christianity are fond of saying that the Church ought to be made up of perfect people, saints, and complain that she includes so many faulty persons, sinners, and pseudo-Christians. It is the standing argument against Christianity, and it is one that betrays noncomprehension or forgetfulness of the nature and essence of the Church. The Church exists before all else for sinners, for imperfect and wandering beings. Her origins are in heaven and her principle is eternal, but she operates on the earth and in time, among elements submerged in sin. Her first business is to be merciful to an erring and suffering world, to save it for eternal life and raise it to the heavens. The essence of Christianity is a union of eternity and time, of heaven and earth, of the divine and the human, and not any separation between them. The human and temporal are not to be despised and rejected but enlightened and transfigured.

In the early days of Christianity there was a sectarian movement called Montanism, which claimed that the Church ought to consist exclusively of righteous and godly beings and that all others should be rejected by her. She was for the Montanists a community of those who had received special gifts from the Holy Spirit and by far the greater part of mankind, being sinful, was to be completely repudiated by her. Ecclesiastical consciousness condemned Montanism and upheld the Church as the home of sinners who repent. The saints are the Church's bulwark and buttress, but she does not depend on them alone, for the whole of mankind—a mankind seeking salvation—contributes in varying degrees to her perfecting. The Church on earth is the Church militant struggling against evil and iniquity. She is not yet the Church glorified or victorious. Christ himself spoke with tax collectors and sinners, visited their homes and ate with them, and the Pharisees criticized him for it. His Church has to be like him. A Christianity that extended its recognition only to good people would be a pharisaical Christianity. Compassion, forgiveness, love for one's neighbor with all his shortcomings—these are the works of Christian love and the means toward its perfection. To accuse Christianity of having to do with sinful people, those who might dull the Church's image, this would be hypocrisy and pharisaism.

Montanism is an example of false maximizing. It is spiritual pride, false morality, ultimately a lack of love. The falsehood of maximizing consists in requiring the most from others but not from oneself. We accuse them of not achieving a perfection of goodness that we have not even considered ourselves. Those who have attained holiness are not in the habit of accusing others or judging them. Christianity, the religion of love, unites strictness toward oneself with compassion and love for one's neighbor. The charges of our contemporaries are only pretexts for their animosity against Christianity, attempted justifications of their own treachery toward it. They are hiding behind a false morality.

Christianity must not be confused with Tolstoyism, which is an abstract moralism. Tolstoy criticizes the historical so-called Christianity radically and cruelly, and his criticism is not without justification, for it is founded on fact. He claims that the Christian religion was professed as an abstraction, without any actualization of it in life and conduct. For him our Lord's moral teaching constituted the whole of the Christian religion: he was ignorant of or opposed to its hidden mystical sides. He believed that everything depends on the truth of a concept, and that once it was understood it was a simple matter to put it into practice. If one recognizes the true law of the master of life—that is, of God—it will be easy, by virtue of that recognition, to actualize it. Tolstoy did not recognize our freedom or see the evil lurking in the depths of human nature. He imagined the source of wickedness to be in the consciousness instead of in the will and its freedom. Accordingly, he did not recognize the help of divine grace for the overcoming of evil, but looked rather for a modification of consciousness. Jesus Christ was for him not a savior and redeemer but a great educator for life, a moral legislator. Tolstoy thought Christianity was easy to put into practice because it is simpler, more advantageous, and wiser to live according to a law of love than according to the world's law of hatred. He imagined that Christ teaches us "not to do silly things." He attributed the blame for the fact that the religion of Christ is not made real in life to theological teaching that concentrates attention on our Lord himself, building up all things on the redemption accomplished by him and on divine grace. Tolstoy attacked the Church at her foundations.

He was right to demand that Christianity be taken seriously and that Christ's precepts be translated into action, but he was mistaken in believing that this is easy and that it can be done simply by means of an enlightened consciousness, without Christ our Savior or the grace of the Holy Spirit. In asking people to make this attempt Tolstoy fell into the error of moral maximizing. For the rest, he did not succeed in realizing in his own life the doctrine that he upheld. The only Christianity that he recognized as authentic was his own personal brand, which found the majority of people guilty of immorality because they did not renounce their private property, because they did not work with their hands, because they ate meat and smoked, among other failings. But he was not strong enough to achieve moral maximization for himself. Love became for him a law without grace, a source of indictment. Tolstoy had a well-balanced critical faculty. He could diagnose sin and describe well the unchristian character of his contemporary society and culture, but he did not see Christianity itself, hidden behind the sinfulness, imperfections, and deformities of Christians. Pride in his own reason prevented him from becoming Christian inwardly. Christ remained an external teacher and could not be welcomed within. But Tolstoy was a man of genius, great in his search for divine truth. Many who have neither his genius nor his thirst for truth attack both Christianity and Christians without trying to realize any perfection in their own existence, and without the problem of the meaning and justification of life causing them any suffering.

## VI

It is a mistake to suppose that it is easy to live according to our Lord's commands, and to condemn his teaching because Christians do not practice it. But it is also a mistake to suppose that there is no need to realize the fullness of Christianity in the whole of life. At every moment of his existence the Christian ought to seek a perfection like to that of his heavenly Father and to lay claim to the divine kingdom; all his life is subject to the words "Seek first the kingdom of God and his righteousness, and all these things shall be given to you."

The fact that our nature is sinful and that the ideal is in every way unattainable on earth must not paralyze our striving after perfection or quench our longing for the Kingdom and righteousness of God. We must try to apply divine truth without worrying about how it will be realized in the fullness of life. The truth of Christ must be so realized, though little may be accomplished on earth, though a person may give but an hour of his life to it. And the right way is found in the effort to fulfill it and to find the heavenly kingdom without criticizing our neighbor.

Christianity is entering upon an entirely new era. Henceforth it will be impossible to live the faith only externally, to stop short at fulfilling rules and observing various rites. Believers will have to take the full realization of their faith more seriously. They will have to defend it by their own personalities, by their lives, by their faithfulness to Christ and his principles, by meeting hatred with love.

In the Orthodox Church today the better elements, those most sincere and enthusiastic, most capable of self-sacrifice and faithfulness to our Lord, are coming to the front, while she is being abandoned by those who were Orthodox only outwardly or from habit, without understanding of their faith and what it committed them to. It may be said that the age of a confused Christianity and paganism is at an end and that a new and better one has begun. Christianity had become a dominating, established state religion, and the Church was tempted by the sword of Caesar. She even used it against those whose faith was not in agreement with that of the rulers. It was for this reason, because Christianity had become associated with the idea of persecutor rather than that of persecuted, that many judged it no longer to be the religion of the cross. It was too often interpreted as a sanctification of pagan customs that did not call for any real illumination and transfiguration. The time has now come when Christianity is persecuted anew, and a greater heroism, a greater expiatory love, a more complete and conscientious confession of the faith are asked for from Christians. We shall no longer be a stone of offense in the path of our faith.

## VII

The Christian faith tells us to seek first the Kingdom of God and divine perfection, but it will have nothing to do with daydreaming, utopias, or false imagination. It is realistic and the Fathers of the Church are always appealing for spiritual sobriety. Christian consciousness has a clear perception of all the difficulties that beset the way of perfection, but it knows that "the kingdom of Heaven has been subjected to violence and the violent take it by force." Christianity teaches us to work from within to the outward and not vice versa. The perfect life, whether individual or social, cannot be attained through any program imposed externally. Spiritual rebirth is essential and it proceeds from freedom and grace. Compulsion will never make good Christians or a Christian social order; there must be an effective and real change in the hearts of persons and of peoples, and the realization of this perfect life is a task of infinite difficulty and endless duration.

The negation of Christianity due to the shortcomings of Christians is essentially the ignoring and misunderstanding of original sin. Those who are conscious of original sin see in the unworthiness of Christians not a flat contradiction of the worth of Christianity but a confirmation of it. It is the religion of redemption and salvation, and is not forgetful that the world finds pleasure in sin. There are many teachers who claim that the good life can be compassed without any real overcoming of evil, but Christianity does not think so. It insists on this victory, a rebirth. It is radical and more exacting.

Many historical persons and institutions were decked out with Christian emblems that they did not deserve. There is nothing baser than lies, simulation, and hypocrisy, and this state of things provoked protest and revolt. The state bore the name and symbols of Christianity without being effectively Christian, and the same could be said of everything else—science, art, economics, law, the whole of "Christian culture." There were even those who tried to uphold the rich and great of this world and the social exploitation of man by man by an appeal to Christianity! The pagan consciousness still lived on in many in Christendom. Such a person was called to take his part in the building up of Christian life, but meanwhile the old evil passions continued to stir within him. The Church influenced him interiorly but could not alter his nature by force. The process had to be inward and hidden. God's kingdom comes imperceptibly. A vast amount of hypocrisy, falsehood, convention, and empty rhetoric accumulated in Christendom, and insurrection against it was inevitable. The revolt against and rejection of Christianity often represented simply a sincere wish for the outside to be like the inside. If there is no interior religion then there should be none exterior. If the state, society, and culture are not Christian then they should not be called so. There is no need for sham and lies. Such a protest has its positive side in the hatred of falsehood and love of truth. But along with its truth and sincerity, its protest against lies and hypocrisy, came a new lie and a new hypocrisy.

Starting from the premise that people and society were in fact only superficially and imperfectly Christian the stage was reached where it was affirmed that Christianity itself is untrue and a myth, that the failure of Christians means the failure of their faith. The critics then began to flatter themselves that they had reached a higher level, a greater perfection, a more authentic profession of faith. Thus anti-Christian hypocrisy took the place of Christian hypocrisy, and the adversaries of Christianity esteemed themselves, as such, more virtuous and enlightened and understanding of truth than mere Christians can be. Actually, these people were led astray by the worldly view that denies truth because it is more impressed by its perversions than by its reality. In that they have lost the sense of sin, they are inferior to Christians.

Nietzsche fought Christianity passionately because he looked only at degenerate and outward Christians. As for the Christian faith, he never began to try to understand it.

The Christian world is undergoing a crisis that is shaking it to its foundations. The day of sham, outward, rhetorical religion is past, and henceforward it will be impossible to wed the externals of Christianity with a deceitful paganism. An age of effective realism is beginning that is tearing away the veils that hide the primordial realities and bringing the human soul face to face with the mysteries of life and death. Social conventions, political and governmental forms have lost all significance. People want to penetrate to the depths of life, to learn what is essential and what is useful, to live in truth and righteousness.

Under the influence of contemporary upheavals souls are born thirsting above all for an unobscured and undeformed truth. We are tired of falsehood and conventions and all the forms and appearances that have taken the place of reality. We want to see the truth of Christianity, shorn of the deceptions that bad Christians have imposed on it. We want to come to Christ himself. The Christian renaissance will be above all an appeal to Christ and to his truth freed from all human perversion and adaptation. Our renewed consciousness of the permanent fact of original sin need not weaken consciousness of our responsibility toward the work of our Lord in the world nor nullify efforts to forward work. To make the truth and commands of Christ real sometimes seems a desperate, impossible undertaking, and Christianity itself tells us that it is a task that cannot be achieved by our unaided human powers. But what is impossible for man is possible for God. He who believes in Christ knows that he is not alone: he knows that he is called to realize the truth of Christ in company with Christ himself, his savior.

*Father Cyprian (Constantine Eduardovich) Kern (1899–1960) received degrees in both law and theology at the University of Belgrade in 1925. He was one of the founders, along with Fr. Nicolas Afanasiev, of the Fraternity of St. Seraphim of Sarov, an association of Russian émigré students devoted to the church. He became a monk and was ordained a priest in 1927. The rest of his life was given to teaching and pastoral work in Serbia, in Jerusalem with the Russian Mission, and at Mother Maria Skobtsova's hostel in Rue Lourmel. From 1936 until his death he was a professor at St. Sergius Theological Institute in Paris and pastor of a parish in the suburb of Clamart. In the years after World War II he and Fr. Afanasiev established the still-running week of study, prayer, and fellowship that gathers Christians of the East and West at St. Sergius. He was a teacher of important figures in the next generation, including Frs. Boris Bobrinskoy, Alexander Schmemann, and John Meyendorff. Father Kern's 1947 study* The Eucharist *was formative for Fr. Schmemann's development of liturgical theology and liturgical renewal. Father Kern's adherence to the tradition, along with his ability to criticize its decline, are both in evidence in the following selection. The accommodated, theologically impoverished models of pastoral behavior and service in the Russian church are sharply contrasted with the biblical models of the pastor and disciple.*

# TWO MODELS OF THE PASTORATE: LEVITICAL AND PROPHETIC

The historical study of the mutual relations of the Old Testament's levitical and prophetic institutions does not fall within the purview of this essay. This would belong to the subject of biblical archeology and history. Thus the systematic exegesis of the relevant texts and books, both legalistic and prophetic, has no bearing on my theme. I will refer to those texts only when they can serve to substantiate the basic thoughts of my theme and shed a biblical light on that which is especially relevant to these two concepts. It should be remembered that there is no part of this article and not a single mention of the levitical name that should be understood as some kind of a diminishment of this sacred Old Testament institution. It should not be forgotten that the levites were part of a divinely established institution and any attempt to remove them from their prominent place would be a violation of something sacred.

In this connection it is important to make one more caveat in clarifying our theme. The expressions "levitical" and "prophetic" in the sense and in their mutual relationship used by me are not just mine. I am appropriating them from one of the most original minds of nineteenth century Russia, Bishop Porfirii Uspensky, who in his time was the authoritative expert on the Church. In his mind these expressions had an especially specific meaning. They are seen not so much in their literal, Biblical historical meaning as an institution for service to God, but as a special *terminus technicus* (technological term) as a characteristic of a particular temperament, as a specific key in that service. In saying

First published in *Zhivoe predanie*, trans. Alvian Smirensky (Paris: YMCA Press, 1937).

"levite" or "prophet" I thus presume, so to say, to describe a pastoral style. A levitical and a pastoral designation in this case is used to define specific categories of spirituality. These are not institutions of religious practice but are religious and psychological types.

Pastoral theology takes note of types of pastoral practice. For example, we make a distinction between a rural priest, an urban priest, a missionary, a teacher in a theological school, a catechist, etc. Do levitical or prophetic approaches describe special ways of sacred service? No. A levitical and a prophetic style of pastoral service can manifest itself in any of the above-mentioned categories. Furthermore, pastoral theology makes a distinction between good and evil pastoral activity. These are qualities of pastoral service. A question arises: is a "levite" synonymous with a bad pastor? Not at all. A levite can function with very deep, sincere, and pure motives. We do not see a levite as necessarily a mean, negligent, avaricious, or an unworthy pastor. A levite is not necessarily stupid, but the style of his service will still be a synonym for a certain spiritual backwardness.

It is time to raise the question: What are these types of pastoral practice? What are their substantial differences?

A levitical type, in this special meaning, is one from a priestly caste, one who is conventional, formal, narrowly nationalistic, inert, and uncreative. In Old Testament times the Mosaic Law priesthood was hereditary and exclusive. There were sufficiently legitimate historical precedents for this. Christ's preaching and ministry inaugurated something new. A new vine was planted. The Word of God and truth were no longer the property of a particular people but were preached to the whole world and to all creation. The God-man and high priest himself gave the example and opened a new way to the priesthood. He did not select his "little flock" from influential families and tribes, nor did he gather his apostles because of their special status. Here is the beginning of the new and not hereditary priesthood. The apostles, hierarchs, Fathers, and teachers of Christianity came into the Church from all walks of life to proclaim eternal life. A shoemaker and a shepherd became bishops. A refined philosopher and a lawyer became Christian apologists. Ordinary laymen became guardians of holy things and bearers of truth. No wonder the words of the apostle Peter that Christians are "a chosen race, a royal priesthood, a holy nation, called into destiny" are so often mentioned and commented upon by the fathers. This universal priesthood of Christians, not the hierarchical but spiritual, was frequently mentioned in the first years of the Church's life. For this reason an exclusive priestly caste is totally out of place in Christianity.

Bishop Porfirii says:

The holy fathers and teachers of the Church, Dionysius Areopagite, Ignatius, Tertullian, Chrysostom, Basil the Great, Gregory, and Augustine did not inherit their altars and cathedrals from their fathers. Nicholas the wonder worker, Spyridon,

Lucian the presbyter and martyr did not study in the academies such as we have. There were bishops and priests in Russia long before the establishment of seminaries. (*Book of My Life*, vol. 3, p. 95)

Until the time when, because of historical circumstances, the priesthood locked itself into a caste, it was more free and alive. Having become locked up, it acquired and expanded its inherent deficiencies. It narrowed its path. It backed away from its flock. It unwittingly transformed itself into a clerical estate and appropriated exclusive prerogatives for itself, presuming itself to be the Church.

This engendered the mistaken view of sacerdotal service not as an "example of virtue but as a means of livelihood; not as a service subject to responsibility but as an authority not subject to accountability" (*Third Oration* of Gregory the Theologian). Pastors who are levites at heart jealously preserve the exclusiveness of their caste and cannot tolerate the appearance of a priesthood outside of their caste.

A characteristic mark of the levites is their conventional stamp. It became a problem in that caste's environment. This conventional image is very close and familiar for Russians. The strong, rooted, centuries-old Russian social establishment ensured a stagnation everywhere, in every stratum of society. It was especially deeply rooted within the clerical milieu. We all remember, or in any case, have heard about that dense, nearly impenetrable clerical society. Who is not nostalgic for those pictures, long lost to the past, and which are found nowhere in the West and not even among our Orthodox brethren in the Balkans and in the Near East? This static, dear to the heart way of life is gone. We can regret its passing. We can be nostalgic about it, but in no way can or should we artificially restore it, as if it is an essential attribute of clerical life and work. Convention is a witness of a degree of an incarnation or a manifestation of a particular spirit in life, but convention that is artificially constructed can in no way recreate the spirit of the past. For this reason convention is sterile: it is afraid of anything new and is capable of quenching real progress, replacing the substance with form.

Thus, to presume the need for some kind of a narrowly conventional state as essential for priestly service is to sin against the very essence of the evangelical concept of the pastoral office. It is an attempt to confuse the living pastoral vocation with levitical formalism.

Personal convention arose within the framework of a common social convention and is an essential part of it. And here is another characteristically levitical trait—its subordination to specific lifestyles, perhaps an adherence to a particular structure, a conformism with an evident social evil. Many bitter words of condemnation have already been directed by Old Testament prophets against this failing of pastors. In contrast to this, the more vivid examples of what has not been in conformance with the fallacy of the well-known social order, we find in the face of the "fiery and flaming" prophet, and the one "clothed with camel's hair and girded with a leather belt"—Elijah and John the Baptist. The earliest successors of the apostles were of similar indifference to earthly goods and honors of this world, those about whom an early source says: "They live in their own countries but as aliens. They have a share in everything as citizens, and endure everything as foreigners. Every foreign land is their fatherland, and yet for them every fatherland is a foreign land. . . . They busy themselves on earth but their citizenship is in heaven. They obey the established laws, but in their own lives they go far beyond what the laws require" (*Letter to Diognetus*, vol. 5: 10). These were whom Chrysostom called "the angelic society" and "newly-born" (Acts) because they still retained the purity and the fervor of the evangelical temperament. The Christian church presented great and splendid examples of its pastors' struggles against social evils and those lifestyles followed by royalty that, on the strength of their authority and power, impinged upon the sacred character of the church. The daring defenders of the church against such abuse contributed their names to the glorious list of the church's witnesses and martyrs. From apostolic times until now, they serve as our inspirers and examples: Ambrose, John Chrysostom, Philip of Moscow, Arsenii Matsevich, Metropolitan Benjamin, and others.

Nonetheless, at the same time numerous other servants before the altar, positioning themselves in the service of the system and becoming submissive before secular falsehoods, became witnesses to the sad impotency of levitism. Many people hostile to the church frequently entertain this aberration: today's Christianity has subjected itself to the service of particular forms of state powers, a capitalistic structure, and thus the church has somehow allied itself with wealth. The poverty of apostolic times has been forgotten as well as the less-than-privileged status of the primitive Christian church, as was the "holy poverty" of Francis of Assisi and the venerable Sergius of Radonezh. There are numerous admonitions and criticisms made by many of today's writers about this deficiency. One cannot but agree with this, and pastoral conscience does not permit one to contradict them.

It is interesting that this deficient tendency can easily and subtly operate concurrently with the most sincere and outstanding pastoral endeavor.

Great and notable ascetics, whose personal monastic, spiritual, and pastoral lives were without reproach, at the same time endorsed many things within a socially evil system. They excused what was inadmissible and justified evil, thus becoming servants of what was false. A personal ascetical life was not infrequently mixed with a service to, or a political accommodation with, forces of social evil. This obscured the purity of the pastoral way by distorting it and by submitting the Kingdom of God to Caesar.

According to the Fathers, priestly service is incomparably higher than royal service (Chrysostom, *Sermon 3*, "On the Priesthood")—"The worthiness of priesthood is beyond measure" (Ephrem the Syrian, "Sermon on the

Priesthood")—but throughout history the priesthood, to great distress, not infrequently lowered itself to the service of the traitorous interests of the police. Frequently the Semitic priesthood, in their accommodation to the forms of the state's ways in order to preserve its shaky authority, actually lowered its own status in seeking protection for itself from the state. For example, this is how the missionary pastors, members of the Missionary Assembly, behaved in seeking the support of the secular armed forces against sectarians and schismatics (Archbishop Anthony Khrapovistsky, *Works*, vol. II, p. 303). The pastor who teaches with reliance upon punitive police powers distorts his apostolic ministry to zero and violates the Gospel. The pastor who accommodates himself to the establishment, no matter which kind, and defends social evil, is no longer Christ's servant. "Am I now seeking the favor of men, or of God? Or am I trying to please men? If I were still pleasing men, I should not be a servant of Christ," writes St. Paul (Gal 1:10; 1 Thes 2:4–6).

The self-contained and ossified Old Testament levitical institution of scribes gave birth to the concept of the "tradition of the fathers," followed by Talmudism. It is of no purpose to think that Talmudism is an achievement of the Hebrew tradition alone. Alas! It has penetrated and has broadly spread itself into Christian religious psychology as well. It should be remembered that Christ the Savior has not so fervently remonstrated against any sin or human failing as he did against Talmudism, that legalistic, bookish approach to God. The most profound failures and distortions of the human soul found the possibility of forgiveness but the Talmudic ossification of the Living Truth found only a bitter rebuke and severe denunciation. Why? Because this was a sign of slavery, of spiritual cowardice and a lack of faith. The Talmudist believes that one is saved through form, length of prayers, this or that potion, the quantity of olives, dates, and figs, and not divine mercy. It is precisely this that kills the life of the Spirit. A true submission to the Spirit, in spirit and in truth is distorted into a dead, formalistic service, in a performance of rites and an obsession with rubrical detail. This perhaps is one of the more frightening particularities of the levitical style.

As in any religious life, as well as in Christianity, there are elements that are eternal and that are transitory. The confusion of these two concepts, the canonization of transient forms, the designation of something that is simply old as something eternal and as such, immutable, is precisely a witness to this levitical inclination toward Christian Talmudism. In the life of any religion, as long as it has not finally died, there were and will be conflicts and struggles between the two directions and trends: conservative and creative, static and dynamic, Old-Ritual-levitical and the boldly prophetic.

In Christianity this Talmudism is a remnant of that trend in the Church, which already in the first century would creep to the surface and somehow try to grab and hold back the gradually receding Old Testament Law. The struggle between the Judaizing, narrowly legalistic attitude with the broad, universal, and creative approach was not resolved at the Apostolic Council in 51 A.D. It has always been present in the Church. There had always been pastors and laity who would seek their salvation in form, in the letter, in petty prescriptions of the *Ustav*, a manual prescribing minute details of liturgical rites, fasting, etc. developed in monasteries, whether this related to fasting, prayer, or to something else. There was always the desire to replace the essence of the Good News, to shackle the spirit, to elevate sacrifice over mercy, to strain at the gnat of the *Ustav,* and swallow the camel.

Everything that is being described is by no means, and not even in a small measure, an attack on the holiness of tradition and the legacy from the past, since Christianity is a living reality and not something doctrinaire or bureaucratic. But it is alive only in the Church, only where grace and heritage from the past abide. Without a loyalty to the past, Christianity is incomplete. Thus, by the way, it must be pointed out that the desire to turn back to absolute primitive Christianity, to toss aside the centuries-old and living experience of the Church is unsavory and essentially incorrect. "Back to Christ" means to turn away the whole of the Church's tradition. This would be a dissipation of all the riches in the Church's treasure house: those mystical and ascetic experiences, liturgical theology, iconography, etc. In other words, it would be an impoverishment or a rejection of Christianity. The Church and her life do not reflect only primitive Christianity, no matter how tempting it may be for us. That life reflects the fullness of the total experience of the humanity of God in all the ages. Yet the rejection of every approach to that tradition and experience, which is Talmudic or formalistic, is in no way a contradiction of, or an irreverence toward, that love and loyalty toward the Church's tradition and experience.

The formalistic and Talmudic approach is precisely what kills the living heritage of the grace-filled Church. Talmudism and the primacy of form shackles the creative impulse, does not adapt to the eternally revealed Truth and practically forbids the Church to live. This Talmudism impinges not only on the parochial, liturgical, and administrative lives of the Church; it goes further. It does not think. It does not live by the Spirit. It refuses to acknowledge theological creativity. It is like the people of the Old Testament who told the prophets "Do not prophesy" (Am 2:12), or "Prophesy not to us what is right" (Is 30:10). For them revelation had come to a stop. They said, "Truth, which is necessary for our salvation, has been revealed in full. The Church can exist and live on the wealth of its spiritual capital accumulated over the ages. Everything has been given to us in the Gospel and the Fathers. Anything else comes from evil and is not needed."

Here one forgets that thought cannot avoid thinking. Man's mind, according to St. Gregory the Theologian, cannot avoid moving toward the Great Mind, that man has not been created just to be a passive recipient of prepared and ready-made truths from on high, but that he himself participates in revelation, he himself seeks and creates. Creativity is one of the attributes of man's spirit, which reflects the image and likeness of God. New life continues to be created in the Church.

The pastor-levite is afraid of this in the Church. He wants to put a stop to its life-flowing source. He himself does not think. He is afraid to think and forbids others to think. He is completely immersed in a deep and placid hibernation. He is oblivious to any of the cries of contemporary questions raised by a dangerously sick, suffering, and disturbed humanity. Nothing disturbs him in his spiritual hibernation. He is unaware of anything that goes on around him and only wants one thing: how to remain in his dormant and inert state as long as possible while justifying himself in that by this he is somehow "guarding" something.

The pastor-levite likewise wants to settle on the ossified forms of the expressions of faith. He speaks in some kind of a pseudoclassical preacher's jargon, larded with Church-Slavonic expressions that are difficult for the faithful to understand. He is afraid of the living, commonly understood language. The levitic school and the manual of ecclesiastical rhetoric in the spirit of the homilies of hierarchs such as Filaret and Innocent forbid him from speaking otherwise.

The pastor-levite introduces the Talmudic spirit in the celebration of divine services. The form and the letter are more valuable to him than the sincere, prayerful attitude coming from the heart. He is afraid to make of divine service something more comprehensible and accessible to the faithful. He is a slave of the rooted, petty patterns in the sacred ritual; for example, the reading of the Word of God in a well-known stereotype, with rolling vocal cadences, in an attempt to impress the listeners with his lower and higher registers, which may be completely incomprehensible to the faithful. He loves pomp and theatrical nuances and believes these to be the sense and meaning of Orthodox church service. The spirit of Talmudism tries to justify itself with its love for ritualistic traditions, but that love does not go beyond an empty formalism: it becomes a ritual for the sake of ritual and external esthetics at the price of comprehending the prayer's meaning. The New Testament Talmudism is mistaken if it thinks that form and ritual engenders a spirit of prayer. If the prayerful spirit is absent, if the priest does not have the prayer within him, then no book of rubrics can create a prayerful atmosphere. The book of rubrics can be compared here to "the way we do things." As such, it generates a particular attitude but in itself it is nugatory. It is nothing more than a monument or a record of a particular way of prayer and its development, and a regulating symbol of liturgical life and practice, but of itself it creates nothing, nor can it bring to life a fading light.

The levitical spirit also confines itself into narrowly nationalistic frameworks. It overlooks that salvation has been proclaimed to all, that in the Gospel there is neither Jew nor Greek, that there is no place for chauvinism in the Church. Becoming a slave to forms of social structure, canonizing and justifying man-made superstructures and barriers, the levitical spirit is likewise enslaved to national fetishes. The idea of a truly Catholic Church embracing all tribes and peoples is alien to it. The levite does not discern in the miracle of the fiery tongues at Pentecost how "all began to speak in strange tongues with strange doctrines, by the strange commands of the Holy Trinity," how in the divine symphony of tongues all the people give one mighty accord to the glory of God's name. He cannot rise above his ethnic, provincial interests and tastes. He still crawls about within the boundaries of Old Testament concepts and is incapable of rising to the level of the whole world. This spirit of pagan love only toward his own people and language stands in the way of the levite's ability to pray in Church if the singing there is not according to his accustomed style and not even in his own language. Here, that narrowly ethnic spirit at one time made the Greeks burn Arabic service books and Bulgarian *antimensions* (altar cloths), while the Slavs burned the Greek ones. The whole idea of the universal oneness of the Church is alien for the levite. He is quite pleased with what he has. He makes no effort to learn about the life and faith of his coreligionist brothers or to pray with them with one mouth and one heart, even if in different languages. He is not disturbed by the estrangement of Christians and the scattering of the flock. The problem of uniting the scattered bits and pieces of Christianity does not concern him, nor does he think about it. The sight of the present rending of Christ's robe leaves him indifferent. He is not disturbed that the Church remains shattered in the face of militant atheism. Divided along dogmatic questions, among tribes and nations, along the differences of the calendar and of customs, according to jurisdictions and names of hierarchs, the Church today stands as a reproach to all, and especially to pastors. It is especially sad and painful to see this division of Christ's seamless robe where it would seem there should be no place for it: at Jerusalem's holy places, at the Lord's sepulcher, at the foot of trembling Golgotha, where at one time the Roman soldiers dared not to tear Christ's robe. The pastor, who is indifferent to this, who is not sick at heart, and who does not fervently pray for the union of all has failed to overcome that levitical spirit within himself. He has not been able to rise to the level of Christ's high priestly prayer, "that they may all be one" (Jn 17:20).

The priesthood of the levitical tradition, in other words, has fallen into a deep slumber. It fell asleep even before the Divine Logos ascended upon the earth, and it has neither awakened nor was it capable of hearing how that Logos, having become incarnate, proclaimed a new Truth and a new commandment for all people—and most certainly and primarily for the pastors, who are called to carry out that commandment.

What, then, is a "prophet" as a type and a role model for a pastor in the Church?

It is not that which the Church designated and canonized as a specific type of righteous individuals in the Old Testament. Although the term is taken from the Bible, it is given a somewhat different meaning, more akin to the types found in early Christian times. A prophet in that sense is not one who foretells the future. He is a bearer of the creative spirit who does not hesitate along the path of his pastoral activity, always hungers and thirsts for communion with the Source of righteousness, sensitive to everything that takes place in the world, not compromising with the deeply rooted evil and falsehood no matter by what authorities of this world they may be sanctioned. These are pastors who are conscious of being priests of God in the highest, of the Living God, themselves living expressions of the faith. It is those pastors who sense and experience the tragedy of Christianity and of their own calling.

An Old Testament prophet was rarely a priest (Ez 1:3; Jer 1:1; 1 Chr 24:20). These were two parallel institutions of the religious establishment. But the New Testament priest must also be a prophet in the spirit of his pastoral calling. He cannot be otherwise. The Old Testament levite becomes a priest as a birthright. A prophet is called directly by God. Neither the privilege of caste nor the accomplishments of the forebears could elevate him to the level of his service. "I am no prophet, nor a prophet's son," they said (Am 7:14).

The Old Testament prophet denounced the shortcomings of priests, kings, and people by his flaming rhetoric and his lifestyle. He was sent from on high as a kind of corrective for the inadequate examples of the priesthood. The priest of the New Testament, as a prophet, must constantly hear that divine voice as a corrective within himself.

The Old Testament prophets were directly called from all levels of society and from different places (kings, shepherds, etc.), and were inspired by the Holy Spirit. Christ's pastors receive that same grace of the Holy Spirit at their ordination "which always heals that which is infirm and completes that which is wanting."[1] If those ancient prophets heard the voice of God and communed with God, then the New Testament prophet-priest communes regularly with the Lord himself in the sacred mystery of the Eucharist. Doesn't he hear the Lord's voice? The ancient prophet was not afraid to open his ears and his heart to the knowledge and discernment of the Divine Truth. Must the New Testament prophet-priest be afraid of this, he who is given no lesser measure of the grace of that same Holy Spirit, no matter how awesome, out-of-place, and disturbing that Truth may be? The prophet of old preached the idea of moral renewal and an internal rebirth (Is 1:10, 6:7; Hos 6:1, 12:3, 6, etc.) and condemned social evil and the injustices of the powerful, stirring his people and priests awake. He was an uncompromising guardian of truth. Must not the New Testament prophet and priest be no less than that? Has he not been called to carry out his service toward the mystical transfiguration of the world?

In the Old Testament God gave Moses the institution of priesthood and the ritual of sacrifice. The Levites were the custodians who carried out those prescriptions. The prophets in their merciless chastisement of the Levites did not condemn the ritual and sacrifice. They rose up against the manner of carrying out these rituals and sacrifices. They fulminated against the priests who "have done violence to my law and profaned what was sacred to me. They make no distinction between the sacred and common" (Ez 22:26 ); against "you priests who despise my Name" (Mal 1:6); who "give direction in return for a bribe" (Mi 3:11) ; "who care only for themselves" (Ez 34:2); and who "feed on the sin of my people, they are greedy for their iniquity" (Hos 4:8). Thus the New Testament pastor must constantly engender within himself the prophet's relationship toward sacrifice, prayer, and the rules of the Church, and not the perfunctory levitical treatment of the sacred.

The Old Testament prophets were servants of all the people. Naturally, they stood on the level of the national Hebrew understanding of revelation and the idea of the divinely chosen Israel. One must not forget that there also were prophets who rose above this narrowly national level. The Lord called some of them for service beyond the confines of the Hebrew people (the prophet Jonah) and opened up broader horizons for them (Zec 7:12–13). But they were incapable of rising to the idea of service to the whole of mankind. This became the lot of the New Testament pastors. Here the pastor must not dare to turn back to the Old Testament concept and lock himself within nationalistic boundaries. The task of the Christian pastor is broader and he must sacrifice his ethnicity, his customs, and his prejudices in favor of broader, universal service. Patriotic tendencies, no matter how exalted they may be, cannot be above the Evangelical, universal aims. Nationality must be subordinated to the universal, Christian transnationality. If the pastor is unable to do this he is once again a slave to levitical atavism.

Bishop Porfirii said:

In all of Europe there is a great spiritual crop failure. The mediocrity and the deep hibernation of spiritual forces replace the stimulation and the flow of gifts in the sphere of certainty, goodness, beauty and truth. Russia is exhausted by spiritual poverty. Where are our prophets who would nurture Russia with inspiring words, inclined towards faith, poetry and the beauty of the spiritual world? Where are our prophets who, in God's name and that of the Gospel, would preach freedom to the enslaved? Where are the apostles? (*Book of My Life*, vol. 3, pp. 238–239).

But the prophetic spirit and style is so uncommon in the general level of the spiritual bourgeoisie. They seem like harsh discordant sounds. They disturbingly force themselves into the quiet murmur of comfortable and serenely happy Christianity. Such people are looked upon as utopian simpletons. So, the question arises: Is prophetic service possible today? Is it not a specific variant of the Old Testament or early Christian religious practice?

If one views religious life as something completely fixed and immobile, sees Christianity simply as an accumulation of completed maxims, and pastoral calling as merely the task of preserving traditions and established rites and forms, then the prophetic inclination and a fervent spirit is but an anachronism and any effort to attain this is a futile, pitiful, and dangerous attempt to return to a life that has long ago gone by the wayside.

But if Christianity is not dead, if the Church is alive even now, if our Liturgy still has that force as it had in the early days of the Church's life, if the divine, miraculous grace is still efficacious through the priest and he sanctifies nature, restores the sick, has power over evil, blesses and transforms this world obscured by sin—then we cannot be dead in our faith nor dare to be other than fervent in spirit. In such a case we pastors cannot but be inspired with the spirit of Elijah, Isaiah, the forerunner John the Baptist, the apostle Paul, and the prophets of the *Didache*. I repeat: to be a prophet does not mean only to foretell the future. It means to be bold and vibrant before God. It means not to make peace with the reigning evil. It means to awaken the dormant religious consciousness, to be responsive and deeply sensitive to all problems that are so burdensome to mankind. If the spirit of the apostles and prophets is dead within us then we are merely like a caste of levites and priests offering fiery sacrifices.

Sensing a cooling of spirit in their Christianity and the ossification of empirical forms in their church, the apostle Paul writes to the Thessalonian community: "Do not despise prophesying" (1 Thes 5:20). In that prophetic spirit he saw the boldness of faith, the deposit of authentic service, and he wanted to see the same in his heirs and successors in service to the Incarnate. He was not mistaken in his concerns. Just as in times past Israel told its prophets: "Do not prophesy truth to us, tell us flattering things, have illusionary visions" (Is 30:10; Am 2:13), so the spirit of bold service before God gradually began to diminish. Form began to triumph over substance and only a pale shadow of the Gospel remained. They began to forget and fear that prophetic spirit. To be sure, it is much less disturbing without it. There is no need to be fervent. One need not seek. One can find contentment within the comfortable confines of established ways. In this there is a tremendous temptation. The early Christian community, in the poignancy of its religious inspiration, continued to live in the spirit of prophetic service and was not afraid of it. The *Didache* allowed "the prophets to give thanks as much as they wanted to," that is, literally, "to make Eucharist," to pray liturgically. St. Justin Martyr, the philosopher, likewise testifies that the priests presided and prayed liturgically as much as they could—that is, as much as they were inspired with strength. This shows that they clearly saw and felt the authentic power of faith in their religious inspiration. This was like a criterion of the authentic religious life. There was nothing false or artificial or distorted in this kind of a spiritual path.

In one of his *Orations* (42, the "Farewell") about the miracle of Pentecost, St. Gregory Nazianzus makes an excellent characterization of the state of the spirit in the just-enlightened and grace-filled apostles: "this was the power of the spirit and not the frenzied mind." All service of the Christian Church was centered here. The Christian as such, and especially the pastor, must be filled with the force of the Spirit, that prophetic Spirit. He cannot be otherwise. John Chrysostom was not afraid to say: "We become prophets when God reveals to us that what the eye has not seen nor the ear heard (1 Cor 2:9). In the baptismal font, you become king, priest, and prophet" (*Sermon 3* on II Corinthians).

It probably will not be out of place to say that there has not been a more crucial and responsible time for Christ's Church since apostolic times to this day. The signs of catastrophe and the image of the apocalypse of our era are sufficiently clear for everyone except those who are still blind [ed. note: This essay was published in 1937]. The Lord does not tolerate and strongly condemns a lukewarm faith (Rv 3:16). In our times especially, there can be no dead faith, dormant spirituality, or deafness with respect to what is taking place in the world. There is a shifting of immense strata of what once was firm and stable for centuries. Mobs arise against the church but large caravans of lost strangers also find their way back. The prophet's words stand vividly before today's pastor: "Behold the days are coming, says the Lord God, when I will send famine on the land; not a famine of bread, nor a thirst for water, but of hearing the words of the Lord" (Am 8:11), and he must realize that to quench that hunger and thirst demands a priesthood of a prophetic type. Pastors must be fully armed prophetically to meet today's challenges in carrying out their service. There are many pastoral paths before us and each one of these is blessed and each one demands zealous workers. The path taken depends on individual capabilities and inclinations as well as upon the needs of the church that sends them to be her representatives. But no matter how they will carry out their task, they must do this in the spirit of the Good Shepherd, not looking backward to the secure, peaceful, stable levitical service, but bearing in mind the tragic circumstance of our times and daring to meet the challenge.

But first of all, do not dampen within yourself that religious pastoral inspiration. Go forward following the steps of the prophets and the apostles. Do not fear that youthful fire burning in them. Do not quench it. Do not be tempted to cuddle up to the traditional comforts. Do not fall for esthetics at the cost of spirituality. Do not be afraid, being inspired by the fervent Spirit, not to appear as a contemporary type. Be utopian. Be a fool. Don't be tempted by the comforts of the mediocre spiritual bourgeoisie. Remember the words of St. Gregory Nazianzus that I cited earlier, and serve not with a frenzied mind but with the power of the Spirit.

"Do not quench the Spirit nor do away with prophecy" (1 Th. 5:19). We tried to bring out in this essay just what the prophetic spirit is and what it means to be a prophetic and not a levitical pastor.

## NOTE

1. *Service Book of the Holy Orthodox Catholic Apostolic Church*, translated and compiled by Isabel Florence Hapgood, "Ordination of Priest," p. 316. (New York: Association Press, 1922).

Born in the second generation of Russians settled in France, Fr. John Meyendorff (1926–1992) had as his colleague, both at the St. Sergius Institute in Paris and at St. Vladimir's Seminary in Crestwood New York, Fr. Alexander Schmemann. Trained in Byzantine studies, church history, and theology, he and Fr. Schmemann were for decades the most sought-after Orthodox teachers internationally. In addition to specialized work on Gregory Palamas and Byzantine theology, Fr. Meyendorff became an important voice both in contemporary ecumenical work and inter-Orthodox activities. Along with Fr. Schmemann he worked for the granting of autocephalous status to the Orthodox Church in America (OCA) by the Patriarchate of Moscow in 1970. His voice was heard as an editor of the national church newspaper in editorials on numerous issues, never flinching from difficult matters such as interchurch squabbles and political compromise by churches, including that of Russia against dissidents and the belligerent, divisive actions of the Russian Orthodox Church outside Russia. He succeeded Fr. Schmemann as dean of St. Vladimir's, and continued in the same spirit of renewal and openness as his colleague and predecessor. Fr. John was able to visit Russia after Gorbachev's glasnost policy opened up the country. He was present there during the dangerous days of the coup attempt in 1990. Throughout his career, Fr. Meyendorff was committed to the ecumenical movement and adamantly opposed to the concept of the Orthodox churches being "diaspora" groups dependent on and intrinsically linked to their "mother churches" in other lands. His books continue to be used as significant sources.

Requested to present a paper on the church and the ordained ministry to a commission working on the merger of the major Lutheran bodies in the United

States, Fr. Meyendorff produced this succinct statement of the church's nature and structure, "Church Ministry: For an Orthodox–Lutheran Dialogue." His debt to Fr. Afanasiev is acknowledged and his wide learning is most evident throughout this essay. Given in an ecumenical context, it suggests both his openness to the other churches as well as the distinctive contributions he believed the Orthodox Church could make to them.


## FOR FURTHER READING

Meyendorff, John. *The Byzantine Legacy in the Orthodox Church*. Crestwood, N.Y.: SVSP, 1981.

———. *Byzantine Theology*. 2nd edition. Bronx, N.Y.: Fordham, 1973.

———. *Byzantium and the Rise of Russia*. Cambridge: Cambridge University Press, 1981.

———. *Catholicity and the Church*. Crestwood, N.Y.: SVSP, 1983.

———. *Christ in Eastern Christian Thought*. Crestwood, N.Y.: SVSP, 1975.

———. *Imperial Unity and Christian Division: The Church 450–680*. Crestwood, N.Y.: SVSP, 1989.

———. *Living Tradition*. Crestwood, N.Y.: SVSP, 1978.

———. *Marriage: An Orthodox Perspective*. Crestwood N.Y.: SVSP, 1975.

———. *The Orthodox Church*. 4th edition. Crestwood, N.Y.: SVSP, 1996.

———. *Orthodoxy and Catholicity*. New York: Sheed & Ward, 1966.

———. *Rome, Constantinople, Moscow*. Crestwood, N.Y.: SVSP, 1996.

———. *Witness to the World and Vision of Unity*. Crestwood, N.Y.: SVSP, 1987.

Meyendorff, John, ed. *The Legacy of St. Vladimir*. With John Breck and Elena Silk. Crestwood, N.Y.: SVSP, 1989.

Nassif, Bradley, ed. *New Perspectives on Historical Theology: Essays in Memory of John Meyendorff*. Grand Rapids, Mich.: Eerdmans, 1996.

# CHURCH AND MINISTRY: FOR AN ORTHODOX–LUTHERAN DIALOGUE

The history of Christianity is rarely envisaged in a global—or "catholic"—perspective. The Reformation in particular is most often studied in the light of its immediate roots in Western Christendom—as a reaction against medieval Latin structures, the papacy in particular, and as anticipated in the conciliarism of the early fifteenth century. An Orthodox historian is bound to look at the momentous events of the sixteenth century in the light of the even earlier and, for him, more fundamental rupture, which split the Christian world in two halves: Eastern Orthodoxy and Roman Catholicism. And when he adopts this wider—and for him quite natural—perspective, he recognizes inevitably that Martin Luther and other Reformers were not in direct conflict with the Orthodox Church, but with a papacy that had already been seen in the East as having somewhat perverted the Christian message. The Reformation then appears to him as a consequence of the original schism between East and West.

Today, in attempting to rebuild Christian unity, we look for a possibility to reverse the process of separation. In the light of this new approach, the schisms of the past often acquire a new historical dimension—that of lost opportunities—which can and should serve as lessons for the future. Obviously, the opportunity that was lost in the sixteenth century consists in the absence of the Orthodox East in the tragic struggle within Western Christendom.

This paper was originally presented at a theological convocation on ministry and polity by the Lutheran School of Theology at Chicago, 6–11 February 1983, and was published in *dialog* 22 (Spring 1983): 114–20.

I believe that it is possible to make this affirmation without indulging in simplistic Orthodox triumphalism, simply by recognizing that the Reformers faced and rejected a Catholic tradition that in their time had already lost its original balance.

Actually, the Reformers were not quite oblivious of the Christian tradition of the East, and used its witness in their antipapal polemics. Luther himself appeals to the "Greeks"—in conjunction with the Bohemian Hussites—as being more faithful to the Gospel than the Romanists, especially in their eucharistic practice.[1] More significant still is the prolonged effort of Melanchthon and other Tübingen theologians to establish contacts with patriarch Jeremiah II of Constantinople from 1573–1581.[2] However, at that time East and West lived in different worlds, not only politically and culturally but also spiritually and intellectually. The contacts could not really jell into a significant dialogue. Both Romans and Reformers tried to use the East in their polemics against each other, while the East itself remained passively frozen within the Muslim occupation of the Middle East, or, in Russia, in a state of cultural infancy, having only recently emerged from the Mongol conquest.

What is sad, however, is that the opportunity missed in the sixteenth century has not yet been picked up in our time. Throughout the nineteenth century relations between Lutherans and Orthodox in Eastern Europe were largely dominated by the ethnic and cultural constituencies of both traditions—Germanic on the one side, Slavic on the other—and were limited to academic encounters. In the twentieth century, in spite of the worldwide ecumenical movement, the academic and ecclesiastico-political dimensions have never been really transcended. Even in the United States the very traditionalism of both the Lutherans and the Orthodox tends to reduce contacts to a level not very different from that which existed in Europe.

However, as Lutheranism is now overcoming the limitations of immigrant history and defining its confessional and ecclesial unity within the realities of American society, and as Orthodoxy also begins to move in the same direction, the true in-depth encounter becomes spiritually inevitable. We speak the same language, our young people go to the same schools, and we all face the same divided, secular, and disoriented world as we seek Christ's justice and truth. It is, therefore, less likely than before that cultural reasons will remain decisive in perpetuating misunderstandings between us. Clearly, history itself—and, indeed, the Lord of history—call us to the basics of the Christian faith: can we or can we not confess them together, and what would be the implications of such a common confession?

In a sense, this indispensable return to the "basics" makes it easier for me to approach the topic of the ministry. The problem cannot be solved within the categories and concepts used during the Reformation–Counter Reformation struggle, but must be based upon a fresh reading of the New Testament and the early Christian tradition.

## THE ORIGINS OF THE EPISCOPAL MINISTRY

As a collection of writings composed on different occasions, by different people, and for different immediate purposes, the New Testament does not use a consistent terminology for the ministry. Furthermore, the conditions under which the Christian communities existed in the apostolic age were different from ours. This is why the simple use of prooftexts has generally led to dead ends.

However, while Jesus did not leave the Christian communities with detailed institutional directives, the extraordinary fact remains that by the middle of the second century there existed a uniform pattern of church structure, adopted by all local churches. This basic unity—which did not exclude some diversity in forms—can be explained either by an unlikely, extra-Christian influence decisive enough to be universally accepted without controversy, or *by the very nature of the church herself.*

It is my strong belief that the latter is indeed the case and that, therefore, the present ecumenical debate about ministry is not a matter of pure historical research, but fundamentally a debate about ecclesiology. What we are after is not a ministry mutually recognized by otherwise separated denominations, holding different interpretations of the New Testament data and diverse views of the church, but a consciousness of belonging to the one Church of Christ and an agreement on what this Church is in her very being. Once this inner consciousness and agreement are recognized it is, of course, possible to speak of formal imperfections in the empirical life of the church and its ministries, and also of legitimate diversities, which existed already in apostolic times and are also inevitable today. But a recognition of basic unity should precede acknowledgment of diversity. Such an understanding of the ecumenical debate may seem utopian, but in my opinion it alone can lead to true unity.

Formal evidence about the life of the Christian communities in the first century is extremely scarce. It can be affirmed, however, that the fundamental spiritual realities were for these communities an anamnesis or "remembrance" of the death and resurrection of Jesus as saving events, and an eschatological anticipation of the coming of his kingdom. This anamnesis and this anticipation were both realized in the eucharistic meal: "For as often as you eat this bread and drink this cup, you proclaim the Lord's death until He comes" (1 Cor 11:26, RSV). It is in the eucharistic meal and through it that the Church was truly herself, as the Church of God , and it is, therefore, within the framework of the eucharistic assembly, gathered every week on the Lord's

Day, that the internal structure of the Church had to take its shape.[3] Indeed, if the Eucharist was a reenactment of the Last Supper, someone had to sit in the place of the Lord and pronounce the words he commanded his disciples to say. On the other hand, the Eucharist was also a participation in the forthcoming messianic banquet of the kingdom, as it was seen by the author of Revelation: "a throne stood in heaven, with One seated on the throne! . . . Round the throne were twenty-four thrones, and seated on the thrones were twenty-four elders (*presbyteroi*)" (Rv 4:2, 4, RSV).

There is no doubt that when Ignatius of Antioch, who was martyred under Trajan (A.D. 98–117), described a local Christian community and compared the bishop with the Father and the presbyters with the apostolic college[4] (*Trall.* 3:1), he had precisely this vision of church order, based not on some legal transmission of powers from Christ through the apostles to the bishops, but rather upon the nature of the local eucharistic community: "Get close to your bishop," he writes, "That is how unity and harmony come to prevail. Make no mistake about it: if anyone is not inside the sanctuary, he lacks God's bread" (Eph 5:1–2). The connection is clearly established between "unity and harmony"— that is, between essential qualities of the church and the functions of the bishop within the eucharistic assembly. Indeed, "you should regard that Eucharist as valid which is celebrated either by the bishop or by someone he authorizes. Where the bishop is present, there let the congregation gather, just as where Jesus Christ is, there is the catholic church" (*Smyrn* 8:1–2).

Similar citations from Ignatius, familiar to students of the early Church, could be easily multiplied. Sometimes historians have interpreted them as showing that the author was a revolutionary reformer, establishing a new ministry—the "monarchical episcopate"—in a church that had inherited a much more diversified ministry from apostolic times. But nothing in Ignatius supports the idea that he was a revolutionary. He writes as if his correspondents were fully familiar with the episcopal ministry, and we know of no adverse reaction from any quarter against his vision of church structure. That structure became the standard model everywhere. No scheme is able to explain the existence and the general acceptance of the "Ignatian" episcopate in the early second century more convincingly than the sacramental, or eucharistic, approach to early Christian ecclesiology. This approach was not invented by Ignatius but was rooted in the very nature of the early Christian communities.

The New Testament writings use a variety of terms to designate the leadership of the Christian churches. The terms *episkopos* and *presbyteros* in particular are used interchangeably and apply to the entire body of elders who, in the churches founded by Paul, exercised functions of leadership in each local church. However, the Pauline epistles also mention *proestamenoi* ("presidents")—"those over you in the Lord" (1 Thes 5:12), a title that refers to those who preside at the eucharistic assembly. Moreover, in the pastoral epistles, the function of "presidency" begins to be definitely associated with the *episkopos* (1 Tm 3:4–5; 5:17). The role played by the apostle Peter as head of the original community in Jerusalem, and his succession in the person of James, provided a personalized—"monarchical"—image of the later "episcopal" ministry. As Peter together with the apostles led the Church in Jerusalem, so James, after Peter's departure, headed it together with presbyters. The model of the Church of Jerusalem, in its anamnetic and eschatological dimensions, was in fact necessarily a model for New Israel everywhere. Thus, in Ignatius the "presbyters" around the bishop represent the senate of the apostles. Also, quite importantly, not only in pre-Constantinian patristic literature (especially Cyprian), but also in the medieval Byzantine authors, Peter was always seen as the prototype of the bishop in each local church.[5]

The term "Catholic Church" applies in Ignatius—and in all contemporary sources—to the local eucharistic community: each church is, indeed, the Church of God in its fullness because what gives that fullness is God's presence, the Body of Christ indivisibly manifested in each Eucharist. This understanding of Catholicity, however, is not congregationalism; Catholicity implies unity with past (apostolicity) and with the future (eschatology), and also unity in faith and life with all the other churches that share the same Catholicity. Local churches are identical in their faith, and therefore always interdependent. Although celebrated locally, the Eucharist has a cosmic or universal significance. The church is always the same Church of God, although she "sojourns" in different geographic locations.

The unity with the past is a unity in the faith "once delivered to the saints" through Christ's witnesses, the apostles. Hence, "apostolic succession" is a succession in the faith of the apostles, witnessed in the continuity of the Eucharist. It is not simply a continuity in beliefs or in convictions: the faith is taught within the Eucharist, and it is there also that it is received and maintained by the entire people of God, by the power of the Spirit. It is such a conception of apostolic tradition that Irenaeus, in the second half of the second century, opposed to the secret or esoteric conception of tradition held by the Gnostics.

The link with the apostolic past presupposes unity also in the space between the local churches. This unity is manifested in the *identity* of their apostolic faith, also well described by Irenaeus. No local church possesses the exclusive privilege of preserving apostolicity, although, in fact, some churches did enjoy more favorable historical conditions and received particular charismata. These special gifts were then used to help others, and were to be "received" or recognized as such by all the other churches. After the third century, the most normal way of maintaining and manifesting unity in faith was found in the councils of bishops who, together with the people, defined the faith that was then "received" by churches not represented at a given council. In this process, the guiding principle was always obedience to the Spirit of God, not to majority opinion by democratic vote.

These basic principles of early Christian ecclesiology provide a framework for contemporary discussion. I refer to them because they contain both the limits and the potential of dialogue leading to an eventual mutual recognition between churches that have been separated for centuries and are not called to recognize each other again within the same Christian faith.

## ORTHODOX ATTITUDES IN HISTORY

One of the most obvious and important conclusions provided by the evidence from the early Church is that there is no recognition of orders or ministries as such, but of the *church* in which these ministries are exercised, and of the *faith* held by that church. It is interesting to note that schisms of the third and later centuries led to prolonged discussions as to whether the baptism of heretics or schismatics was to be recognized. The issue of the ministries was treated almost as an afterthought. The central problem was whether the Novatians, the Donatists, the various categories of Gnostics, and the later heretics could or could not baptize and thus add new members to the one church. A community using a recognizable baptism would necessarily be considered as possessing a recognizable ministry: sacraments and faith were seen as inseparable.

In practice, no really consistent attitude was ever formulated. In his letter 188, St. Basil of Caesarea, after writing several paragraphs setting forth his rejection of the Encratite baptism, surprisingly adds: "But I know that we have received the brethren Izois and Saturninus into episcopal rank, who were of that party. Therefore we can no longer separate from the Church those who have joined their company, since through the acceptance of the bishops we have published a kind of canon of communion with them."[6] Historically, we know practically nothing of Izois and Saturninus, but the somewhat paradoxical attitude of St. Basil toward them and toward the issue of reconciliation with dissident communities clearly shows that the real issue was whether such communities could be considered churches or not. It is on the basis of that decision that the particular—and pastoral—issues of baptism and the ministries can also be solved.

It can be shown, I think, that Basil's attitude represented a model for later generations. The evidence of an *agreement in faith* between the local churches was the necessary sign of, and the condition for, church union. In the late fourth century, for example, the reunion between the Nicaeans and those who, in the East, were reluctant to accept Nicaea for terminological reasons (and who represented a majority of those who were at various times considered "Arians"), occurred by an agreement in faith, followed by sacramental communion. Before such formal corporate reunion occurred, individuals were accepted either through baptism or through anointment with chrism or through simple confession of faith (cf. Trullan Council, AD 692, canon 95). The matter of ministries was never debated per se, and its resolution came each time in the context of a complete agreement in faith between churches.

Throughout the centuries there have been variations in the practical policies of the Orthodox Church in matters of reunion with non-Orthodox Christians,[7] but, behind these practical inconsistencies (which have parallels in the history of Western Christendom), there was ecclesiological continuity: the *faith* remained as the ultimate sign of "apostolic tradition," expressed particularly in the episcopal ministry but also in other basic components of the canonical, sacramental, and liturgical tradition.

This consistency of the Orthodox, vis-à-vis a different approach to episcopacy within the Anglican communion, manifested itself clearly in the various conversations and statements concerned with Anglican orders during the period between World War I and World War II. Throughout those conversations the Anglicans were particularly—if not exclusively—concerned with having their orders "recognized as valid" on the basis of an uninterrupted chain of consecrations going back to the apostles. The Orthodox, on the other hand, while admitting the existence of such an uninterrupted chain within Anglicanism, kept expressing concern for the unity of faith. Some autocephalous Orthodox churches favored the non-reordination of Anglican ministers, but only "in case of the union of the two churches,"[8] and excluded any intercommunion before full dogmatic unity should be achieved.[9] Eventually, in 1948 in Moscow, most Orthodox churches signed an even more negative statement on the issue, referring to the absence of doctrinal agreement[10] with the Anglicans.

Clearly, the bottom issue in those debates was the refusal of the Orthodox to accept "apostolic succession" (understood as mechanical continuity) as the only criterion of ecclesial and sacramental reality. They always denied that the church was somehow created simply by the fact of episcopal succession, but rather insisted that the true episcopate existed only within the true Church. Apostolic "succession" has no reality outside of apostolic "tradition," and the guardian of apostolic tradition is the whole church, although the bishops within the church are its most responsible witnesses. It does seem to me that, on this point, further dialogue with Reformation theologians is both possible and desirable.

## THE MINISTRY AND THE CHURCH TODAY

In the history of the modern ecumenical movement, no initiative has come closer to a full theological and practical approach to this issue than the consensus document on "Baptism, Eucharist, and Ministry," worked out by the Commission on Faith and Order of the World Council of Churches. This text is currently under study by all member churches.[11] Certainly, the document does not solve all the problems, and we cannot discuss it in detail here. It is generally acknowledged, however, that in this ecumenical consensus the contribution of the Orthodox members of the commission has been substantial. One of the most important of such Orthodox contributions is, in my opinion, the *ecclesiological setting* of the document. For instance, it is affirmed that "ordination is an ac-knowledgment by the Church of the gifts of the Spirit in the one ordained, and a commitment by both the Church and the ordained to the new relationship" (par. 44). The necessary consequence of this *ecclesial* character of ordination—an act of the whole church and not simply the passing on of some powers from one individual to another—lies in the concluding paragraph of the document concerned with an eventual "mutual recognition." This "mutual recognition" would not be a simple recognition of "ministries," but a mutual recognition of *churches*: "The mutual recognition of *churches and their ministries* implies de-cision by the appropriate authorities and a liturgical act, from which point unity would be publicly manifest. . . . The common celebration of the Eucharist would certainly be the place for such an act" (par. 55, italics mine).

It is at this point that the reason for the Orthodox objections against any form of *inter*communion between yet divided churches becomes apparent. In inter-communion there is an unavoidable lack of true, mutual commitment to Catholic unity, and a peculiar reduction of the sacramental reality either to a mechanistic act of bestowing grace or to pietism. Within such a reduced Catholicity there can-not be any mutual recognition of ministries. The Orthodox, in their rejection of intercommunion, are often accused of stubborn confessionalism. It would be fairer to recognize in their attitude on this particular point an authentic concern for true Catholic unity and a reluctance to accept substitutes for it.

Actually, just such mechanistic or pietistic reductionism in medieval Christian-ity was vehemently objected to by Martin Luther,[12] who opposed to it his under-standing of the faith as a response to the Word of God, confessed also in the sacra-ments. Between the Orthodox and the Lutherans, therefore, the real issues are the content and the implications of that faith, and particularly whether the sacraments involve a sacramental *structure* of the Church herself, whether this basic structure goes back to the apostolic witness, and what are its permanent, unchangeable el-ements. But there is a common starting point: the apostolic succession of the min-istry is not an institution above the church, but a part of the *apostolic tradition,* which is a continuity in the apostolic faith, held by the people of God and sealed by the gifts of the Holy Spirit, promised by the Lord for his church.[13]

If one accepts the principle that the unity of separated Christians can only be achieved through their recognition of each other as members of the one church, and if that unity itself is indeed to be described as an inner sense, an inner commitment—spiritual, doctrinal, sacramental, institutional—to the one church, then the entire theological methodology of the ecumenical quest be-gins to transcend the particular form of confessionalism that emerged in Eu-rope after the Reformation: the definition of church membership by the ac-ceptance of this or that historic confessional formula (Augsburg, Westminster, etc.). The church catholic is never bound by such historical "symbols." The councils of the early church never produced exhaustive "confessions," but rather condemned individuals or doctrines that were seen as incompatible with the apostolic tradition. The apostolic truth itself was always considered inexhaustible in human words. The catholic church holds that living faith is that which is expressed in Scriptures and maintained by tradition. The goal of ecumenism should be the recovering of that experience of a common faith.

In America, confessionalism further evolved into "denominationalism," where church membership is in fact defined by even more mundane categories: ethnic background, social status, etc., even if pro forma reference is also made to doctrinal traditions. It seems to me that the present trend toward unity within American Lutheranism can become a really significant event of Christian reintegration if, by transcending denominationalism, it moves in the direction of a renewed church consciousness. However, from an Orthodox viewpoint, there is also a danger that in reaction to the somewhat sectarian confessionalism of those Lutherans who stay outside of the union the new church will, on the contrary, evolve toward relativistic denominationalism.

The Church can never be a "denomination" or a "confession." Her "being" is not determined by accidental historical events or situations, but by the *apax*-event of Christ's death and resurrection, and by the *coming* kingdom. This is why Catholicity is possible only within the apostolic faith (because the apostles witnessed to the Resurrection) and in expectation of the eschatological fulfillment. In order to be authentically "Catholic," one must transcend—or at least be free from—the contingency of the present, by accepting the acts of God both past and forthcoming. This looks a little impractical, but Catholicity transcends practicality, as it must also transcend history, geography, and culture. It is fully manifested only in the Eucharist, which is, as we have seen earlier, both a memorial and an anticipation. But this transcendent nature of the church's being is also liberating: the good news of the Resurrection of Christ liberates humanity from historical, geographic, or rational determinism. It makes us free by faith.

The issue of the ministry can therefore be ultimately reduced to the question of whether one defines it as a projection of secular, historical realities, such as power, efficiency, social justice (e.g., equality of the sexes), or as a function within the eucharistic assembly. In the latter case, the ministry is apostolic, unchangeable, and eschatological in nature. The bishop presides at the assembly, as Peter presided over the church of Jerusalem after Pentecost, and as the one sitting on the throne in heaven, described in Revelation (4:2ff).

In practical terms, the Faith and Order document on "Baptism, Eucharist, and Ministries" reaches the conclusion that "the threefold ministry of bishop, presbyter, and deacon may serve today as an expression of the unity we seek and also as a means for achieving it" (para. 22). However, it also recognizes that "churches maintaining the threefold pattern will need to ask how its potential can be fully developed for the most effective witness of the Church in this world" (para. 25). This is a mild and diplomatic way of raising the question of whether the traditional structure, where it exists, is being used in accordance with its own nature and purpose. Can one say, for example, that the pope and bishops opposed by Luther in the sixteenth century were performing a ministry that was really identical with that described by Ignatius of Antioch?

Of course, one may be able to argue that the original functions of the *episkopos*, as head of the local eucharistic community, would be modified with new requirements of the *episkope* as they emerged after the third century, when the bishop began supervising not one but several eucharistic communities. Perhaps this was a necessary development, securing in particular the necessary unity of the local churches on the regional and even the universal levels—a condition for a meaningful Christian witness in the world. But what about the power structures of feudal or imperial origin that began to be used as standard references to define episcopal authority? What about the rise of papal primacy? What about purely titular bishops, consecrated without election by, or responsibility for, a concrete local church?

Such questions are indeed applicable not only to the Roman Catholic and Anglican traditions but to the Orthodox as well. They emerge inevitably in the mind of any Protestant conditioned by his own history and observing the historical realities of "Catholic" Christianity. How often, instead of transcending history, "Catholicity" was—and still is—invoked to justify surrender to worldly categories! The Orthodox theologian might observe in defense of his church that none of these medieval or postmedieval developments in the exercise of the episcopal ministry was ever elevated to the level of formal doctrinal definition or commitment (as the papacy was in the West), but he will still face great difficulty in presenting the actual realities of contemporary Orthodoxy as unequivocally consistent in practice with those of the early Church.

It is obvious, therefore, that if one is to move in the direction of Christian unity, the issue of the ministries should be approached both in the light of their God-established apostolic origin and in the light of the various ways they have been exercised in history. It is only a fundamental agreement on the nature of the Church, and a common experience of it, which can lead to mutual recognition. Agreement needs critical study of one's own past and present but, first and foremost, a vision, a common discovery of the "realized eschatology" which makes the Church the Church.

## NOTES

1. "Pagan Servitude of the Church," in *Martin Luther: Selections from His Writings*, edited by John Dillenberger, pp. 261–62 (Garden City, N.J.: Anchor Books, 1961).

2. The most accessible edition of the Greek version is *I. Karmisis, Ta dogmatika kai symbolika tes Orthodoxos catholicos ekklesias*, 1–2 (Athens: 1952), 375–489. German text and commentary can be found in *Wort and Mysterium. Dokumente der Orthodoxaen Kirchen zur ökumenischen Frage* 11 (Herausgegeben von Aussenamt der Evangelischen Kirche in Deutschland, Luther-Verlag, Witten, 1958).

3. The method, which consists of looking into the original sacramental nature of the Church for the real origin of Church structure, has been developed by the Orthodox theologian Nicolas Afanasiev. See particularly *Tserkov Dukha Svyatogo/L'Eglise du Saint-Esprit* (Paris: YMCA Press/Cerf, 1971–1975). See also, "The Church Which Presides in Love," in *The Primacy of Peter*, edited by John Meyendorff, pp. 91–144 (Crestwood, N.Y.: St. Vladimir's Seminary Press, 1992). The name of Nicolas Afanasiev is therefore attached to what is generally called "eucharistic ecclesiology." There is no doubt that the thought of Afanasiev was influenced by Rudolf Sohm's opposition between the spirit and the law in understanding the structure of the early Church, and therefore in discovering continuity not in legally defined institutionalism, but in "spiritual" consistency. The works of Sohm were quite popular among Russian theologians before the Revolution (see the Russian translation of Sohm's *Kirchenrecht* [Leipzig, 1892] by the famous Paul Florensky in cooperation with A. Petrovsky, Moscow, 1906). However, Sohm's charismaticism received in Afanasiev the correction of sacramentalism. More recently, and independently, the centrality of the Eucharist for the understanding of the early Church and for the solving of contemporary ecclesiological problems is developed by John Zizioulas. See particularly, "Apostolic Continuity and Orthodox Theology: Towards a Synthesis of Two Perspectives," *St. Vladimir's Theological Quarterly* 19: 2 (1975): 75–108; and *Being and Communion* (Crestwood, N.Y.: St. Vladimir's Seminary Press, 1985). See my *Orthodoxy and Catholicity* (New York: Sheed & Ward, 1966), 1–16.

4. *The Epistles of St. Clement of Rome and St. Ignatius of Antioch, Ancient Christian Writers*, volume 1, translated and annotated by James A. Kleist (S. J. Mahwah, N.J.: Paulist Press, 1946).

5. Cf. texts gathered in John Meyendorff, "St. Peter in Byzantine Theology," in *The Primacy of Peter in the Orthodox Church* (London: Faith Press, 1963).

6. Saint Basil, *The Letters*, with an English translation by R. J. Deferrari, III, pp. 20–21 (Cambridge, Mass.: Harvard University Press, 1962).

7. On this subject see the recent article of Bishop Peter L'Huillier, "The Reception of Roman Catholics into Orthodoxy: Historical Variations and Norms," *St. Vladimir's Theological Quarterly* 24: 2 (1980): 75–82.

8. Statement of Constantinople, 28 July 1922, in E. R. Hardy Jr., *Orthodox Statements on Anglican Orders*, p. 4 (New York: Morehouse-Gorham, 1946).

9. Statement of Cyprus, 7/20 March 1923, in Hardy, *Orthodox Statements*, 9.

10. For a more detailed and technical discussion of this issue see Th. O Wedel, ed., *Ministers of Christ* (New York: Seabury, 1964), especially my article, "The Bishop in the Church,"150–65.

11. WCC Faith and Order Paper No. 111 (Geneva, 1982).

12. There is also a remarkable, clear criticism of such reductions in Gustaf Aulen's *The Faith of the Christian Church*, translated by Eric H. Wahlstrom (Philadelphia: Fortress Press, 1960), 366–68. On the positive side, Orthodox theologians often find themselves at home with the often reemerging tradition of sacramentalism and patristic scholarship within Lutheranism; for example, G. L. C. Frank, "A Lutheran Turned Eastwards: The Use of the Greek Fathers in the Eucharistic Theology of Martin Chemnitz," *St. Vladimir's Theological Quarterly* 26: 3 (1982): 155–71.

13. Cf. the definition of "apostolic succession" as "succession in the apostolic tradition," in WCC's "Baptism, Eucharist, and Ministry," part IV, 34–35.

# DOES CHRISTIAN
# TRADITION HAVE A FUTURE?

*To the ongoing crisis of Christian tradition, Fr. Meyendorff provides a calm, insightful analysis in this essay, one free of prejudice toward other Christian churches, and in fact open to them as part of a common quest. His understanding of tradition is one that is dynamic, enlivened not only by the new challenges of our time and tradition's extension of the Gospel to these, but also made alive by an eschatological dimension—the presence of Christ and the kingdom of heaven.*

Our society today is witnessing a remarkable revival of traditionalisms. I use the word "traditionalism" in the plural, because today's pluralistic and secular society inevitably searches for its roots in a variety of ways. The unifying American dream of a new world—pure, Christian, and ultimately free from the corruptions of the old—is, of course, still alive, but it is being challenged by innumerable groups searching for their identity elsewhere. Partly inspired by the growth of Black community consciousness, and emulating the revived identity of the Jews, other ethnic groups are being led to assert themselves as separate cultures and traditions. In the past, all these movements would have been considered un-American, and certain conservative elements of American society obviously still look at the "ethnics" with dismay and latent disapproval. However, institutions try to react constructively, and universities encourage ethnic

This was originally delivered by Fr. Meyendorff at the eighth annual Thomas Verner Moore Lecture, sponsored by St. Anselm's Abbey, at the Catholic University, Washington, D.C., on 26 September 1981. It was first published in *St. Vladimir's Theological Quarterly* 26: 3 (1982):139–54.

studies. Thus, the idea of cultural pluralism is being integrated into the American dream itself.

I am referring to these facts only to focus our attention on the contrast between the revival of traditionalism in secular society and the obvious crisis and confusion present in our notions about the Christian tradition. We are, in fact, in the midst of a crisis of Christian identity. Indeed, any collective American identity is inseparable from tradition: one can be a Chinaman, a Jew, or an Irishman only by an association with the past history of the Chinese, the Jews, or the Irish. Similarly, one is a Christian because one identifies first of all with the historical person of Jesus Christ and also with Christians of past ages. But here confusion comes, because of competing interpretations of who Christ was and what he preached, because of divisions among Christians and—specifically in our time—because of a crisis in the institutions whose function it was and still is to teach and maintain the Christian tradition. The result is that secular traditions are readily honored and respected, and people die for the preservation of their national and cultural traditions and are venerated as heroes for doing so; but if someone presents himself as a "traditional" Christian, or simply refers to the authority of tradition, he is identified as a conservative who refuses the necessary "updating" of the Christian faith. In a sense, among Christians, "tradition" has become a bad word.

The problem lies also in the fact that, in the light of the Christian faith, tradition is not a very simple concept. It is certainly not mere respect for the past. This complexity itself has led to reductions and simplifications, of which I will be speaking today. It also leads many Christians today into confusing secular and religious traditional values, which eventually reduces Christianity to being a mere external adornment, used by fundamentally secular ideologists of the Left or of the Right.

In my attempt to discuss these issues—speaking not as a sociologist or a psychologist, but only as a historian and a theologian—I will try first to define tradition not only in terms of the past to be preserved but in terms of the future to be anticipated and prepared. Second, I will make a historical excursus into the second century of the Christian era, because at that time the situation of the Church was, in certain extraordinary ways, similar to our own. Finally, I will speak of our present ecumenical situation and touch upon the approaches to the issue as they appear in the three major Christian families—Roman Catholic, Protestant, and Orthodox.

## TRADITION AND ESCHATOLOGY

As distinct from Platonism and other forms of static philosophical idealism, the Bible reveals actions of God in history. The world has a beginning and an end, determined by God. Also, the Bible is incompatible with ontological dualism:

since God created the world himself—and not, for example, through the mediation of some inferior demiurge (as the Gnostics used to think)—this world, whether "visible" or "invisible," is good and is destined to salvation. However, the Bible also affirms an existential dualism between "this world," which finds itself in a state of rebellion against its Creator, and "the age to come," when God will be "all in all" (1 Cor 15:28).

Thus, in this period of time between the beginning and the end, humanity in general, and each human being in particular, is offered the opportunity of reasserting his loyalty toward God and of struggling against the "prince of this world"—the "tyrant" or "usurper," who controls creation through the power of death. And the New Testament tells us that, in a sense, man can prepare, anticipate, and even provoke the end, that the end, although fully determined by God, also awaits man's readiness to meet it.

One might ask, perhaps, at this point whether this eschatological approach has anything to do with tradition. Indeed it has, because in the Christian revelation alpha and omega do coincide, and because life and truth coincide. Without eschatology, traditionalism is turned only to the past: it is nothing but archeology, antiquarianism, conservatism, reaction, refusal of history, escapism. Authentic Christian traditionalism remembers and maintains the past not because it is past, but because it is the only way to meet the future, to become ready for it. Let us recall the meaning of the Christian eucharistic celebration: it is, indeed, a memorial of what Jesus did in the past, but it is also performed "until He comes," it is based on the expectation of his coming. In the eucharistic canon of St. John Chrysostom, immediately after the words of institution, the Orthodox Church specifically remembers "all those things which have come to pass for us: the Cross, the Tomb, the Resurrection on the third day, the Ascension into heaven, the Sitting at the right hand, and the second and glorious Coming"—as if the Second Coming had already occurred! And the interior design of ancient Christian—and also Romanesque and Byzantine—churches always places at the very center an eschatological image: the Pantokrator, or the image of an empty throne, prepared for the one who is coming. The Eucharist not only remembers, it also prepares, awaits, and anticipates.

In later centuries, this eschatological dimension was largely forgotten. How many of our modern church buildings reflect it? Who preaches about it? No wonder that a true sense of tradition was also lost.

One should note, however, that even if one were to recover the eschatological content of the Christian faith, it could be understood in different ways. Following are three examples, which are directly relevant for the Christian attitude toward the world and which qualify all aspects of Christian ethics.

The first is that eschatology can turn apocalyptic: *The kingdom of God is coming soon; there is nothing to expect from history; Christians can do nothing to improve human reality; even the smallest social cell—the family—is only a burden and is of no justifiable concern.* The Church here is reduced to a "remnant," which can only appeal for its Lord—"Come, Lord Jesus!" (Rv 22:20). No real mission or responsibility for society or culture is then or even desirable. God is seen alone as the Lord of history, acting without any cooperation, or *synergia* (cf. 1 Cor 3:9). The new Jerusalem is coming from heaven "all prepared" (Rv 21:2), and we have nothing to contribute to it. It is understandable that sometimes Christians adopt such an apocalyptic eschatology, especially when they find themselves in hostile societies and are deprived by force of any possibility of influencing the world around them. Such was the case of some early Christian communities, and this is reflected in the New Testament itself. Similar situations exist even today, for example, in communist countries. In such particular, extreme situations, apocalypticism is perhaps legitimate. But clearly, apocalyptic eschatology, since it sees no *future* for Christianity (except the *parousia*), is not concerned about the past either: it does not admit any tradition, any culture, any progression or regression in humanity's quest for God. And, of course, it has been rejected by the Church as a *permanent* interpretation of Christian eschatology. Indeed, the Church believes that the "new Jerusalem," the kingdom to come, is not only a free gift of God but also a seal and a fulfillment of all the positive, creative efforts of mankind to "cooperate" with the Creator throughout the entire process of history. This is why, when the Roman state accepted Christianity, the Church welcomed the opportunity and the responsibility that fell to her, in spite of all the risks and temptations it entailed. Since that time, the idea of Christian tradition has become inseparable from what we call Christian culture. On the opposite extreme of apocalyptic eschatology stands the humanistic and optimistic understanding of history: the belief that the historical process is controlled by man and that it can and should be understood in a rational theory of progress. In this approach, history indeed has a meaning, and there is also necessarily a place for tradition, which is understood primarily in terms of an interplay between "progressive" and "reactionary" trends. This optimistic belief in progress can be called a "post-Christian" phenomenon (the importance it attributes to history would be difficult to imagine, for example, in a society dominated by a Buddhist set of values). Since the time of the Enlightenment, this optimistic eschatology has been dominant in Western society and, in the twentieth century, has spread even to China in its Marxist form. Whether or not it still calls itself Christian, this type of "eschatology" identifies the new Jerusalem with human achievements, understood in secular terms. Its tragedy resides in its fundamental utopianism. Indeed, it ignores basic realities of human life, such as death and sin, which occur both on a personal and a societal level and cannot be overcome by social progress alone. It conceives of an endless civilization which, if realized, would be as horrible as the eternal survival of a human being dominated by sickness and old age. Accepting the idea that the human person is subject to necessities of historical determinism, it destroys the main content of Christian hope: that Christ's resurrection has liber-

ated man from dependence upon "powers and principalities" ruling in the
fallen world, that death has no power, that man is no longer a prisoner of social, physical, or historical conditioning.

Clearly, this eschatology, based on the optimistic idea of human progress and,
in fact, suppressing the human freedom of ultimate self-determination, is incompatible with the idea of Christian tradition.

The third type of eschatology is based on the biblical concept of prophecy.
Both in the Old and the New Testaments, the prophet does not simply fore-
cast the future or announce the inevitable. The biblical prophet issues either
a promise or a threat. Generally, the two are combined. But prophecy always
places man before an option, a choice between two types of personal or social behavior. He is *free* to choose, but the prophet has informed him of the
consequences. Such an eschatology has been called conditional eschatology,
and it constitutes the only theologically acceptable basis for the idea of tradition as well.

Indeed, what we call holy tradition is the history of the right choices made by
human beings confronted by the prophetic Word of God, responding correctly
in the concrete historical circumstances of their time. They are those whom we
call saints. Accepting tradition actually means to live in the communion of
saints, who lived in the past but have also prepared the future. Their correct
choices have concerned Christian doctrine or Christian life. We may be living
in different historical circumstances, and the options that confront us may not
be identical with theirs, but the effort to remain in communion with the saints
is a necessary and crucial element of the Christian faith itself, because that faith
is concerned with history. This concern for the "communion of saints" has
sometimes also been called "Catholicity in time." Without that aspect of
Catholicity, "Catholicity in space"—that is, the external, geographic universality of the Church—has very little meaning. Also, quite importantly, the saints of
the past cannot be fully understood by us without our awareness—at least
partial—of the true content of the options they faced. Knowledge of history
and—I would say as a historian—the use of historical methods of research are
essential for separating truth from legend, content from form, essentials from
futilities, holy tradition from those human traditions that Jesus condemned before the Pharisees.

The idea of tradition is therefore inseparable from eschatology—the "conditional eschatology" revealed to us in Scripture. It was inevitable that this eschatological dimension would be somewhat obscured with the establishment of
Christianity in the Roman Empire in the fourth century, and throughout the
medieval and postmedieval periods. However, particularly in Eastern Orthodoxy, it never disappeared completely. It appears most clearly in the writings of
the second century, as the second and third generations of Christians were cop-
ing with the problem of finding criteria of true doctrine in the face of the challenge of the competing Gnostic traditions.

## TRADITION IN THE SECOND CENTURY

Based upon the historical event of Christ's resurrection, the Christian faith depended entirely upon the eyewitnesses of Jesus. Indeed, Jesus himself did not write anything, but only established a *community* of disciples, chosen by him and entrusted with the ministry of being his witnesses. By the second century, all the members of that original community had died, and many were claiming to be their successors in the preservation of the authentic teachings of Jesus. Those whom we call the Gnostics included a variety of groups, carrying on a variety of traditions. One of their common claims was that they had secret, esoteric connections with Jesus through the mediation of covert teachings transmitted from one person to another and reserved for an elite group of spiritual leaders ("gnostics"—"people who have knowledge").

What means did Christians of the second century have to verify the teachings that were handed down in this way? Although apostolic writings were in circulation, no New Testamental canon had yet been universally accepted: there was no formal basis for accepting the teachings contained in the Gospel of Matthew, or John, and rejecting those found in the Gnostic Gospel of Thomas. The Church had no defined magisterium, or central headquarters, where authoritative decisions could be made in matters of doctrine or discipline. There was no way in which a Christian could say: "I believe this teaching because it is in the Scriptures," or because "the magisterium of the Church has defined it." And, nevertheless, precisely during that period, tradition not only proved itself to be an effective reality in the Christian Church, but also received its most convincing, most permanent—though sometimes paradoxical—definitions.

Two major Christian personalities played a particularly important role in this regard: St Ignatius of Antioch (died circa 107) and St. Irenaeus of Lyons (died circa 202). It is not my intention to make a detailed presentation of their understanding of Christianity, but only to point at those aspects of their thought that have a permanent and, indeed, contemporary relevance for our understanding of Christian tradition.

For Ignatius, the structure of the Church is defined in terms of the Eucharist and, therefore, eschatology. Gathered for the Eucharist, the local community becomes the Catholic Church—not a part or a segment, but the plenitude. Indeed, "Wherever Christ Jesus may be, there is the Catholic Church"(*To the Smyrneans*, 8).[1] The constant appeals of Ignatius to his correspondents to be "obedient to the bishop" are based not on some external or formal power of the episcopate, received through some legal delegation, but upon the fact that the bishop presides at the Eucharist and manifests, during the eucharistic meal, the presence of Christ, or even of God the Father. Interestingly, Ignatius never mentions an "apostolic succession" of the bishops. The apostolic college is rather represented by the *presbyterium*—the group or college of elders who sit around the bishop during the eucharistic celebration, just as the apostles sat around Jesus at the Last Supper. Obviously, the Eucharist is seen by Ignatius in the same eschatological terms that appear in the book of Revelation, where the twenty-four elders ("presbyters") surround the throne during the angelic singing of the *Sanctus* (Rv 4:4–11). The gathering of all around the Eucharist, presided over by the bishop and the presbyters, is, for Ignatius, the source of true teaching, as opposed to that of all splinter groups. The truth appears as a vision, as direct experience received in the local eucharistic community, that expresses the "Catholicity" or fullness of the divine presence.

Almost a century later, Irenaeus envisages the Church on a more universal scale—the threat of Gnosticism was a common threat to all the local churches. He does not, however, depart from the principles of the Ignatian perspective, maintaining the Ignatian idea of eucharistic Catholicity in each local community. Addressing himself to the Gnostics, he writes: "Let them either change their opinion, or refrain from making those oblations. . . . Our opinion is consistent with the Eucharist, and the Eucharist supports our opinion"(*Against Heresies*, 4: 18: 5).[2] But, at the same time, he brings in the idea of what I called earlier "Catholicity in space":

> Having received this preaching and this faith, the Church, although scattered in the whole world, carefully preserves it, as if living in one house. . . . Neither do the churches that have been established in Germany believe otherwise, or hand down any other tradition, nor those among the Iberians, nor those among the Celts, nor in Egypt, nor in Libya, nor those established in the middle parts of the world. . . . Neither will one of those who preside in the churches who is very powerful in speech say anything different from these things . . . nor will one who is weak in speech diminish the tradition. (*Against Heresies* 1: 10: 2)

At the same time, Irenaeus bases his polemics with the Gnostics on the idea of "Catholicity in time," and this brings in the notion of the apostolic succession of the bishops. He uses this argument primarily to refute the Gnostic claims of having preserved the true teachings of the apostles through secret, mysterious traditions, transmitted by word of mouth from one individual to another. The Church, on the contrary—according to Irenaeus—preserves tradition publicly, with bishops preaching it in the framework of their sacramental, eucharistic ministry within the community. Such is the meaning of apostolic succession: it is not a mechanical "validity" of ordination, but faithfulness in transmitting apostolic truth. "The tradition of the apostles, made clear in all the world, can be clearly seen in every church by those who wish to behold the truth. We can enumerate those who were established by the apostles as bishops in the churches, and their successors down to our time, none of whom taught or thought of anything like these mad ideas [of the Gnostics]" (*Against Heresies* 3: 3: 1).

Irenaeus is very specific in affirming that the tradition is kept in *every* church. Indeed, his ecclesiology is the same as that of Ignatius: each local eucharistic community is "Catholic" and possesses a fullness of grace and divine presence. But, in order to illustrate his point, he refers to the succession of bishops in "the very great, oldest and well-known" church of Rome, which possessed already in his time an "outstanding preeminence" in the West, where he was writing (*Against Heresies* 3: 3: 2). Immediately afterward, however, he also points to the apostolic succession in Smyrna and in Ephesus.

It is my conviction that the teaching of Ignatius and Irenaeus on tradition, with its sacramental and eschatological context, provides the essential basis for our own understanding of Christian tradition. Actually, the spiritual, intellectual, and social confusion that reigned in the late Roman empire is not without analogy in our own post-Christian world.

In later centuries, the concept of tradition was often reduced to legal categories of authority demanding obedience, and gelled into institutions inspired by political systems. The episcopate itself progressively—but very early on—detached itself from its original meaning and function in the local eucharistic assembly, and became a medieval administrative institution with jurisdiction over large geographic areas, including many local eucharistic communities (or "parishes"). Emperors took the initiative in gathering "ecumenical councils," whose decrees were applied as state laws. In the West, to counter imperial power in the Church, the papacy itself assumed political power and gradually developed into the unique and obligatory criterion of true tradition. All these later developments overshadowed the original concept of tradition as it was understood and expressed by Ignatius and Irenaeus.

But is it possible today to transcend the historical past? Clearly not. Ignatius and Irenaeus cannot provide us with exact institutional models for the Church of today. However, without preserving or recovering the essential—eschatological and eucharistic—dimension of their understanding of the Church, a concept of Christian tradition today is impossible. Without such a recovery, it is impossible to distinguish holy tradition from purely historical, human, and therefore, changing forms of Christian life and belief. It is also impossible to transcend the opposition between conservatives and liberals, traditionalists and progressives, and to discover the sacramental continuity, throughout the centuries, of the communion of saints.

Of course, the theological question of whether a holy tradition exists at all, as distinct from human and humanly conditioned traditions, is a problem in itself, which is solved differently in the various confessional groups.

## THE CONTEMPORARY ECUMENICAL SITUATION

In raising the question "Does Christian tradition have a future?" one inevitably faces the fact of Christian disunity. If there is any issue upon which Protestants, Roman Catholics, and Orthodox have been historically divided, it is precisely tradition. Nevertheless, the present situation has been significantly modified not only by the ecumenical movement but also by drastic changes occurring within each of the three major families of Christians.

Contemporary Protestantism, in spite of its confessional and cultural pluralism, is united by its historic origin in the Reformation, which implied the rejection not only of the medieval Latin tradition in its doctrinal authority but also of the very idea of *any* authority other than Scripture. One of the major achievements of the contemporary ecumenical dialogue has been the recognition, among many Protestants, that no society can exist without tradition, and that the Reformed Christianity of the sixteenth and the following centuries is no exception. There is an increasing awareness of the role of tradition among Protestants, and there are, indeed, Protestant traditions, as expressed in "confessionalism" or "denominationalism." The principle of *sola scriptura*, the common acceptance of Scripture as the only ultimate criterion of Christian truth, cannot and did not produce ecclesial unity in history or doctrinal unanimity among the communities of the Reformation. Traditions still divide them today. This creates a very ambiguous situation, which appears particularly in the history of debates on this issue within the World Council of Churches. Indeed, within that body occurs a meeting not only among various Protestant groups, but also among such defenders of the idea of tradition as the "high church" Anglicans and, of course, the Orthodox.

On the one hand, many Protestant theologians begin to admit the utopian character of Christianity without tradition. On the other hand, partly because of their original prejudice in favor of the *sola scriptura* principle, and partly because historical experience confronts them with the fact that the emphasis on tradition is, in practice, divisive, Protestants tend to identify tradition as a purely human—and therefore necessarily *relative*—element in Christianity. One inevitably holds some tradition, but one is justified in doing so only if one is fully tolerant of any other tradition as well. This acceptance of pluralism, often coupled with a definite relativism in doctrine, is particularly proper to American Liberal Protestantism: the various "denominations" are seen as being of purely historic origin and, as Reinhold Niebuhr has shown, reflect the social and ethnic history of American society.

Of course, within the Protestant community there is a unifying factor, the Bible, admitted by all. However, modern methods of biblical exegesis have uncovered its "human elements" as well, and therefore relativity, and therefore pluralism. Some modern ecumenists are even quite happy with an exegesis of the New Testament that makes sharp distinctions between a "Pauline," a "Johannine," or a "Lukan" Christianity, all equally legitimate, and whose discovery allows the legitimate coexistence of different Christian traditions as separate groups or churches. And, of course, if one defines a certain biblical doctrine as historically relative or socially determined, one can also easily challenge biblical authority for the solution of basic contemporary issues (for example, the role of women in the church).

There is also a reaction against that liberal trend: fundamentalism—the blind and often naïve acceptance of a literal inerrancy of the biblical texts, which implies refusal of history and of any form of cooperation between God and man in the act of revelation. The Bible is transformed into something it has never pretended to be: a universal informational textbook about history and science.

What is lacking on both the liberal and the fundamentalist sides (which, of course, do not exhaust all of Protestant thought today) is the idea of communion between God and man in the sacramental and eschatological fellowship of the Church—a fellowship where Catholicity or consistency in time is possible, where unity in space is desirable, and where the Bible should and can be properly and harmoniously understood both in its divine elements and in its human context.

In Roman Catholicism—as, of course, in Orthodoxy—tradition is a central reality in the existence of the Church. Furthermore, it stands at the very center of all the debates that have taken place since Vatican II. It has also been discussed for centuries between East and West. And these differences on the meaning of tradition actually led to the medieval schism between Rome and Orthodoxy. I have mentioned earlier that, already in the second century, tradition was recognized as the inevitable criterion of Christian identity vis-à-vis the Gnostics. Later, the innumerable debates on the Trinity, on Christology, etc., that took place throughout the centuries could only be solved through reference to tradition. However, just as all parties involved referred to scripture, so they all also invoked tradition. This was true of the Arians, the Nestorians, the Monophysites, the Iconoclasts and, indeed, of both the Greeks and the Latins when they clashed with each other over such issues as the Latin interpolation into the Creed (the *Filioque*) or various other theological, disciplinary, or liturgical issues. Generally speaking, the East insisted that all these problems be solved in their very substance through conciliar debates. They saw the apostolic tradition as entrusted to all the churches, who could therefore express it authoritatively only through consensus or conciliarity. This was not democracy, but rather a mystical belief in the full reality of Christ's and the Spirit's presence in each Eucharist, and therefore a belief in the collective responsibility of the entire people of God for the preservation of the faith.

Humanly speaking, however, this was admittedly not a very realistic approach to the issues. It allowed controversies and debates to last for centuries, and emperors to interfere in church affairs, seeking—generally without much success—to impose solutions by force. The Latin West gradually became realistic. Building upon the ancient respectability and prestige of the Church of Rome, it developed the idea that the bishop of that city—where the Church was founded by the apostles Peter and Paul—was the heir of Christ's promise to Peter: "You are Peter, and on this rock I will build my Church" (Mt 16:18). In that capacity, he was the final and ultimate criterion of true tradition, so that every conflict, every debate, every conciliar settlement ultimately depended upon a solution by him.

It is not my intention to engage here in a discussion of the origins and legit-imacy of the Roman primacy, but only to point out its crucial importance for the understanding of tradition. First of all, I would point to the fact that—contrary to the antipapal polemics of all times—papal authority did not result from some ambitious, power-seeking plan of the pope to take over the leadership in the universal Church. If the Eastern belief in consensus of the churches was founded, as I said earlier, upon a mystical and eschatological perception of the Church, so was the belief in the special charisma of Rome. Indeed, it was not plainly described in Scripture, and not *clearly* sustained by early Church his-tory. All informed Roman Catholic historians and theologians today recognize that the medieval papal authority was the result of a doctrinal and canonical *de-velopment*, which consisted in a gradual recognition by the Church of the fact that God had granted to his people a permanent leadership, able to regulate and to unify the local churches within a single, universal, disciplinary, and doc-trinal structure.

Ultimately, the conflict between East and West resides in two conflicting spiritual perceptions of tradition. Is a solution possible today?

The "Constitutions" of Vatican II and the profound changes that took place within the Roman Catholic Church in the past two decades have all involved both the theory and the practice of tradition and, therefore, touched upon re-lations with the Orthodox Church. This process has been happening on differ-ent levels. Some effects were negative and divisive, while others present hope-ful signs for the future. I will note three examples.

The first is the breakdown of monolithic discipline, which characterized the Roman Church in the past, and has led to much confusion precisely because tradition had been identified too exclusively with authority: papal, episcopal, priestly. Traditions were now rejected because they were seen as imposed from outside. This led to new approaches to the Liturgy, to the faith, to discipline. Seen with Orthodox eyes, some of these approaches were welcome—such as the use of the vernacular in the Liturgy—while others were clearly divisive and negative (for example, secularization of the Liturgy, suspicion against doctrinal consistency, etc.).

A second example comes on the level of theological thought. Post–Vatican II Roman Catholic theology, even if one excludes extreme cases like Küng's, is ad-mitting much more widely than before the historical relativity of doctrinal for-mulations. It tends to subject tradition to a radical hermeneutical reinterpreta-tion, similar to the critical exegesis introduced by nineteenth-century Protestant scholars in the study of the Bible. The decision of an early Christian council, or the statement of a pope, is seen as relevant (or only "probably rele-vant") in its own time, but meaningless today. This approach, based upon mod-ern existential thought and linguistic analysis, allows for various degrees of rel-ativism in approaching tradition. And, it raises many problems. For instance, historical relativity in understanding the Old Testament Scriptures is built into the very nature of the material; indeed, for Christians, the value of the Old Testament itself is *relative to* the coming of Christ, which was being *prepared*. In the New Testament Church, however, the *real presence* of Christ is a saving givenness, a *liberation* not only from sin and death, but also from any historical determinism. The relativization of truth is therefore impossible; the living truth is manifested fully in Christ. Although *words* and *expressions* used by ancient or medieval councils are historically conditioned, their content and meaning are not. Tradition, therefore, is to be seen as *consistent* throughout the centuries. But where is this consistency to be found if all doctrinal definitions are of relative value? Some would perhaps say that unity in history is primarily to be found in the *authority* that defines the truth, which can contradict itself in order to meet different historical situations. But then there is really no longer any hope of discovering a single Christian tradition. The problem of unity can only be solved by the acceptance of a common authority—a direct return to the absolutism of the medieval papacy—which would only be called to admit greater pluralism within its jurisdiction.

Thirdly, on the highest level of Roman Catholicism—that is, the papal pronouncements themselves—there is also a new search for a reinterpretation of tradition. I will mention only one example, which is of great importance for the relations between Rome and Orthodoxy. On the occasion of the 700th anniversary of the Second Council of Lyons (1274), Pope Paul VI made a formal statement calling that council a "council of the West" that mishandled the affairs of the Eastern Church. Until that statement of Paul VI, the Council of Lyons was generally accepted in Roman Catholicism as an "ecumenical" council that sanctioned union with the East and approved the addition of the *Filioque* to the Creed. Its categorization as only a "council of the West" would, of course, imply that it has no ecumenical authority. But if this is the case, other councils— for example, Florence, or Trent, or Vatican I, or Vatican II—or formal doctrinal statements by popes that were never accepted by Eastern Orthodoxy, are *also* reduced to the level of Western historical theologoumena, which Eastern Christians are under no obligation to accept.

Obviously, if this line of approach is pursued, the entire problem of the relationship between Rome and Orthodoxy appears in a new perspective. If holy tradition is defined not in terms of papal approvals—which were doubtlessly given to the Western pronouncements listed above—but in terms of reception by the entire Church, what exactly is the status of these pronouncements? And what about contemporary papal pronouncements? If these can all be ignored by Eastern Christians, can they also be formally criticized and denied? And if this right of criticism is given to Eastern Christians, is it not also obvious that Western Christians can oppose them too? Indeed, are the categories of East and West really applicable in our time, as they were in the Middle Ages? We are living in a small world, where cultures and traditions can no longer be seen in isolation from each other. Christian tradition must be present *as such*—in its universal existential significance—if it is to be accepted by our contemporaries.

What is the position and the contribution of the Orthodox Church in the inevitable debate on the nature of tradition? This position can be described both negatively and positively. In the negative sense, the Orthodox East has never been obsessed with a search for objective, clear, and formally definable criteria of truth, such as either the papal authority or the Reformed notion of *sola scriptura*. In a way that is often puzzling for Western Christians, the Orthodox, when asked positively about the sources of their faith, answer in terms of such concepts as the whole of Scripture, seen in the light of the tradition of the ancient councils, the Fathers, and the faith of the entire people of God, expressed particularly in the liturgy. This appears to outsiders as nebulous, perhaps romantic or mystical, and in any case inefficient and unrealistic. The Orthodox themselves defend their position as sacramental and eschatological. But are the other, supposedly clearly defined criteria more realistic and less mystical? Is not the belief in papal infallibility also a mystical belief?

The practical result of the "nebulosity" with which tradition is defined in Orthodoxy is the deep sense that the entire Church—and not only the "authorities," whether patriarchs or even councils—is responsible for tradition. Of course, an "ecumenical council" would be seen as the highest form of witness to the truth. But the Orthodox always point out that some councils of the past have been convened as "ecumenical" but were eventually rejected by the church.

In practice, the absence of formal criteria or authorities, and the common responsibility placed upon all, leads historical Eastern Orthodoxy to a very conservative attitude. There is no ecclesial authority that would be able to *impose* changes or reforms, not only regarding doctrine but even in Liturgy or discipline. Changes, nevertheless, do take place, but they always require a slow process of "reception." In situations where the entire body of the Church lacks enlightened knowledge of the issues, both conservatism and changes are, of course, quite dangerous. Historically, Eastern Christianity has often fallen into a state of frozenness, where refusal of change is equated with traditionalism. On the other hand, as a reaction against conservatism, some rush into a race of progressivism, competing in this with Western Christians.

The most obvious and most significant challenges to Orthodox traditionalism today are, of course, the challenge of the socialist totalitarian society of Eastern Europe, where the largest numbers of Orthodox Christians live, and the opportunity offered by the relatively recent establishment of Orthodox churches in Western societies or in the Third World. Although quite different in nature, the forces—in both of these situations—challenging a church that is so sacramentally oriented, so immutable doctrinally, so firm in referring to consistency with the past, are very strong indeed. The odds against the very survival of the Church in such circumstances seem overwhelming. Nevertheless, there are obvious signs of survival, progress, and renewal.

My paper has not given an answer to the question raised in its title: Does Christian tradition have a future? Perhaps no direct answer is possible. Actually, the New Testament itself gives no rosy picture of the success of the Christian message in history. Rather, it orients our minds and our hearts toward the *eschaton*, when, according to the promise, Christ will be all in all. This is why I began my paper by recalling the early Christian eschatological basis for the notion of tradition. Christian tradition cannot be reduced to the preservation of ideas and concepts, or to the definition of external, juridical structures serving to preserve the concepts. Both concepts and structures may be needed in history, but their role and significance are *relative*. They might and should change, but not their content, which is revealed in the mystery of Christ as new life, as liberation from both conceptualism and the law, and as an experience of the unchangeable, who was incarnate of the Virgin Mary and became flesh—an indelible part of his own creation and of human history.

## NOTES

1. *The Epistles of St. Clement of Rome and St. Ignatius of Antioch*, *Ancient Christian Writers*, volume 1, translated and annotated by James A. Kleist, S. J. (Mahwah, N.J.: Paulist Press, 1946).
2. St. Irenaeus of Lyons, *Against the Heresies*, volume 55, translated and annotated by Dominic J. Unger, O.F.M. Cap. (Mahwah, N.J.: Paulist Press, 1992).

*Alexander Men (1935–1990) defies easy categorization. His parents were secular Jews and when his mother converted to Christianity, naturally she had her son baptized. Alexander was raised and formed in the "catacomb Church" that resisted both the Bolshevik regime and the accommodation of the Russian Church. Blocked from a career in science because of both his Jewish background and active Christian faith, he studied theology privately and was ordained a priest in 1960. Married with two children, he served in several parishes until settling into the one at Novaya Derevnya, outside the city of Moscow, close to the famous Sergius-Trinity monastery. For almost twenty years he preached, taught, and continued basic education in the faith through a series of books on world religions, the Bible, and the Liturgy, all published abroad under pseudonyms and brought back surreptitiously into Russia. With Gorbachev's opening up of Soviet society, Fr. Men almost immediately became a sought after lecturer and TV commentator. Many intellectuals and artists rediscovered Christianity through his lecturing and writing and flocked to his parish and to him personally for baptisms, confession, marriage, and pastoral care. On his way to the train from his home in Semkhoz to celebrate Sunday Liturgy at the Novaya Derevnya Valley church on September 9, 1990, he was attacked from behind and died of ax blows to his head after crawling back to the gate of his garden. His attackers were never found or identified, many believing them to have been right-wing extremists. Fr. Men's ability to present the living tradition of the faith in a way that connected it to contemporary issues made him, along with the others represented in this collection, part of a singular voice in the Orthodox churches. His work continues in his writings, several collections of which have been translated into French,*

*English, and Italian versions. His vision is sustained in Russia by a number of organizations that promote religious education and outreach to young people and the distressed.*

*The selections here both bear the vibrancy of live delivery, as is also the case with his taped and transcribed liturgical sermons and conversations at house meetings after Saturday vespers. In these talks on the Creed, also taped and transcribed, Fr. Men not only presents catechetical basics but integrates these into the demands of contemporary life.*

## FOR FURTHER READING

Hamant, Yves. *Alexander Men, A Witness for Contemporary Russia, A Man for Our Time*. Translated by Steven Bigham. Crestwood, N.Y.: Oakwood/SVSP, 1995.

Men, Alexander. *Awake to Life! Sermons from the Paschal Cycle*. Translated by Mariete Sapiets. Crestwood, N.Y.: Oakwood/SVSP, 1996.

———. *Christianity for the Twenty-First Century*. Edited by Elizabeth Roberts and Ann Skukman. New York: Continuum, 1996.

———. *Conversations on Christ and the Church*. Translated by Alexis Vinogradov. Crestwood, N.Y.: Oakwood/SVSP, 1996.

———. *Orthodox Worship: Sacrament, Word, Image*. Translated by Colin Masica. Crestwood, N.Y.: Oakwood/SVSP, 1999.

———. *Seven Talks on the Creed*. Translated by Colin Masica with Olga Trubetskoy. Crestwood, N.Y.: Oakwood/SVSP, 1999.

———. *Son of Man*. Translated by Samuel Brown. Crestwood, N.Y.: Oakwood/SVSP, 1998.

# FIFTH TALK ON THE CREED

We move on to the mystery of the Divine Spirit, or the Spirit of God, concerning which the "Symbol of Faith" has this to say: "I believe in the Holy Spirit, the Lord and Giver of Life, Who proceeds from the Father, Who with the Father and the Son is worshipped and glorified, Who spoke by the prophets."

Let me translate this into plain Russian: "I believe in the Holy Spirit, who brings life, who issues forth from the Father, who we worship in the same way as the Father and the Son—one Divinity, who speaks through prophets."

In fact, already in the Old Testament, in ancient times, when a mysterious power overcame an ordinary man, calling him to service, he went out to preach, like the great pastoral prophet Amos went, who was neither of the priestly order, nor a servant of the Temple, nor, so to say, an officially appointed prophet who had this duty. He was simply a herdsman and farmer. Yet once the Spirit of God came over him, he subsequently wrote: "When the lion roars, who does not tremble; When the Lord speaks, who will not be a prophet?" That is to say, this is a power that takes a person beyond himself. A power that works in such a way that a human being is enabled to do more than he normally can.

When we say "spirit" we often imply by this something incorporeal, almost impotent. On the contrary, in the language of the Bible the Hebrew word *ruach* or the Greek word *pnevma* signifies "power, storm, wind, hurricane, breath." And "breath" is "life." The Spirit is power. The Divine Power, or the Holy Spirit.

---

Translated by Colin Masica with the assistance of Olga Trubetskoy from *Seven Talks on the Creed*. Crestwood, N.Y.: Oakwood/SVSP, 1999.

The word *holy* is equivalent to the word *God*. Both words need clarifying. In the Bible, in the Old Testament, the word *holy* often designates not our notion of a righteous man, but someone special, standing higher than this world, sacred. We could even say it means something inviolable. Therefore God, first of all, is called Holy. In this sense he is other than the world, the absolute Other. And man must remember that he is radically distinct from everything with which we come in contact. So, when the prophets speak of the "Spirit of God," this means the Spirit of Holiness, the Holy Spirit. Is this an impersonal power? No. Notice the first lines in the Bible itself, where we read that when the Lord fashioned the universe, the earth was without form and void. Darkness signifies the primary material, the primary structure of the cosmos. The Spirit of God, as it were, "hovered," in the Russian translation "floated," over the water, but really this verb means something like "warmed." It was used to describe a bird that hovered over its nest or hatches its eggs, or warms its fledglings. He brings life to the universe.

If God as Father is the first principle of everything, and God as the Logos, as the Word, is the Creator of everything that has been created, it is God as Spirit that is its preserver, supporter, and the power constantly abiding in it. And of course this power, indisputably, is divine, and personal.

When the prophets came forward under the impetus of the Spirit, they themselves were astounded that things were revealed to them that not only were not comprehensible to them, but even contradicted their innermost thoughts and feelings. There took place tragic battles between the will of the prophet and the voice of the Spirit of God. Battles, because in the biblical revelation the personality of the prophet was never suppressed; he did not dissolve in the ocean of the absolute.

On the contrary, he stood before God, as a personality before the One who is beyond the personal. And here there transpired a dramatic struggle and voluntary agreement. A man receives the Spirit of God within himself. Therefore God "spoke by the prophets."

Can we say that there have been no prophets since those ancient times? No. It is sufficient to remember that at the beginning of the nineteenth century, St. Seraphim of Sarov, one of the glorified saints of Russia, said that the chief aim of the Christian life is the acquisition within oneself of the Holy Spirit, or, as he expressed it, the "gaining" of the Spirit. It means this is possible for us as human beings. And we know of people of great wisdom, ascetics, righteous men and women, public figures—they might be illiterate, or great writers—who acted as prophets, through whom the will of God was revealed. They were giants of moral power, of social protest, they went against the current. What was it that assisted them? It was the influence of the Spirit of God on history. For example, probably many of you are acquainted with the historiosophical concepts of Leo Nikolaevich Gumilev, who noted that the birth of new nations, new formations in the human race, is inescapably connected with the appearance of a so-called "impassioned" group, a white-hot epicenter, consisting of the kind of personalities that go in advance to meet risk and even perish, and thereby move the development of history forward.

So, we have a basis for thinking that there are influences of the Spirit of God on history. The Spirit of God is manifested in talents and gifts. It is very mysterious and odd. We don't always understand where it is coming from. The history of mankind bears witness that from time to time peoples, civilizations, or separate individuals are given precisely this gift of the Spirit, and everything depends on how they receive it and on how they realize it. It can be realized in a completely false direction. It is here that both reason and conscience, and a clear, precise awareness, ought to help a person, because a human being possessed by the Spirit of God is not a sleepwalker, a Pythic oracle, a creature that has lost its senses. No. The Spirit of God does not extinguish human reason, but on the contrary, illuminates it. If a person does not permit reason to function and thinks that it is possible to live only by irrational, intuitive impulse, he or she can get lost. One may dissipate the spiritual gift of passion, destroy it, or turn it in entirely the wrong direction.

How has this played out in history? I think you can estimate it fairly well. There have been people seemingly possessed by the idea of saving others, of helping others—the Russian revolutionaries of the nineteenth century, for example. Certainly they had passion, certainly this was a moral impulse, a high impulse, but they didn't take the time to think about how all this could be done. So they rushed ahead blindly; it was entirely a blind impulse, a mad, destructive impulse. "Call Russia to the ax." Well, they did call it to the ax, and the result was extremely lamentable.

Then it was they who became victims of this perverted impulse. They themselves turned into new oppressors and slave-masters. Spiritual comprehension demands sober analysis. Therefore the apostle John says, "My brothers, do not believe every spirit." They might be pseudomorphs of the Spirit of God.

It is very important for us to remember and to know that Christ, when he was telling his disciples that he would visibly depart, depart from this world, promised them that the Spirit of God would continue his mission on earth. He would be the Protector, the Intercessor for the community of the Church, the Paraclete. *Paraclete* in Greek means defender, intercessor, comforter, as he is called. "I will send you, I will ask the Father to send you this Comforter. He will direct you to all truth." Thus, the Church is created by the power of the Spirit of God.

Here we have a difficult problem in front of us.

## WHAT DO WE CALL THE CHURCH?

A small bit of philological information: the Russian word "church" [*tserkov*] comes from the Greek word *kyriakon*—"the house of God," whence also

*Kirche*, English *church*, etc. There is another Greek name for the church—*ekklesia*, which means "people's assembly." This term was used to translate the Ancient Hebrew word *kakhal*, "community," or the Aramaic *kekhal*, "community of people." From *ekklesia* come the French word *église* and the Spanish *iglesia*. What is this all about? When you read fiction or journalism, or some sort of historical literature, often the word "church" [*Tserkov*] is met with as the designation of some kind of institution, some kind of establishment, like a political party. According to this model, so to speak, which we have become accustomed to seeing in the course of our whole life, we think that this "party" must issue some directives, and have some ideological basis or ideological appraisals of everything in the world. Therefore I am often asked here and in other places where I talk with people, "But what is the position of the Church regarding UFOs?"—or something else. As if the church had some kind of laboratory, a structure, or shall we say a "trust," which works out an ideological position with regard to all phenomena in the world—including cosmic phenomena. This is a kind of notion of an ideological apparatus, a notion of, so to say, an authority structure, which can be overthrown, and then return to power, and not accidentally. Christians themselves are guilty in this, because in certain periods of history the Christian community in fact underwent sclerotic alterations, and began to be reminiscent of some kind of ideological party. Naturally, along with all the consequences that proceeded from that—with the suppression of dissent, with fanaticism, with a quite powerful bureaucracy, with the immobility and clumsiness of this apparatus—there went, so to say, a great measure of conservatism.

But, when we read in the "Symbol of Faith" about the Church, which is moved by the Spirit of God, the "Symbol" absolutely does not mean this historical reality. According to the Christian point of view, the Church is a divine-human organism. A divine-human organism, or the Body of Christ, as the apostle Paul teaches us.

It is a certain spiritual community in which Christ continues to work, in which the Spirit of God lives and which exists by this Spirit. How did it come into being? Christ created it, but he did not formalize it, he did not give it any structure. He only said, "You are Mine, you are My community." Every member of it had to be a bearer of his Spirit. Soon after the events in the Gospel another important event took place—the birth of the Church. It happened like this. It is described in the book, *The Acts of the Apostles*. The disciples of Jesus from Galilee were gathered in Jerusalem according to his command. They were praying there together. It was the Jewish holiday of *Shavuot*, or Pentecost, as we call it, because it was fixed at fifty days after Passover/Pascha. Until this time the disciples kept quiet, perhaps were even timid. They did not come forward as some new spiritual religious force. They also went to the temple to pray with all the others; they lived in their semidomestic commune. There were a few hundred persons there. Perhaps the entire Church was no larger than us, gathered here today. But at one point, when the holiday was in full swing, this group of apostles and disciples went out into the streets of the city and began to glorify God in a strange manner.

They spoke and almost sang. It was an astounding doxology. They spoke in some incomprehensible tongue. But, on the other side, people who had come together for the pilgrimage from all the ends of the earth recognized it, and understood this speech. How? We don't know. But the meaning got through to them all. This was an extraordinary phenomenon. Some decided that they were simply drunk; others could not understand what was going on. Then Peter stepped forward and said, "No, brothers and sisters. This is not madness, nor are they drunk."

The Spirit of God had descended on the apostles. And had led them forth to preach the Gospel. It is from *this* moment that the Church was *born*, preaching and proclaiming Christ crucified and risen from the dead.

It resembles its founder, the God-Man Jesus Christ. But there is a huge difference. If the human principle in him was free from evil and from sin, the human element of the Church is earthly; it is not free from sin. The Church consists of the same kind of people as all the rest, but she is the seed, the basis, as it were, the kernel of the future humanity, which must come together in spiritual unity, in the greatest diversity, in the greatest openness and the greatest freedom.


## WHAT DOES MAN SUFFER FROM?

From alienation, from loneliness, from being crushed by the crowd or by himself.

The Church is not the crowd; it is a spiritual unity, when all are transparent to one another. At the same time it is what the Russian philosophers of the last century called *sobornost'* (i.e., in contrast with collectivism), in which the personality disappears, and with individualism, in which the personality has an exaggerated and excessive development. Under the term *sobornost'* theology understands a unity which does not kill personality. It is one of the special properties of the Church. She is the continuation of the life and activity and witness of Christ on earth. She carries within her his treasures, and sows them like seed throughout the world. But we always should remember that as soon as the members, the bearers of the Church, depart from the spirit of Christ's love, they automatically cease to be its representatives. Therefore it is abundantly clear that ecclesiastical institutions by themselves, so to say, this whole "structure," does not automatically guarantee faithfulness to Christ.

Of course, some of you may ask, "Then what do we need the institution for? Why not let there be free communities without any hierarchical structure?" and so forth.

You know that the more advanced an organism is, the more differentiated it is: only the simplest have nothing but a nucleus and protoplasm. An advanced

organism is distinguished by the complexity of its component elements. Therefore the apostle Paul says, "In the body various parts and organs serve its unity."
Therefore, being simultaneously not only a spiritual but also a social organism,
the Church has to have some kind of social structure. Otherwise she cannot live.
This is simply a necessary condition, for the Church just as for any association.

Now let us turn to her attributes, or more accurately, her characteristics,
which we find in the "Symbol of Faith." *[I believe]* in one Holy, Catholic, and
Apostolic Church. This is our main theme today. First of all, why is the Church
one? Because we are looking at the oneness of God. This is a mystical oneness.

You are thinking, then there is no point in the revelation to mankind of the
Divine Tri-Unity, there is no point in God revealing himself as Creator, as Logos, and as Spirit. No, quite the contrary. It has a direct practical significance
for our life. It is not abstract metaphysics, not abstract dogma.

I remind you once more how deeply Andrei Rubliev and his presumed
teacher, St. Sergius, understood this. When ancient Russia found itself in a difficult situation, during the Mongol yoke and internal strife among the princes,
of spiritual crisis and decline, what could oppose this disintegrating world?
Love. But what kind of love? First of all, divine love. St. Sergius named his little church in honor of the Holy Trinity. It was the first Trinity church in Russia.
Why? Because, as the ancient text says, the St. Sergius wanted the people,
through contemplating the unity of the Holy Trinity, to overcome the evil division of the world.

On the night of his Mystical Supper, before his death, Christ prayed, saying,
"May they all be one, as You O Father are in Me and I in You. Let them also all
be one." That is, the unity of divine love that is primary, in the Trinity, is the
prototype for us, for our unity, our mutual interpenetrating, our mutual inter-
permeability, our mutual openness to one another. When people are capable of
being, to use philosophical language, "immanent" to one another, in reality, we
are "transcendent" to one another—that is, each one of us is a closed system.
Even people who love one another penetrate from heart to heart only with difficulty. So you see, God calls people to a new path—one of mutual interpenetrating. When Rubliev painted his "Trinity," he portrayed in a practical way,
with colors and lines, this invisible mystery of love, this circle, which beckons
and calls man to change his model of the world.

The aggressive, embittered, disintegrating existence of man—a pack of
wolves, of solitary wolves (it only seems that they are a real pack)—is opposed
by the Catholicity *[sobornost']* of love of the Holy Trinity. Therefore, as Christ
is one, as God is one, as the Spirit of God is one, the Church is one. When Christ
began to speak about the Church, he told Peter, "I will build My Church on a
rock, on a stone, on you, and the gates of hell shall not overcome it," because Peter was the first to confess him as the Messiah. "The gates of hell" means the
powers of the nether regions, the powers of death. And he did not say, "My
churches"; he said "My Church," using the singular to refer to one substance.

But here you might ask me, "But how is it one?" When out of the more than 1.5 billion Christians that are on earth, about 900 million are Catholic, 90 million are Orthodox, and the rest are Protestants. And the Protestants divide into countless groups—Lutherans, Evangelicals, Baptists, Pentecostals, etc. Where is the unity here? This question is a very complicated one, but we don't need to think that a mechanical unity can substitute for spiritual unity here.

These divisions, which have taken place in the Church over the course of the centuries, do not reflect the nature of the Church itself. They reflect cultural, political, national, and psychological barriers, which people have not been capable of surmounting. We must note that when the old Roman Empire attempted to unite and identify itself with the whole of Christianity, the Eastern provinces opposed this. They broke off. The so-called pre-Chalcedonian churches were formed—the churches of the Copts, of the Ethiopians, of the Syrians. The grounds were dogmatic ones, but it was really a reaction of the Eastern borderlands.

But in spite of that, until the tenth century the Church remained essentially one, and not divided. Everywhere there were churches with their own heads—a pope in Alexandria, a pope in Rome (*papas* means "father"), in Constantinople, in Antioch, and other major centers. But after the fall of the Western Roman Empire, in the parts, the "halves" of the former Empire, different social and cultural conditions arose. In the East, the absolutist imperial power was retained, and all the ancient structures of slaveholding, etc. were also retained, and the ecclesiastical leadership, the ecclesiastical community, and the ecclesiastical structure found itself under the control of the state, a rigid control. This has been the fate of the Eastern Church over the course of 1500 years down to this day.

In the West, the Empire collapsed. Barbarians flooded into Italy. Only one structure remained—the authority of the Church—as a basis for the rebirth of a future culture. The Roman Church felt independent of the state, because in general there was no state; there were the newly arising barbarian kingdoms, which warred among themselves, fell, and sprang up anew.

The Western Church became, so to speak, masculine, bellicose. When the Byzantine emperors tried to take control of it and subject it to their authority, the Roman pontiff turned to King Pepin in the name of the apostle Peter—to the barbarian King Pepin. The latter moved his detachments to Rome and did not allow Rome to be seized and subjected. He then set aside for the Roman pontiff, for the pope, a part of the territory of central Italy. For what purpose? So that no emperor or king could take the Roman bishop under his control with his bare hands.

Thus arose the papal state, which existed until the year 1870. Then it was abolished as a result of the uprising led by Garibaldi, and reestablished in 1929—no longer in its previous dimensions, but symbolically, 108 acres in all. In compensation for its loss of statehood, this territory is not subject to any government.

I have been on this Vatican territory. When you enter, there is a border guard in old-fashioned costumes, designed by Michelangelo, and you are crossing an international boundary. Such was the destiny of the Western Church. But the Eastern Church, subject to the Emperor, kept moving away from it more and more. There were different cultural paths. Conflict between the East and the West had an effect on the Church and ended with the patriarch of Constantinople excommunicating the papal legate (envoy), while the papal envoy excommunicated the patriarch, and this is considered the formal beginning of the division of the churches, occurring in the year 1054. It is true that today, after 1000 years, the patriarch of Constantinople and the pope have called back this document and have publicly burned it as a sign that this conflict is over. But alas, after 1000 years of separated existence, many dogmatic and other peculiarities have accumulated that make unity a complex problem. Later, a schism took place in the Western Church, and the Protestants appeared. They began to subdivide in their turn.

## SO WHAT IS THE CHURCH?

The Church is a complex formation. First of all, it is that Church which was founded by Christ. This means, coming without interruption from the apostles. Such is the Orthodox Church, the Eastern Church. Such also is the Catholic Church, the Western Church. In the practice of the Orthodox Church, we recognize the hierarchy and the sacraments of the Catholic Church, that is, we recognize it as a church, albeit separated from us. They, in their turn, call us "separated brethren." The same thing obviously can be said about the ancient Oriental churches—the Armenian, the Ethiopian, the Coptic. It gets more complicated when we come to Protestantism. But in the broad sense of the word, we may consider any community a church that confesses Jesus Christ come into the world in the flesh, crucified, and resurrected.

The history of conflicts and discussions has shown that when people argue, they only become hardened in their positions. Theological polemicists have not been able to bring the churches closer. Something else has brought them closer. Now, when they know more about the West in the East, and the West knows more about the East, rapprochement proceeds through quite different channels. For example, the Western Church is beginning to honor our saints. I have seen an enormous amount of literature about Russian ascetics of the past and present. In every Catholic church in Italy I have seen a representation of the Vladimir icon of the Mother of God and other Orthodox icons. They relate to us very openly, as if gradually departing from the idea of division.

In our church there are various points of view in this regard. From complete rejection, which was formulated by Alexander Stepanovich Khomiakov: he thought that Christianity was only the Orthodox Eastern Church while the

Catholic Church was no longer Christianity. But at present the Orthodox Church does not share that point of view. If we receive a Catholic priest into our ecclesiastical jurisdiction, he becomes Orthodox; no one reordains him. His priesthood is considered real. All his sacraments—baptism, communion, and everything that he has performed, were real. Hence the logical conclusion that we recognize the Catholic Church as part of Christianity. Only by getting well acquainted with one another can we understand the causes of the divisions and often see to what extent they were far removed from genuine spirituality and a "sense of Church."[1]

## ONE HOLY, CATHOLIC, AND APOSTOLIC CHURCH: WHAT DOES IT MEAN?

One holy, Catholic, and apostolic church: Does it mean that she consists of saints? Yes. In apostolic times all believers called themselves that—saints. Not in the sense in which we use this word now, but in the sense that they were special people dedicated to God. Although the Church lives in the world and is wholly immersed in it, on the other hand she is the ship of God, floating on the sea, an ark. In any case the Christian is separated from the world. He is separated in some respect. There is here a kind of secret dialectic. Both in the world, and not of this world, both openness, and closure.

To explain this simply is impossible; it can be understood only in practice. Only in practice can you grasp what this means—to be with all and like all, and at the same time to be separate, to be inside your ark.

One more thing. Dedication to God is imitation of Christ. Christ was the healer, Christ was the sacrifice, Christ was the heart that is devoted to human beings, and he was the witness to the truth. "I came in order to witness to the truth." The Church is the same. If members of the Church betray this, they cease to be expressions of the Church. Sometimes the reproach is made, "But isn't this similar to the Communist party? They say that the party's ideal has been perverted, that the ideal was thus and such, whereas it has become different in real life." No. No. This is not similar, because such a radical difference does not exist in political history, where we could say that in the beginning there were people who wished to respect culture, respect all human beings, the value of personality, the right of religious belief, freedom of conscience, freedom of the press. It was not like that. As soon as our revolution began, all of this came crashing down in an hour. If we look at the past, in the nineteenth century, when the Marxist circles were being formed, there was no "superfluous" democracy in them either. No, that was not at all characteristic of them. There is no point in speaking of perversion here. Everything was as it was intended. Everything proceeded in the appointed direction and bore its fruits. But those fruits turned out to be bitter ones: for everyone, including those who cultivated them. This has no connection with our theme.

Meanwhile, the distance between the Gospel and, for example, any kind of religious-fanatic-inquisitor is infinite, because there is nothing even comparable here. The external regalia, as we might call it, of this inquisitor means nothing more than the crosses on the wings of fascist airplanes, for it is only an external symbol. The content is absolutely otherwise.

"In one Holy, Catholic [*Sobornaia*], and Apostolic Church." *Sobornaia* is the Church Slavonic translation of a Greek term, in the original *Katholiki*—the Catholic Church. *Catholic* means "universal," gathered from the whole world. Not something separate, or pertaining to a particular epoch, or national, or ancient, or modernized, but universal—that is, really its place is everywhere. There are no barriers, no limitations. While creating national cultures or influencing them, the Church remains supranational, supraethnic, suprahuman, embracing all. The universal Church, that is, in its primordial sense.

We may, of course, ask, "Well, how are we to understand the 'Russian' Orthodox Church, the 'Georgian,' and so forth?" These are all national embodiments of the Church. Are they necessary? Yes, of course. The Church influences the creativity of man, in the moral, social, and artistic spheres. The Christian religion lies at the base of the world of people, including "nations." The creativity of nations is a great calling before God. You know that when civilization becomes depersonalized it ceases to be creative. Therefore in every culture there has to be created its interpretation, its refraction, of Christianity. The more multifaceted it is, the more fully the Church expresses itself. If we look at African churches, we shall see there patterns peculiar to the folk tradition of the Africans—Madonnas with black faces, representations of Christ in ebony wood. Indian churches with Christ represented as seated in the lotus position. Every culture, including those of the North American Indians and the Eskimos, creates its own aspect of the Church, and this in no way diminishes its unity. This was providentially prepared by the sociocultural unity of the Roman Empire that already existed. Christianity was preached in the Roman Empire, and the Roman Empire took in a multitude of peoples, who in general did not lose their identity, but at the same time were mutually connected by *koiné* Greek as an international language and by Roman laws and the concept of Roman citizenship.

Finally, the *apostolic* church. In a simplified form this presentation is connected with the idea that the apostles appointed their successors, and the successors, others; that a laying-on of hands took place, and thus down to our time. It did in fact happen like this.

Even if there wasn't, in the literal sense, a transmission of apostolic rights (historians argue about this), the living continuity was always maintained. It was there before the books of the New Testament arose. It was the basis of the Church, the basis for choosing from various books, namely, those that corresponded to the tradition of the apostles. The oral tradition was the source according to which everything proceeded. This means the Church was founded on the apostles. There were first, the twelve; and later, the seventy who were her founders.

Moreover, Christ used the number twelve with a purpose. According to the Bible, twelve is the number of the elect. In ancient times, there were twelve patriarchs, the founders of the people of Israel, which at one time was the Old Testament Church. As if to continue this line, Christ chooses twelve apostles as progenitors of the New Testament Church of Christ. Therefore the whole Church stands, as represented in the Apocalypse, on the shoulders of the apostles as on a rock. And one more characteristic of the Church comes in here. *Apostle* means "envoy," the envoy of Christ. The Church should be the envoy of Christ in the world. When she carries this out, then she is real. The Church bears his voice. She is the preaching Church. Preaching in the sense that she bears witness to the treasure that has been entrusted to her, to the living Christ, to his presence in the world, to the living Spirit of God, who is present here. Not because the wisest or the strongest people are gathered in the Church, but because the Spirit of God speaks through them, because he is the chief—at times hidden, and at times manifest—power in this world.

At all times and no matter what events take place, the Church is always this same voice. Her tradition, leading from the apostles, is simultaneously the criterion of testing what in the real, empirical, earthly church belongs to Christ and God in the Truth, and what is alien, transitory, perverted, human.

## WHAT IS THIS TRADITION OF THE CHURCH?

The tradition of the Church is, first of all, her principal dogmas. There are very few of them. Many people who have recently been converted suppose that there is a colossal collection of dogmas. No. That which has been stated in the ecumenical councils is dogma. The rest is freely accepted or rejected by whomever it pleases.

## WHAT IS THE AXIS OF TRADITION?

The axes of tradition are the teachings and revelation of God that are in written form—the Holy Scripture—the Bible. Therefore, do not imagine that the Bible is something opposed to tradition. It is in fact the fixed tradition of the Church, and through the Bible we test how much we have departed from or how much we are in agreement with the will of Christ and with the Holy Spirit. This is the way that a question here is resolved.

Thus a person, upon entering the Church, and living in her, has received not only a refuge, but also a calling. Being a Christian is a profession, to put it in ordinary language. It means doing in the world something quite special, doing something for the eternal One. And although our life is ephemeral, although it is short and often insignificant, participation in eternity, involvement in it, makes it full of nonephemeral content.

When we enter the Church, we find there Christ and the Holy Spirit, who is acting in her. And just as though the Lord Jesus was buried and the seal was on his grave he conquered death, so also the Church, more than once, it seems, has been destroyed either by external enemies or by internal ones, unworthy Christians who have defiled her essence, degraded her, and misinterpreted her; but she has risen anew each time and will always arise.

In the Apocalypse of John the Church is called the Bride. "Bride" is an image taken from the Old Testament. "The Bride" is the community that awaits its divine bridegroom. And this means that the foundation of everything here is built on love. Love is life, love is the greatest mystery. As we draw near to God, we reveal him within the Church as infinite love, as the meaning of our entire existence, as its beauty, as its fullness.

There is a final thing I want to tell you. Time and again I am asked, "The teaching of Christ is excellent. The *Gospel* is magnificent. But *why* do we need the Church here? There is so much that is negative in it." Yes, there has been the negative side. There has indeed. But before saying this and rejecting the idea of community, we should remember that this is after all Christ's Church. He founded it 2000 years ago. He said that the gates of hell would not overcome her. He is present in her always unto the end of the age.

One more thing. If it is so, this means that Christ did not wish us to reach the truth in isolation, each one by himself in some sort of separate and isolated little world, but that he wanted us to do this together, despite the difficulty, for any human society contains within it the danger of temptations, frictions, scandals. But that is what he wanted. Once more I repeat, this was his will, his Church, his Spirit, which abides in her even today.

Thank you.

## NOTE

1. *Tserkovnost'*—a peculiarly Russian concept which is difficult or impossible to translate; roughly, it is "the feeling of the Church as it is supposed to be." Tomas Spidlik—or his translator, Anthony P. Gythiel (*The Spirituality of the Christian East.* Kalamazoo, Mich.: Cistercian Publications, 1986), after making a similar comment, translates it as "a sense of Church" and says it "amounts to the consciousness . . . that no one may believe he is saved unless he is saved together with others" (p. 352–53). (Translator's note)

# SIXTH TALK ON THE CREED: ON THE NICENE, THE CONSTANTINOPOLITAN SYMBOL

Today we are approaching the end of the "Symbol of Faith" and next time we shall talk about its last lines. Today I will dwell on the statement, *I confess one baptism for the remission of sins.* What does this mean?

The word "baptism" in Greek means "ablution." A holy ablution in deep antiquity signified a turning point in the life of a person, a washing off from his or her soul and body of some dark elements, both physical and spiritual. Water was employed here as a symbol of purity. Meanwhile, today we know that water is the wonder of the universe. Life exists on the Earth only thanks to water. The waterless deserts of the moon or of other planets in the solar system are correspondingly lifeless. Think about this a little—our life is sustained by water, our organism consists of 70 percent or more of water. Life arose in water; a particular molecule, structured in a particular manner, imparts to the element of water exclusive properties necessary for life. Now we also know that not only did it help in the creation of life, but in some mysterious manner is able to hold information. Water possesses some kind of peculiar memory. So, the intuition of the peoples who employed water in religious rites, in ablutions, was not mistaken.

In the time of the Old Testament the custom arose that when a pagan, a member of a different nationality, converted to faith in the One God, he went through a ritual of ablution, of holy washing. Often this took place in the river

Translated by Colin Masica with the assistance of Olga Trubetskoy from *Seven Talks on the Creed*, Oakwood Publications, 1999.

Jordan or at Siloam—a spring or pool that existed near the Jerusalem Temple. Part of it exists even to this day.

Why did the ablution take place in the Jordan? The Jordan from ancient times was considered a sacred river and, simultaneously, the boundary of the holy land, dividing it from the mountains of Moab and the eastern deserts. This holy ablution was a sign of the pagan's joining the true faith. Later John the Baptist appeared, about whom you all know. He summoned the people to perform a holy ablution—*mikme*, or *baptizma*—in the River Jordan. It wasn't heathen that he required this of, but true-believing Israelites, because he emphasized that the coming of a new era of the Spirit, when the Lord himself would come to earth demanding from the people, even those who had been brought up in the true faith, a turning point in their inner life—repentance, renewal, and consciousness of themselves as so unworthy that they had to go through the holy ablution just as the heathen did.

Holy ablution was also employed by the contemporaries of Jesus Christ, the semi-monastic order of Essenes. They did this several times a day. Finally Christ the Savior himself used the ritual of water ablution—baptism—as a sign of the mystery of entry into the Church of Christ.

This entry can take place only once. Therefore we say, "I confess *one* baptism for the remission of sins." That is, an adult person, coming to baptism, should understand it as reconciliation with God, as entry into the holy land of Truth, Good, Purity, and Faithfulness. That is why baptism is not repeated. It is unique.

How is this sacrament performed? Before telling you about this, l should explain to you what the word *sacrament* signifies. Among the sacred rites of the Church there are some, some particular ones, when the entire Church calls on the Holy Spirit to come to the spot where people are gathered. Out of many sacred rites of this sort the Church in the West in the fourteenth century selected seven principal ones. What does the number seven mean? In the Bible this is a symbol of fullness or completeness. It hints at the fact that there are really more than seven sacraments. The seven are the key ones. This was formulated for the first time in the thirteenth century by Thomas Aquinas. Later it was accepted in the Eastern Church as well. Today our church recognizes seven sacraments. The first, the introductory sacrament, as it were, is baptism. In any sacrament there are two features, two elements—one is the divine gift, the power of the Lord that comes to us, and the other is our response. Therefore a sacrament is a divine-human phenomenon, an intersection, as it were, of two worlds, the presence of the deity with us and of us with him—copresence, unity.

Moreover, a sacrament is the blessing or hallowing of man and of nature as a whole, because man is also nature. Man is the head of nature, its meaning, its spiritual center, the focus of all creation. At the blessing of the water with which the sacrament of baptism is accomplished, life is blessed—life itself, the miracle of life. This is after all an astonishing wonder. For some reason it cannot touch people who have been brought up to reject miracles. Just take a look at how the buds on the trees open. How in the spring the petrified branches, seemingly dried up from freezing, suddenly fill with sap, how the grass springs up on the ground, how life arises again. How it matures, how a bird is born from an egg, how man is born, how everything is created. Why does this take place? Why doesn't a helium plasma simply rage on the earth to this day, some kind of storm that kills life? What happened? Who set in motion thousands of laws so that they would come together in order to create life on earth, and man? This is a miracle indeed.

But there is also a second miracle. Spiritual birth. Christ said, "He has not yet come to faith who has not experienced a new birth." One time it is necessary to break the husk, the armor, that surrounds our soul—hidden inside, obsessed with itself, coiled up, like the embryo of an infant. When this shroud is opened, the soul also opens, like wings on a butterfly emerging from a cocoon.

Spiritual birth. Many people have been close to this, but then have become frightened by the shock to their soul and have drawn back into ordinariness, into everyday life, again returning to their usual spheres. God knocks on the heart of every person, and this is the most important moment of his or her life. Our task at that moment is to open the door to him, so that he does not pass us by. Thus, in baptism we encounter the will of a human being to enter the enclosure of the Church, to receive blessing, forgiveness, and the divine sign— "Come to me."

Finally, let us examine water as a symbol of human life. Baptism is divided into two parts, which are usually are united, and at the time when we are going to baptize those of you who have not been baptized and are coming on Holy Saturday, we will perform the baptism. Customarily both the "catechizing" [oglashenie] and the baptism are done together. But when I baptize one person, separately, I often separate these two parts. The priest asks the person whether he is ready for baptism, whether he desires to unite himself to Christ, whether he renounces Satan and his works, and every demonic evil—all evil is demonic. Then the one newly baptized recites the Symbol of Faith.

It is namely this "catechizing" that I have separated out, because it should be accompanied by discussions, and by reading of the Holy Scripture. But inasmuch as we have been meeting several times already, for us this has as it were taken the place of this catechizing as a preparation.

Then comes the sacrament of baptism itself—the person is received into the bosom of the Church, of the universal Church of Christ. But you will ask, "But why do they baptize children? Obviously children do not come because of their faith." Well, that's how it took shape historically. Christianity, having rejected the pagan custom of the consecration of an infant, of its entry into human society, into life, somehow did not create an analogous, sufficiently important ritual, and mothers began to bring their children to get them baptized. This was approximately in the fifth century.

Just as the state grants an infant citizenship—accepts him into its bosom, although the infant at this point still has no idea of this—and just as he becomes a beloved member of the family, although he is not conscious of this yet because he has just been born, so also an infant is received into the family of Christ's Church. This is, as it were, a baptism in advance, stored up for the future. At the same time the presence of the godparents signifies that they pledge to bring him up in the Christian faith, that the choice has been made by his parents even if not by him. For at this age a human being is not yet separate from his parents.

The second important sacrament is the sacrament of Communion. It is a sacrifice, but a sacrifice in a special, mystical sense. It is union with Christ. When in ancient times a man brought a sacrifice, he called on God by this to be a participator in his life. Man called God to a meal, for any sacrifice was at the same time a meal, which united the members of the society and also connected them with the divinity. Therefore when the ancient Israelites got together for the sacred meal of Passover, the so-called Seder, they ate bread together, and drank wine; this was a prayer meal, which united them in the Old Testament Church. Christ took this ritual and made it the sign of his real presence with men.

The eternal meal is prolonged, it continues. As Mandelshtam puts it, "The Eucharist is like a prolonged, eternal feast." So indeed, the Eucharist, the Thanksgiving, is a new Passover. That is, whereas then there was deliverance from slavery, here there is salvation, which is given through the coming of Christ to us. We must feel and experience that he is indeed here, that he is with us—who are eternally unworthy of him, far from him, but he is open to us.

Every time the Eucharist is celebrated, the cup and the bread remind us of The Mystical Supper. He left it to us as a sign and a rite. He said, "Do this in memory of Me." On the night before his death on the cross, he took the cup and the bread and said, "This meal—this is My body and blood, that is, it is me myself."

In the old manner of expression "me myself" meant, "I shall give myself to you and when you are together at this meal, I shall be with you, always." Therefore the oldest evidence concerning Christians is always inseparable from this sacrament. It is called "Thanksgiving" because prayers of thanksgiving are read there; in Greek it is "Eucharistia;" or "The Liturgy," meaning "common work." Or *Obiednia*, a popular expression meaning "that which takes place before midday," before "dinner" (*obied*). At the present time it is customary to come to the Eucharist on an empty stomach, out of reverence. It is celebrated every day in city churches, and every Sunday in village churches. First the holy chalice is raised in one place on earth, then the earth rotates. Always, in all countries, everywhere the chalice is raised. At every moment, at every hour. In it is life.

For this is bread, the flesh of the world: The grain of wheat, the blood of the vine, that material thing, that substance, nature, which nourishes and sustains us. For when a human being is nourished, he is connected to nature, he is in communion with it. The element of nature, the life of the cosmos, enters into us through the process of nourishment, is assimilated, is identified with our organism, and through this the energies of nature, the secret and the manifest powers of nature, enter into our body and it grows, it exists, it acquires these energies from nature. This is why the taking of food has always been a religious act, has always been accompanied by prayer. Down to this day we always try to cross ourselves before taking food, and if we are together, to recite a prayer.

A reverent attitude toward food: Christ makes a meal his most heartfelt sacrament, when his heart is given to us. The first Christians in fact celebrated this at a table—a prayer-meal. But when the number of people in the Church grew, this table turned into an altar, which stands in an elevated spot, in the altar-space, and there stand the chalice and the diskos with the bread, the consecration is performed, and then the people partake of the Holy Mysteries— the divine meal of Christ. How astonishing that he did not leave us some kind of philosophical teaching, a doctrine, aphorisms of some sort, but he left us himself through this simple meal, symbolizing life, food, without which man cannot live. And this was not only on the last night before his death on the cross; this was also another time, when he fed the hungry in the wilderness, and then hid himself from them, when they wanted to proclaim him king.

When they were looking for him, he said, "I am the bread from heaven, which came to you, in order to nourish you. The one who is nourished by my flesh and blood will have eternal life." Of course, they did not understand this expression. But the flesh and blood, I repeat, is a man himself. It means that he is our food; by analogy with nature, he sustains our existence—like food, nature sustains every one of us.

The third sacrament—the order has no significance, it may be changed—is the sacrament of repentance or confession. It is a second baptism, as it were, conditionally. Inasmuch as the sacrament of baptism is not repeated, while a person who has received forgiveness through it returns often and by nature to a sinful life, some kind of sign is necessary that he is forgiven anew, that he may approach the holy chalice—and the sacrament of repentance is this sign. It is performed also by the whole Church, but in the presence of the priest, who receives the confession of the person privately. You might ask, Why the witness? Can't I repent before God by myself, so to speak, or somewhere in my soul? But in fact there will be no exploit of overcoming here, because for a person to tell himself how bad he is not so difficult, whereas to say so in the presence of a witness, moreover a witness whom you know, is hard; one has to get over this obstacle, but it is by this that the root of evil is broken. Further, some people are troubled by the idea that by telling a priest about one's sins and failings, his opinion of them might fall. This is a serious error. I can tell you about myself, that once when I was a boy I thought, "How can a priest associate with people, when he knows everything about them? It's like in the Tales of Hoffman: if he knows everyone's thoughts, it is impossible even to live." But when I became a priest, I saw that God works in a marvelous manner and causes me to forget all the sins that I have heard, and to associate with people as if I haven't heard anything from them. Some kind of mysterious, authoritative hand washes from my consciousness and memory everything I have heard from them. And this leads us to the next sacrament, that of priesthood.

The Church is a community of human beings. The Lord Jesus, although he addresses every soul individually, wills that we come to him together. He wants it that way. He created humanity in such a way that humanity could live only together. The Church is a new kind of relationship, the ideal model for mankind. But the creation of the Church is a difficult thing, as you know. As a great social organism, it needs an allocation of different forms of service. The apostle Paul explains this to us in a simple manner. He says that man, having a body, simultaneously has in it various organs, which have different functions. That is, an organism is not a monotonous collection of parts of any kind, an aggregate, but rather a polymorphous unity, which has different aspects. He tells us also, "Are all apostles, are all teachers, do all have the gift of healing?" No, of course not. And the mutual connection among people rests on this. Because, when one talent is given to one person, and another talent to another person, we can serve one another. If we were all uniformly gifted with all the gifts, we would not need one another. We need each other precisely because the gifts are distributed unevenly. As it is difficult to glue smooth surfaces together, it is much easier to glue together surfaces that have some kind of pits and bumps. So it is with a human community.

So, there is a form for the service of the Church, which is first of all the celebrant—*predstoiatel'*—that is, the one who speaks for the community at the time of the celebration of the sacrament of the Eucharist. He is the voice, the hands of the community, giving expression to it in, well, common language, its "fully empowered agent." At the beginning these were the apostles. Later the apostles came to be called bishops. Why was this? "Bishop" means "overseer," "steward." The leader of the community became not only its agent at the sacrament, but also the guide of its life, including even its economic life. So he became the bishop/overseer, while the priest only assisted him in performing all the sacraments, except the sacrament of priesthood.

The sacrament of priesthood and the laying-on of hands is performed only by the bishop. Why is it called the laying-on of hands—*khirotonia*? This is an ancient Old Testament custom—the transmission of some spiritual gift or power through the rite of laying on of a hand or hands. You may see this sacrament in those churches in Moscow where we have bishops serving. For example, in the Novodevichy Monastery priests are ordained quite often. This sacrament is also a miracle, because we priests work not by our own power—we are people just as weak and sinful as any of you. But if we are able to do something out of the ordinary, it is only by the power of this gift, namely, this *khirotonia*, this grace of the priesthood. I am extremely aware of how much it is acting more than I myself act.

I was asked an hour ago in the Institute, where I was delivering a lecture, whether I felt a change in my attitude to the world when I became a priest. I thought a bit, and recollected. I remembered the days of my youth, and I understood that I then had ten times less strength even than when I got to be a middle-aged person. Ten times less strength. How come? This difference between a man of twenty-five and fifty-five? But at fifty-five my capabilities have increased by several orders of magnitude. The grace of God is responsible for this, not I. At this time I even need to cool down in certain circumstances. I remember the first days when I served in the church—I would come back and even have to lie down and rest afterward. Now the thought of this doesn't enter my head, although I do much more serving. So, this is not something human, but something divine.

Our problem as ministers of the Church is to receive all this into ourselves and make it our own.

The question may occur to you (it arose also in the Middle Ages)—what if a sacrament is performed by an unworthy priest? Well, to begin with, I will tell you that we are all unworthy. Second, when the Church says that the sacrament is real and is really accomplished, if it is celebrated by a priest, independently of his moral level, what does it mean? It is not magic or a conjuring trick, not a mechanical performance of the sacrament, but the great teaching of the Church that this sacrament, in a given case, let us say, the Liturgy or baptism, is performed by you, by the entire church. *You* perform it according to your faith. God responds to the voice of the church, and not to the—may we call it— arbitrary word of the priest. That is why, if he is unworthy, but the community, the faithful, the church, is worthy; and it is it, the community, that performs this sacrament, although indeed by the priest's hands. Well, to be sure it is pleasanter when those hands, are, so to speak, clean. But we must remember this all the same—because some people say, "This doesn't suit me, it just doesn't suit me." This is all incorrect. He who is thirsty will drink even from a tin can if water is poured into it.

There is another sacrament that we call Unction; this is the sacrament of oil, or anointing with oil. It demands, as with any other sacrament, faith, but in this case a particular, specific faith, for this is the sacrament of healing, the sacrament of the body. It should be performed over a sick person so that he either gets well or dies. Sometimes death is healing. I have known people who were really open to the action of the sacrament and it lifted them straight out of the grave. Or, on the contrary, they died. That is, it is like a litmus test, like some kind of linchpin. But the subjective side of it is very important, because the person himself participates here. It is called the sacrament of oil, because from apostolic times there has been the custom of anointing a sick person with sanctified oil, with olive oil.

One must only not confuse the sacrament of oil, unction, with anointing with chrism, Chrismation. Why is it called *soborovanie*? Because in accordance with ancient custom, several priests gather—a *sobor*—and pray over the sick person. Remember the film *War and Peace*? When Pierre's father is dying, priests are standing there with candles. They are administering unction—*soboruiut*—to him before his death. Why have I referred to a film? Because nowadays such an anointing by a *sobor* of priests never takes place. It happens just the other way around. There is a mass of sick people and a priest. One, or two of them. We have changed places. So that the *sobor*, the "assembly," is not ours, but yours. An assembly of sick people. Yes, each one may be healed. Really be healed, in the simply physical sense. If this does not happen, it is simply because of our lack of faith. Whoever is ready for it receives healing in the sacrament of unction—and by prayer in general.

Chrismation is a sacrament that, unfortunately, as it turns out, we have somehow let be moved to the rear of the list. It is the sacrament of the joining of the baptized person to the real life of the Church, through the summoning and descent of the power of the Holy Spirit. In the West, and in world church practice in general, this sacrament is performed over adults, teenagers, and children, who consciously, after baptism in childhood, enter the community and the Holy Spirit comes to them. With us, it is performed right at the baptism of an infant, with no transition, and this sacrament, as it were, merges with baptism. Out of a hundred persons hardly one knows what we are talking about here—that after baptism there was also chrismation. I think that with time this will come back into the church. I knew one priest, a well-known theologian abroad, who when he baptized his own daughter said, "When you grow up, then you will go to Russia and they will chrismate you there." Indeed she came to me when she had already become a young woman. Some of us got together, prayed, and performed the sacrament of Chrismation on her. Her father was a specialist in liturgics, a scholar with a famous name. He was one of the few who knew how important this sacrament is in its own right. It is due to the disregard of it that our brothers the Protestant Pentecostals have put some kind of extreme emphasis on this receiving of the Holy Spirit and think that this mystery should be accompanied by certain phenomena, that a person should feel it simply as a shaking, that he should "speak in tongues"—that is, pray in a certain strange manner. Really this is not obligatory. It depends on the person, on his emotional makeup. Sometimes it is possible to experience everything very deeply, but with a great inner restraint. In any case, such a reaction on the part of the Pentecostals came about because of the fact that the mystery of the Holy Spirit got hidden somewhere in the background, without anybody noticing that this had happened. That's in fact the way it turned out historically.

Finally, I conclude with the last of the sacraments, which is really the first—the sacrament of marriage. As the Russian Orthodox theologian Troitsky emphasizes, this is the only one of the seven sacraments that was established not by Christ the Savior, but in the Old Testament, from the beginning. When God created love between a man and a woman, he also created this sacrament. It consists of the fact that the human spirit is structured in such a manner that a certain mysterious—one might even risk saying *mystical*—union of two beings is possible, who become immanent to one another. I ask you to forgive me the use of the philosophical term. The Bible expresses this in simple words, "Let the two become one flesh." One flesh, that is, not only spirit, but the whole being is somehow a kind of striking unity.

Satan is the power of destruction, disintegration, annihilation. God is the power of unification, creation, harmony. Therefore it is even said that God is unification—the greatest miracle. The apostle Paul in fact writes thus: "This mystery is great." The ancient prophets, and after them the apostles, compared this amazing merger of souls with the merger of man and the divine mystery, with the relationship between divinity and humanity. In the Bible nothing is said concerning the begetting of children as a part of this mystery. The commandment, "Be fruitful and multiply" is addressed to living creatures—to animals and to man in the same degree. They have this in common. Reproduction is possible without love. But love is possible without reproduction. Vladimir Solov'iov emphasized this: a very strong love between two persons does not necessarily have to be crowned by the begetting of a human being or even by the begetting of some sort of genius. No, these, in general, are different things. You might ask, "But is this not something ideal? Does this exist in real life?" God created love between people, but we have corrupted it—I am talking about what exists in reality and what has been given to us as a beckoning ideal. It is easy to be a cynic and say that nothing of the sort exists. Very easy. But a cynic is a cynic. He sees only what is on the surface. But in the final analysis just think a little about the fact that the greatest products of the human genius in music, poetry, prose, painting, and sculpture have been connected in one way or another with this great experience of love. Not at all with reproduction. You think about this; I even hesitate to cite examples, because in reality this encompasses everything that has been created by humanity. From Homer and Shakespeare down to our day.

Yes, and the Bible itself, in which there is the Song of Songs, a hymn of love.

If we have trampled and sullied this and made it vulgar, this is our fault, and not the fault of love. If we are unable to love, then we depart from the commandment. True, others say, "Well, is an eternal love, so to speak, possible?" Of course it is possible. But one and the same person—in the end doesn't one get bored with him, tired of him? Only eyes without love can say that there is one person before you. Every year there is another person before you. If you love, you are always discovering in him or her ever new features. Your wife is the way you relate to her, and vice versa. The physiognomies of our loved ones, our husbands and wives, are a mirror of our attitudes to them. That is the reason that Christ placed this ideal before us, for it is the source of fullness of life, of happiness, it is the norm, no matter how we have trampled it down. Finally, there is one last thing that may be added to this. A certain doctor, again a cynic, used to tell me, "Look my friend, this is nothing but hormones, hormones." Well, I suppose that hormones are also not something extraneous to us, they work in us. But are hormones the only thing? I cite you only one example, the clearest one, from my point of view.

Recall the epilogue of Gogol's old-fashioned landlords: Afanasii Ivanovich, a withered little old man—what kind of hormones were there any longer?—long since a widower, and as soon as he thinks of the name of his Pulcheria Ivanovna he bursts into tears. But she has been dead a long time. What is it that connects them—after all they both lived a semianimal life, they ate and drank and slept. But there was love. And it proves to be something that can remain after all the boiling of hormones dries up in a person. On the other hand, a person may be full of physical life, but all of a sudden love disappears. Everything about his hormones is in good working order, but there is no love. So then, the mystery is in something else here. We have to look for the cause of why we can't make it. Of course, this is difficult to do from one side; here it is necessary that the two be considered together. But there is one important thing. Man is egotistical by nature. God created love as the first and strongest natural remedy for egocentricity. When a person stops considering his own ego as the only absolute point of reference in the universe, and when he finds this point of reference in another ego, there is the beginning of the miracle and mystery of love.

Thus we see that the system of church sacraments encompasses life in all its manifestations, and the connection with nature, and food, and love, and correspondingly, toil. If we have nature, if we have the grapevine—then wine and bread—this involves toil. Bread after all does not grow simply in that form. Nor does wine gush out by itself. They are the result of human toil. Everything is united here. Community, brotherhood, mutual aid, the Church. Therefore, when we say, "I confess one baptism for the remission of sins," by this we remember the other sacraments also, which constitute, together with baptism, the one life of the Church.

One mystery, into which we may enter and abide.

Thank you.

Well, the next time we shall talk about the concluding words, *I look for the resurrection of the dead and the life of the age to come*. After that we shall meet at 5 p.m. on the 14th of April in the church—whoever is not baptized. So, that's it. But are there many of you? If so, you won't fit in because I have a small church.

*Paul Evdokimov (1901–1969) was a lay theologian intensely active in ecumenical work and held in high regard by both Catholic and Protestant Christians in France. As an émigré from the Russian Revolution, he was in the first graduating class of the St. Sergius Theological Institute in Paris, later earning doctorates in philosophy and theology. Father Sergius Bulgakov, Anton Kartashev, and Nicolas Berdiaev were among his teachers, and many of their perspectives are to be found throughout Evdokimov's work, most especially the freedom of the Gospel and the kingdom, and the openness of the church to the world in light of the Incarnation—God's coming into human time, flesh, and blood. Paul Evdokimov was close to many other of the writers featured here, especially to Elisabeth Behr-Sigel, Fr. Nicolas Afanasiev, and Lev Zander. For years before his appointment to the St. Sergius faculty in the late 1950s, he directed hostels for those in need: addicted, troubled, and homeless people, immigrants, and students from the Third World. His writing is permeated with the vision and language of the Liturgy, the "primary" theology of the Eastern Church. Many of his most important books have been translated from the French originals, among them* Ages of the Spiritual Life, The Sacrament of Love, Woman and the Salvation of the World, *and the anthologies* In the World, Of the Church, *and* Orthodoxy. *An official observer of the Orthodox Church at the second session of Vatican II, it is thought that he had a significant impact on the council's document on the Church in the modern world. The essay presented here represents his thinking quite accurately. The meeting, even marriage, of the divine and the human in the Incarnation, in the Church and the sacraments, is intensely experienced and expressed in the Eastern Church and the contemporary relevance of this sensitivity is Evdokimov's concern.*

## FOR FURTHER READING

Clément, Olivier. *Orient-Occident, Deux Passeurs: Vladimir Lossky, Paul Evdokimov.* Geneva: Labor et Fides, 1985.

Evdokimov, Paul. *Ages of the Spiritual Life.* Revised translation by Michael Plekon and Alexis Vinogradov. Crestwood, N.Y.: SVSP, 1998.

———. *L'amour fou de Dieu.* Paris: Ed. du Seuil, 1972.

———. *The Art of the Icon: A Theology of Beauty.* Translated by Steven Bigham. Crestwood, N.Y.: SVSP/Oakwood, 1990.

———. *Le buisson ardent.* Paris: Lathielleux, 1977.

———. *La connaissance de Dieu selon la tradition orientale,* Lyon: Xavier-Mappus, 1968.

———. *Le Christ dans la penseé russe.* Paris: Cerf, 1970.

———. *Dostoievsky et le problème du mal.* Lyon: Ed. du Livre français, 1942.

———. *L'Esprit Saint dans la tradition orthodoxe.* Paris: Ed. du Cerf, 1969.

———. *Gogol et Dostoievski.* Paris: Desclée de Brouwer, 1961.

———. *La nouveauté de l'esprit.* Begrolles: Abbaye de Bellefontaine, 1977.

———. *L'orthodoxie.* Neuchatel-Paris: Delachaux et Niestle, 1959. English translation in preparation.

———. *La prière de l'Eglise d'Orient.* Paris: Desclee de Brouwer, 1985. Mulhouse, 1966.

———. *The Sacrament of Love.* Translated by Anthony Gythiel and Victoria Steadman. Crestwood, N.Y.: SVSP, 1995.

———. *Woman and the Salvation of the World.* Translated by Anthony Gythiel. Crestwood, N.Y.: SVSP, 1994.

*In the World, of the Church: A Paul Evdokimov Reader.* Edited and translated by Michael Plekon and Alexis Vinogradov. Crestwood, N.Y.: SVSP, 2000.

Phan, Peter C. *Culture and Eschatology: The Iconographical Vision of Paul Evdokimov.* New York: Peter Lang, 1985.

# CHRIST AND THE CHURCH

There is much talk about the problem of language. Today preachers claim that theological language no longer corresponds to the experience of modern people. Our new civilization brings with it its own vocabulary, words that change the way we speak and shape the ways in which we express the truth. Now if language is changing, the realities described by words, which are in perpetual evolution, remain the same. Every translator, in looking for an equivalent, descends to the root of a given word in order to grasp its precise meaning. A good translation demands a continuity of intelligence, a grasp of the realities being described in order to find the appropriate words for them. Culture is a transmission without any break in meaning. Through multiple linguistic mutations that do not at all change, the substance of the message is communicated. The Bible's Semitic concepts and the Hellenic ones of the church fathers retain all of their freshness, their truths being perfectly translatable into every language, remaining open to heaven while avoiding the closed character of so many philosophical systems.

For a person of average education but free of prejudice, the Gospel is immediately accessible. Its earthy, physical language in the parables is able to effectively convey its enduring message. The obstacle to understanding does not so much stem from the condition of the secularized world, which has always been there. Rather the problem has to do with the secularized human spirit, deprived of the receptive sensibility toward the *symbolic* dimension of existence. This is a

First published in *La Table Ronde* 250 (November 1968): 183–92. Translated by Michael Plekon.

dimension of depth that discovers that what is visible does not at all exhaust the world and that the most ordinary and everyday things are signs of invisible realities. Even at the most sophisticated level, knowledge integrates the cognitive function of reason and the evaluative function of the heart—that is, the knowledge of facts and the grasp of their meaning. It becomes understandable that beyond sensation and perception, beyond above all *direct* conceptual and discursive thinking, there is the sphere of intuition, of contemplation and *indirect* reflection. When we deal with a mystery, meaning is never given directly but is represented through the means of mediators: an angel, a sign, a symbol. All are messengers bearing a secret message.

Neither is a mystery a matter of "faith." To affirm only the existence of the material realm—its eternity and independence—is setting up an absolute, and this is a faith infinitely more complex and difficult than a simple and honest faith in a God who is the creator. Sooner or later one must choose. And with such a decision it is the same as with death. Each one has to do it for himself. "The one who is not with me is against me and the one who does not gather with me, scatters."

The faith the Gospels speak of is rooted in historical events. The disciples on the way to Emmaus "recognized" the Lord in the breaking of the bread. This is the overall intention and meaning of the Fathers who "visited the land of which they speak." Faith is very much like a recognition, and this is why in the *kerygma*, or preaching, of the Gospel proofs are never utilized. Beyond any speculation faith confesses and describes, says "Come and see." Faith communicates the transparent apostolic word for all. "Whoever loves knows God."

The positive encounter refuses with reason archaic formulas, dead theology, words with no reference to life or to the deepest realities of the tradition. All of the grandiose work of the ecumenical councils, the blood of the martyrs, the listening to the Word by the Fathers, remains like a gold-bearing stone marked by a transcendent sign—"it seemed good to the Holy Spirit and to us." There is in the dogmas a metamathematical rigor that the consensus of the Church has confirmed as a sign of the mystery of God. The ecumenical impatience and its impulsive acts relativize the truths of faith instead of assimilating them in a common effort, in search of living words which bring with them the Spirit. The "Eucharist of the intelligence" precedes the "Eucharist of the heart." It avoids the idolatry of the "symbol" which tragically falls outside what is "symbolized" and therefore unity-communion.

Confusion emerges when the same terms point to different realities. Ecumenical encounters center their reflection on the concept of the Church. It becomes more and more evident that here the difference is not in theological formulas that are often and apparently able to converge, but at the existential level of the lived experience of the mystery of the Church. It is located in the ultimate reality of the "symbolized," and it is this interior that must be deciphered.

Like every symbol or sacrament, the Church has her own visible and invisible aspects. She is both "institution" and "event," and it is the inseparable combination of both of these that is called the Church. The visible does not exist except in function of the invisible, its "heavenly" source that gives it all the fullness of a *sensible* historical reality. The purely sociological aspect remains immanent phenomenologically, and does not at all exhaust the hidden reality of the Church. On the other hand it is necessary to say that the "idea" of the Church simply does not exist, but the Church herself exists, and for each member, her existence is the thing most real and known of all that is real and known.

Before this mystery, in the West and especially in Protestant circles, one says, "the Church sins," "the Church needs to repent," "the Church is dead." An Orthodox Christian could not put it in those ways. An Orthodox Christian rather would say, "there is sinfulness in the Church . . . in the Church there is need for repentance . . .there are members of the Church who are dead." This is because for the Orthodox, the Church is a society essentially divine and human, theandric. The Creed does not say, "I know," but rather, "I believe in the Church." If I know the visible, institutional Church, I believe in the invisible, I believe that the Church is the whole Christ (*totus Christus*) that unites the divine and the human and that in the total mysterious reality of the Church the divine progressively deifies the human, fills it with God.

The need to define is always a disturbing sign of decadence, of an eclipse of the light. This is why one finds no formulas about the Church in the time of the Fathers. They lived in its full reality as something brilliant and evident. They did not seek to prove the light that made the day. They did not speculate on the Church, but within they adored God, prayed, and the Church's *lex orandi*, or rule of prayer, was the only yet full witness of "the mystery hidden for all eternity in God."

In order to come closer to their experience it is necessary to locate oneself within the school of the Fathers, to grasp their striking realism that *identified the Church and Christ*. According to St. Augustine, the Church is the whole Christ, the head and the body (*totus Christus, caput et corpus*). Likewise St. Gregory of Nyssa strongly insisted: "If anyone looks at the Church, he looks at Christ" (In Cant. Hom. 13; P.G. 44, 1048). A vessel that contains the relics of martyrs reads: *In isto vaso congregabantur membra Christi*—"In this vessel are gathered the members, the limbs of Christ."

The word *ecclesia* translates *qahal* from the Hebrew, and emphasizes the organic unity of the people of God. When God speaks he always does so to the whole of his people. This is why from the beginning the Christian tradition was a communal church and its unity was a "Christophany," a revelation, a visible manifestation of Christ. The members are not only united but they are *one* in Christ. Their deep connection to each other comes from their Head who is, most powerfully, the source of their integration. The use of the word "body" to refer to the Church is rooted clearly in the Eucharist (1 Cor 10:7) and gives expression to the consubstantial union of Christ with each and every one, "the fullness of him who fills all of creation" (Eph 1:23). Christ progressively realizes this, as St. John Chrysostom says, "The Head will be fulfilled when all of us are united and linked to each other" (P.G. 62, 29). Christ, who by the Incarnation is the God-man, becomes the humanity of God, the Church. The realism of the vision of the Fathers comes from their life in Christ: "Between the body and the head there is no separation . . . the least separation would mean death," St. John Chrysostom again says (P.G. 62, 29; 586). Here, St. John of Chrysostom is expressing God's own wish: "I wish that there should be no separation, nothing between you, I wish that the two should become one."

The tradition of the Eastern Church locates the origin of the Church in paradise, at the time when God "walked in the coolness of the evening," conversing with Adam as with his other self. The mystery of the Incarnation prolongs as well as deepens this "conversation," expressing the pre-eternal desire of God to become one of us, to become human. According to the Fathers, the Incarnation would have taken place even if there had been no fall as the *ultimate expression of communion*. The icon of the Mother of God, the *Theotokos*, holding the child Jesus in her arms, expresses what the Incarnation is. This icon speaks of the exquisite tenderness (*Eleousa*) of the communion between the divine and the human. "God became man so that man could become a god." So runs the saying of the Fathers, and in the letter of Peter the same rationale for the Christian life is given, "so that you become sharers in the nature of God . . . in the holiness of God," in the conditions of divine life (2 Pt 1: 4).

In the texts of Mark 5:9 and 1 Cor. 10:17 we see that evil corrupts, disperses, isolates us, and takes the life out of existence. Over against this, Christ, the bread of life, gathers together, revives, gives life, makes whole. "And as there is one loaf, so we, although there are many of us, are one single body, for we all share in the one loaf," though decomposed into numbers, a legion, the terrible mass of humanity. All are integrated in Christ, made members of him, "of the same flesh and blood as his." In this unity in Christ "the Holy Spirit brings our souls to life and makes the one nature of the Trinity shine mysteriously in us." The Church is thus nothing else but the life of God in the human, "in the community of mutual love." Dionysius the Areopagite calls the Incarnation *Philanthropia*, the love of mankind, and the Divine Liturgy repeatedly calls God the "lover of mankind." Saint Gregory Palamas puts it precisely—"Human eros soars up to the one thing necessary, and God in his love goes out from himself and unites himself to us."

The Lord's promise that "the gates of hell shall not prevail against the Church" only emphasizes the identification of Christ with the Church. "I am with you always, even to the end of the age." Placed at the very center of creation, called the *macroanthropos*, visibly and invisibly the Church transforms all of history into the history of salvation. What then is her message in the light of modernity, in the "historical situation" of today?

According to Lagneau, "Atheism is the salt that prevents faith in God from being corrupted." For Simone Weil, atheism is a purification of the idea of God from every sociological and every theological contamination. A similar purification proposes an "ecumenical dialogue" with the atheist, with every person who has never experienced the living content of the faith because of its historical expression, its "empty shells" that are put in question. If religion constituted the foundation for civilization in the past, this will not be the case in the future except in transcending every manner of representation by which modern humanity feels itself out of step. Our age is that of humanity come of age, adult, and we refuse any understanding of God that is not at the same time an understanding of humanity. Such an epiphany of God and humanity is the ultimate meaning of the Church as Incarnation.

"The tears of repentance keep the waters of baptism flowing." From baptism's purifying washing the Church offers to those who are hungry not "ideological stones" of systems and doctrines, not the "theological stones" of the catechism, but the "bread of the angels," and "the heart of the brother/sister offered as pure food." The higher the vertical of divine transcendence the more it must be rooted, "incarnated" in the horizontal of immanence. The real problem is neither that of God's being nor of his existence, but that of his presence as the One who exists in our history.

The optimism of proofs of God reveals a "substantial boredom" and overlooks the fact that God is not "evident" and that silence is a quality of God, for every proof that would force one to believe is a violation of the human conscience. This is why God limits his omnipotence, rejects all signs, and conceals himself within the silence of his crucified love. It is in this silence, Nicolas Cabasilas says, that God declares his love for us, his absurd, foolish love (*manikon eros*) and his incomprehensible respect for human freedom. "The form under which God extends his hand is the same which makes that hand invisible."

It is because we can say *no* that our *yes* resounds so fully. And it is why God accepts being refused, disregarded, rejected, and abandoned by his own creation. "God presents himself and declares his love . . . pushed aside, he waits at the door. . . . For all the good he does for us he expects nothing in return except our love, in exchange for this he forgives us all we owe him." The Christian may be a miserable creature, but he or she knows Someone even more miserable, this beggar of love knocking at the door of our hearts. "I stand here at the door and knock, and if anyone hears my voice and opens the door, I will come in and dine with him" (Rv 3: 20).

Faith says, "Give up your puny reason and receive the Word; shed your blood and receive the Spirit." The simple calling out of God's name makes him immediately present, the One ignored and yet intimately known by all. God created a "second freedom" and he runs the risk of a freedom that can rise up and is even capable of putting God himself on hold. It is a freedom that can oblige God to descend into death and into hell, to let himself freely be assassinated in order to offer the assassins forgiveness and resurrection, and to in the end be with him in paradise. The Fathers put it this way—God is capable of doing everything, except compelling humankind to love him. The divine omnipotence becomes the life-giving cross, the only response to atheism's questions about freedom and evil.

The freedom to refuse God is willed by God himself. It is a limitless freedom. Any power exerted over human choice makes its destiny conditional. And this is hell to thus speak of divine love, of its heavenly dimension, of the divine vision of humankind immersed in the night of solitude.

It is most urgent to correct the "terrorist" or "penitentiary" concept of God. It is no longer possible to believe in a God without a heart, a God who does not suffer or have any feelings. The idea of an omnipotent and omniscient God closes off all possibility of advance. It is the kenotic passage from Philippians (2: 6–11) that is the keystone and which speaks of the veritable alienation of God from himself. "He emptied himself, taking on the form of a slave . . . accepting even death on the cross." "I am among you as one who serves." The omnipotence of God renounces all power, most of all the "will to power." God does not simply destroy evil and death, he assumes them. "By death he has conquered death." His light shines from the crucified and risen truth. God cannot do other than suffer with us and this suffering is the "bread that God shares with everyone." Jesus, whose life consisted in being the Son, is the last of the just ones to cry to God, "Why have you abandoned me?" He endured the terrible test of being abandoned by God, of losing him, thus coming to know the torments of the atheist and sharing with everyone in this state the fearful loss of the transcendent.

The resignation of the Fathers, the failure of paternalism so well expressed in *The Words* of Sartre: "I knew no one who waited for my soul. I had no creator (a father). I was given only a great master." Young people violently reject the patriarchal forms of the "mandarins," whose power is without any content or authority, leaving them thereby orphans. Christ turns this around and reveals in true fatherhood the sacrificial offering and the Spirit's work of liberation. The fearful and unsuffering God turns out to be the Father who suffers: "The father is Love who crucifies, the Son is crucified love and the Spirit is the victorious power of the cross."

The hunger for brotherhood, for being and for being together, the hunger for communion, and the hunger for unity—this is now deeper and more widespread than ever before. "Life, presence, nothing but presence." The Church has her roots in the destiny of all people. It is from this depth that there comes, according to the Fathers, faith's certainty—secret and hidden—that the love of God will have mercy on us all, even on the demoniac and despairing who slide into Satan's depths and hurl their blasphemies up at heaven.

Sartre said, "Other people. That's hell." Berdiaev said it another way, following Dostoyevsky: "Hell is the destiny of the others." The soul is totally engaged in the destiny of every suffering being for "all are guilty for all." And if we give in to despair, it is God who never despairs—Christ has shown us this, and the Church proclaims and lives it. "If one does not hope, one will only encounter hopelessness." "Jesus is the wound which can never be healed." It is this wound for the destiny of the others that adds something to the suffering of Christ who is "in agony even till the end of time."

The crisis that the world is passing through now is an anthropological one. We are accosted with the ultimate meaning of our fate. It does not have to do with the means of living only, but with the spiritual refusal of being a human robot, only an object. The two dimensions of humanity, the personalist and the communal, are crystallized in collectivism and anarchism, in the reds and the blacks who collide with and seek to exclude each other. The only adequate solution to human dignity is the unity in diversity of the Trinity, the unity of the body in the diversity of human persons. This is the "Catholic" meaning of the Church, which echoes in the words of St. Paul: "In Christ there is neither Greek nor Jew," words which radically transcend every nationality, every suffocating heresy of "filetism," or ethnocentrism, and which set out the whole of humanity as the only brotherhood of the children of God. But the Church also transcends the anonymity of international organizations. The cohesion of the community of the Church allows for the breath of the Spirit who always sustains true personal creativity and true communication, the tangible, concrete face of the brother or sister in the service of all.

"The death of religion," in the end, is the absence of authentic religion and of life-giving encounter with the transcendent. Young people today are searching beyond all heavy and tedious moralism for a passionate adventure, a feast of Encounter where earth and heaven meet. But is this not the continual prayer of the name of Jesus, his presence in people who have become "eucharistic," holy people who risk bringing in again the great joy and sacred play, the bread of suffering providing the wine of the feast? "I ascend to you singing," says St. John Climacus, joyfully.

It is through the sacraments and the Liturgy that the Church surpasses the sociological weight of itself as an institution and embraces everyone with the Pentecostal fire of prayer. Only the Gospel and the Holy Spirit are authentically revolutionary, for the upheaval comes from the love of God himself, which demands the Church to go out of herself and from these "fools in Christ," from the charismatically inspired people possessed of the "sanctity of genius" and who do not cease praying that "all may be saved." Christ and the Church mean exactly the urgent demand for peace in a world full of war and nuclear weapons, for justice where all are threatened by hunger and tortured by racism, where freedom is only a word.

Between the idolatry of the "cult of personality" and the nihilism destructive of all that has value, the Church encourages all to enter the spiritual combat, the stakes of which concern ourselves, and not God. In a surprising awakening of existence, one searches for "the new man" everywhere. The Church puts such a being before us in the figure of Jesus, one perfect in light of the Beatitudes. This is why in Christ every person is a "new creature," capable of supplying what is absolutely new to the city of humankind, to the world.

The apology for, or defense of, the faith in our time is not so much directed toward atheism as toward its own expression, toward theological ideas that disfigure the human face of God. In Marxist countries, people have been called to transform nature by technology. Monastics, for their part, also participate in this transformation, but from their own perspective—namely, in the deification of humanity and the cosmos, in making both "very similar" to God again, as they were created to be. They raise sacrificial prayer for those who do not know how to pray, opening up to these the "communion," the community of the saints, reuniting them in the heart, the selfless love (*agapé*) of the God-man, revealing to them what a person completely remade in Christ looks like—one who has become the tree of life, the spring, a fire, the Church.

Elisabeth Behr-Sigel was born near Strasbourg in 1907, and remains at ninety-six an active lay theologian of the Orthodox Church in France. Her remarkable gifts match an equally remarkable life. Her parents were religiously indifferent (her father Protestant and her mother Jewish), however very positive experiences in church youth groups encouraged her faith, and in 1926 she was among the first women to be admitted to the theology faculty at the University of Strasbourg. She continued studies in Berlin and in Paris where she first encountered the Orthodox Church. Two years later she was received into the Orthodox Church by Fr. Lev Gillet, and in Paris she was part of the first French-language Orthodox parish of the Transfiguration and St. Genevieve, of which Fr. Gillet was the pastor. Father Gillet became a lifelong friend of Elisabeth's, and she wrote his biography in 1994. While in Paris, she also became close to Fr. Sergius Bulgakov, Nicolas Berdiaev, Mother Maria Skobtsova, and S. L. Frank. She became friends as well with two important lay theologians, Paul Evdokimov and Vladimir Lossky, and their spouses. The year before her marriage to André Behr, she served as a lay pastoral associate in a Reformed parish in a small rural village, Ville-Climont, with the permission of Metropolitan Evlogy. The severe shortage of clergy in the years following World War I made such measures necessary. While not licensed to celebrate the Eucharistic Liturgy, she did lead services, preach, and visit the sick and elderly. After World War II, during which she raised three children and taught philosophy in several lycées, Elisabeth returned to her original specialization and began publishing essays on the Russian Orthodox spiritual tradition. After her husband's death she completed a doctorate on the nineteenth-century Russian theologian Alexander Bukharev in 1975 and began to lecture regularly, alongside a growing list of publications. Her active participation in the World Council of Churches (WCC) led to a series of articles now gathered into several volumes, with a particular focus on women, their place in the Orthodox Church, as well as the question of whether women can be ordained to both the diaconate and the priesthood. In her seventies and eighties Elisabeth found herself to be without doubt the most radical and controversial woman theologian in all of the Orthodox churches. She has, with grace and compassion, continued to ask hard questions about how the Orthodox Church, historically grasped by so deep a love for the Mother of God, could have so neglected and even devalued the gifts of women as baptized Christians.

The essay presented here is Elisabeth Behr-Sigel's contribution to the now historical Sheffield Consultation of the WCC on men and women in the church. It is particularly appropriate to hear from her, the friend and colleague of so many other of the authors represented in this collection, on precisely the issue of how tradition is dynamic, living, and a constant source of new insight and action in the church.

## FOR FURTHER READING

Behr-Sigel, Elisabeth. *Discerning the Signs of the Times: The Theological Vision of Elisabeth Behr-Sigel*. Edited by Michael Plekon and Sarah E. Hinlicky. Crestwood, N.Y.: Oakwood/SVSP, 2001.

———. *Lev Gillet: A Monk of the Eastern Church*. Translated by Helen Wright. Oxford: Fellowship of St. Alban and St. Sergius, 1999.

———. *The Ministry of Women in the Church*. Translated by Stephen Bigham. Crestwood, N.Y.: Oakwood/SVSP, 1991.

———. *The Place of the Heart: An Introduction to Orthodox Spirituality*. Translated by Stephen Bigham. Crestwood, N.Y.: Oakwood/SVSP 1992.

Behr-Sigel, Elisabeth, with Bishop Kallistos Ware. *The Ordination of Women in the Orthodox Church*. Geneva: WCC, 2000.

# THE ENERGIZING
# FORCE OF TRADITION

## ORTHODOX TRADITION AS RESOURCE FOR THE
## RENEWAL OF WOMEN AND MEN IN COMMUNITY

**"W**hat *resources*—or better, what *inspiration*—for a renewed human community do you derive from the tradition of your church?" I was asked to respond to this question, in a paper to be presented at one of the plenaries, on the very day I was leaving for Sheffield, because the original speaker was prevented from attending our meeting. It was perhaps rash of me to accept the assignment, and I apologize for the improvised nature of my text. It will be a spontaneous response, there having been no time to think it over and to compose a well-balanced text. As we say in French, *Faute de grives on mange des merles* (which in English would correspond to "Half a loaf is better than no bread").

When reflecting on the topic, I was first of all arrested by the word "tradition" and its meaning. What is the tradition of the church? Quite obviously—but ignored by some—a distinction has to be made between a multifarious tradition and *the* tradition of the Church, a distinction which is not always easy to define. There are popular traditions, family traditions, religious traditions related to the various cultures; and these traditions are not to be discarded as such. Within non-Christian cultures, they have often been seeds of the gospel—*logoï spermatikoi*—preparing for the coming of the one Logos. Among the peoples

First published in *The Community of Women and Men in the Church: The Sheffield Report*, edited by Constance A. Parvey (Geneva: WCC, 1983).

that the Church has evangelized—however imperfectly this has always been done—the popular traditions carry with them elements that belong to the genuine tradition of the Church. But they are not identical with it.

An Orthodox will not consider the tradition—contrary to what was expressed here—as "a collection of experiences and hopes of the past." For him or her the tradition is the very life of the Church, and its continuity is an ever-renewed inspiration. Both are the work of the Holy Spirit. The tradition finds its expression in beliefs, doctrines, and rites, as well as in the popular traditions I have just mentioned. But at the same time it goes beyond them. The tradition is essentially the dynamic of faith, hope, and love. It has its origin in the event of Pentecost and even before that in the encounter of a few women with the risen Christ on Easter morning, and from there it has been propagated like a wave train throughout the world and the centuries. It is a conveyor of energy; it is a ferment unceasingly raising and activating the dough of the institutions; it is the place of an ever-renewed event, a place where each of us in community with all (e.g., the "communion of saints") can meet the Lord of the Church in an ever-renewed way.

Faithfulness to the tradition does not mean sacralization of the past, of the history of the Church. Tradition is not a kind of immutable monster, a prison in which we would be confined forever. It is a stream of life, driven and impregnated by the energies of the Holy Spirit, a stream that unavoidably carries historical, and therefore, transitory elements, and even ashes and cinders. Sometimes it seems to stand still as if imprisoned in a layer of ice, but under the rigid frozen surface the clear waters of spring run. It is our task, with the help of God's mercy, to break through the ice, especially the ice in our slumbering frozen hearts. Then, when our hearts have become "burning within us" again, like those of the disciples of Emmaus, we will recognize the Lord and the Lord will explain to us the passages which refer to himself "in every part of the scriptures" (Lk 24:27, NEB). In us and from us, the tradition will become a spring of living water again. "From this ancient source," says a contemporary Orthodox spiritual father, "we will draw new strength" to respond to the problems of our day.

This renewal of tradition is also our concern as we are gathered here in Sheffield: a concern for a "new community," from which all forms of domination, of slavery, of exploitation exerted by a human being or group on others will be banished—a concern that the church is called to illuminate in the light of the gospel. The church must be the sign and the seed in humankind's history of this new eschatological community.

This aspiration for a "new community" is one of the signs of our time. But is it something really new? Is it not rather a renewed awareness—unfortunately often deviated—of the old baptismal faith, and a deeper understanding of the existential and ethical implications of the grace given in baptism as a participation in the death and resurrection of Christ and through Christ as an access to new life? This grace, which, according to the mysterious design of the Triune God, is extended to all humankind ("Go forth therefore and make all nations my disciples; baptize them everywhere in the name of the Father and the Son and the Holy Spirit," [Matt. 28:19, NEB]); a grace offered to all and gathering all those who receive it into one body, making each one of them individually, whatever his or her race, culture, sex, social status, an equally precious and necessary stone of "God's building" (1 Cor. 3:9, NEB).

"Baptized into union with him, you have all put on Christ as a garment. There is no such thing as Jew and Greek, slave and freemen; male and female, for you are all one person in Christ Jesus" (Gal. 3:27, NEB). This proclamation of Paul, which does not abolish the differences but does away with all the contempt and enmity that may exist between them, has resounded through the centuries. In the Orthodox Church, it is solemnly sung at each baptism and at the great baptismal feasts of Easter and Pentecost. But, you will ask, what about the empirical realities in our so-called Christian societies and nations? As Orthodox Christians, together with all other baptized Christians, we cannot but confess, collectively and individually, our infidelity to the "celestial vision." This is the tragedy of our historical existence that is not yet transfigured by the light of Christ, though already recipient of the first fruits of the new life. *Semper justus, semper peccator* ("always justified, always sinners") as Luther said, a statement that the Orthodox ascetics and Fathers in some sense would make their own. "The whole church is a church of penitents," said one Syrian church father.

Yet we must not yield to a kind of morbid masochism by making a caricature of the teaching and the praxis of the Church, as having as an aim the oppression of the weak by the powerful, as if God had abandoned his people. I am deeply disturbed by a certain way of criticizing, of globally and one-sidedly condemning the historical Church, as has been done even here in this meeting, though I am fully aware of the imperfections, errors, and sins of Christian people. This is a criticism and a condemnation not only with reference to the community to which I belong and in whose depths I perceive the fullness of the Catholic Church—of the *kat 'holon* Church—but also with reference to other ecclesial bodies in which apostles and saints have again and again been called forth by the Holy Spirit.

What I am referring to specifically is the patriarchal model, which should be defined more precisely. The so-called patriarchal model has certainly influenced the institutional structures of the various Christian churches. It has marked their mentalities. The church, while anticipating the kingdom of God, is also a historical reality in this world and therefore has not escaped this influence. The patriarchal model is not *wholly* negative in its ideal view of the family and of society. It does not necessarily simply lack of respect toward women. Within its structures and through a language that seems to remain patriarchal, the Church has brought forth a radically new message.

Saint Paul is accused of having exhorted the wife to be submitted to her husband. But what is ignored is that this recommendation is made in the context of and following a much more general exhortation, one of loving kindness and service. The chapter opens with these words: "Be subject *to one another* out of reverence for Christ" (Eph. 5:21, NEB, italics added). It is true that this verse is often forgotten by the moralists in the church. In the same way, Paul's preaching lifts the union of man and woman, even its fleshly aspect, to the dignity of a sign of the mysterious love of Christ and the Church, for example, of supreme love, a love so deep that each one gives himself or herself up to the other, a love in which there is no room for either dominator or dominated.

In the patristic times, St. John Chrysostom, who speaks very disparagingly of the coquettish and prattling women of his time, solemnly states that the woman can be the "head" of the man, his guide, responsible for his salvation, when she surpasses him in courage and spiritual strength. He also recommends to the husband not to be led to ruling over his wife as over a slave and to ask of his wife, as the mother of his children, not slavish obedience, but the love of a *free* woman. To acknowledge this, to acknowledge that the light of Christ was thus able to transfigure patriarchal customs, does not mean that the Church should perpetuate them. It is the ferment of the Gospel that shatters the old oppressive and outdated structures. I recognize the genuine tradition of the Church in a women's movement that claims that women are to be respected as free and responsible persons. It is in the dynamic of the authentic tradition (and not in ephemeral ideologies) that we find the source of eternal life, the source of our real liberation. In line with the energizing force of this tradition we are called (following the example of the scribe of the Gospel who draws from his treasure new and old things—*nova et vetera*) to invent new styles of communal life, new styles of family life in our society and church.

Driven by the breath of the Spirit swelling the sails of the boat (the Church), borne by the mighty stream of life and grace (true tradition), we shall sail forth with faith, hope, and love toward the new continents that God has designed for us. With discernment we shall make use of the human sciences: psychology, sociology, even of psychoanalysis and Marxist analysis. As interpretative sciences rather than exact sciences, these can enable us to disclose, up to a certain extent, the mechanisms of the behavior of the fallen Adam, the determinisms that hang heavily on a humanity entangled in its anxieties, its egoism, its contradictory desires. Real faith in God, the one who is *altogether other* and in the good news, the radical newness that he proclaims to humankind, need not fear these sciences. Yet these sciences prove unable by themselves, when not accompanied by a deep change (*metanoïa*), to create a new future. They prove unable to haul man out of the cave, in which, according to Plato's profound myth, he is shackled facing the wall. This strength of overcoming is given to the believer who in his or her faith freely clings to the word of God and the vision granted to the Church. The believer receives it in the communion of the saints of all peoples and all times, in solidarity with those men and women still immersed in chaos, but over whom sweeps the wind of the Spirit like a dove (Gen. 1:2, NEB).

What is this vision of a human community that faith opens up in the framework of the historical tradition of the Orthodox Church? To describe it, or at least to suggest its essential features, two icons will perhaps be more effective than an abstract theological discourse, which would also require more time than is available. Unfortunately I cannot present them in a way so that all of you can see them, but some of you may know them.

Icons, as you may know, are those pictures in front of which the Orthodox people pray, because through the pictures of Christ and his saints the believer receives the mysterious presence of him who is beyond all images and in whose image humankind, man and woman, was created. A father of the church reports the following words of a heathen: "Show me thy man and I shall know who thy God is." In the perspective of the Fathers of the Eastern Church, this sentence could also be inverted: "Show me thy God and I shall tell thee what human being thou art called to become." For they say: "God made himself man so that man may become God." This God in whose image man and woman were created, according to the first chapter of Genesis, and in whose likeness they are both called to grow, is neither the impersonal one, the faceless absolute of the philosophers, nor the solitary sovereign of a certain form of theism. He is the one God in three persons of the ancient symbols of Christian faith; he is the "Lord of love," as a modern Orthodox church father has called him. Such is the mystery of communion, of the fullness of personal life entirely shared, given, and received, that a fourteenth-century Russian monk tried to give impression to by creatively renewing an old iconographic theme. Inspired by the Old Testament story of Abraham welcoming three men to Mamre (Gen. 18:1–6), Andrei Rublev, following a traditional allegorical exegesis of this passage, represents the persons of the Trinity as three angels of marvelous youth and beauty sitting around a table. They bow to each other in a most graceful attitude, which expresses both the absence of all constraints and the total giving up of one to the other. They do not touch one another, but their three figures form a circular movement in a kind of dance. One stream of life runs through them. They are distinct and yet one. Each is himself in the very gesture with which he bows his face to his neighbor and in the convergent movement of their heads. In the middle of the table there is a cup. It stands for the sacrifice of the Lamb, "slaughtered from the beginning," the cross of the Son with whom the Father and the Spirit sympathize in the full etymological meaning of this word. Around the three in the center of the picture, trees, cupolas, and roofs can be recognized. They represent the physical universe and the historical world of humankind. They too seem to be caught in the same circular movement. Led by its coryphaeus, Christ, reconciled humanity and together with it the whole world join the divine dance. In the light that emanates from the center, they are not engulfed in the divinity, but, at their level (for example, the level of the creature), they participate in the Trinitarian life. This Trinitarian life—through the ecclesial vision of which the iconographer is the interpreter—appears both as the foundation in which any genuine human community is rooted and the fulfillment to which it tends. The icon transmits a call; it invites us to enter the mystery of communion, without confounding and annihilating personal existence, a mystery of self-denial without servility, of mutual love and giving up in total freedom.

To conclude I would like to mention quickly another iconographic theme: that of the so-called *Deesis*. It is an icon that is traditionally to be seen in every church, above the "royal doors" of the iconostasis. Together with that of the *Trinity* it represents one of the major expressions of Orthodox spirituality. In the center, there is Christ in majesty. Converging toward him and heading a procession of men and women who represent the saints of all ages, there are, on one side, John the Baptist and, on the other, the praying Virgin, the *Theotokos*. Both processions move toward Christ as toward a fulfillment: the fulfillment of humanity in God, in which neither male nor female is denied, but in which their opposition is overcome by their conversion to the Lord in their mutual relationship as well as in their individual personalities.

Meditating on this icon, I read in it a message that we have to make ours more and more and to translate into reality: God, in his infinite respect for and love of his creature, wants to associate with his work of salvation man and woman, or in a deeper sense, the male and female principles. They are represented by John the Baptist, the violent one, whose violence turned inward finds vent in his struggle against the possessive and egoistic self, and by Mary, the humble servant, who by accepting the Spirit as her bridegroom became *Theotokos*, the mother of the *Theos-Anthropos*, the God-Man. The Baptist, as the archetype of the law, in all its strictness, and of bitter and fruitful repentance, prepares the way and straightens the highway. But it is a woman, whose very femininity is a sign of the acceptance of the other, the supremely other, who is the beginning of the new humanity in which God makes himself flesh. "There is not a mother's son greater than John and yet the least in the kingdom of God [for example, the least of those born in Spirit] is greater than he" (Luke 7:27–28, RSV). And it is a woman who represents these "little ones," the "poor" of whom it is said that "the kingdom of Heaven is theirs" (Matt. 5:3, NEB). All this means that the humble acceptance by faith of the divine Word, wondering humility at the mystery of God's love manifested in Jesus Christ, is the evangelical value par excellence, whose symbol, according to scriptural symbolism, is feminine. In this essence the Church, which includes both men and women, is essentially feminine, whereas each of those who compose it is called to take up his or her part in Christ and also the part of the "other" that is in him or her.

What connection is there, you may ask, between the mystical vision expressed by an icon and our daily struggle for a real community of men and women, between all human beings, whatever their race, culture, or economic standing? I believe that the "celestial vision" can be a powerful source of inspiration in the struggle. It will prevent our struggle from getting diluted in a utopian, immanent humanism, or from sinking into the moving sands of violence, sometimes denying the reconciled community toward which we aim. I say that it can be an *inspiration* for and not a solution for the specific problems set by specific situations. The "celestial vision" must inspire action. It does not exempt us from the effort of understanding and analyzing the problems, an effort that must precede and guide any action. The Western temptation is to neglect or to ignore the vision, while the temptation of the Orthodox is to dodge the effort necessary to translate it into the present situation. One finds pleasure in it and it is sometimes an alibi for laziness, a justification for a sclerotic conservatism, pretending not to examine the questions raised by modern peoples both inside and outside of the Church. And yet the apostles and the "Fathers," in their times, did not refuse to respond to these questions. They responded with the spiritual achievement of a "crucified intelligence," as Father Georges Florovsky said, which dared to invent new words and to inspire new attitudes in faithfulness to the evangelical and apostolic nucleus of the ecclesial faith. It is in the same faithfulness, according to the spirit of the "Fathers," that we have to go forth here and now.

*Mother Maria Skobtsova (1891–1945) was born Elisabeth Pilenko in 1891 in Riga, and died in the gas chambers of the Ravensbrück concentration camp March 30, 1945. She compressed many lifetimes of experience into her years. A precocious child, she was a favorite of the well-known ober-procurator of the Russian Church, Constantine Petrovich Pobedonostsev. Gifted in many disciplines, she later on became part of the literary circles of the poets Alexander Blok and Vyachislav Ivanov, among others, in St. Petersburg. She was one of the first women allowed to attend courses at the theological academy there. Involved in politics before and during the revolution, she served briefly as the first female mayor of her family's summer hometown, Anapa, on the Black Sea. She was very nearly shot by Bolsheviks and was put on trial by the White Army as they retreated. Her first marriage ended in divorce, as did her second (to the White Army officer assigned to preside at her trial). The three children she had from the two marriages died young, one daughter from meningitis as a small child, the other daughter as a young adult on the child's return to Russia. Her son would die in the slave labor camp of Dora, along with her chaplain and friend, Fr. Dimitri Klepinine. First intent on bringing education to impoverished Russian immigrants in France, she quickly learned that the needs of the poor during the Great Depression were far more basic. Eventually she requested monastic tonsure and spent the rest of her life running hostels for the destitute, unemployed, homeless, and confused, as well as a nursing home for the elderly poor. These became her "monastery in the world," as her bishop predicted. On top of scavenging food in the Paris market district and preparing it for her charges, listening to their troubles, and attempting to locate them work, she continued a vigorous*

*intellectual life. She was a participant of several discussion circles and continued to publish in the leading journals of the Russian emigration, particularly* Put' *(The Way). The first English edition of an anthology of her writings has been published by Orbis Books. The following essay, written in late in the 1930s, is deeply rooted in her own experiences of deprivation and loss, particularly that of her daughters. In retrospect, we can read in it the end she herself would have: arrest and imprisonment in the Ravensbrück concentration camp. After surviving several years there, she took the place of another inmate and went to the gas chamber on 31 March 1945, just weeks before the camp's liberation. This reflection of suffering and death as birth to eternal life is therefore anything but theoretical; it is a meditation on her own struggle.*

## FOR FURTHER READING

*Mother Maria Skobtsova: Essential Writings.* Translated by Richard Pevear and Larissa Volokhonsky. Maryknoll, N.Y.: Orbis Books, 2002.

Hackel, Sergei. *Pearl of Great Price: The Life of Mother Maria Skobtsova.* Crestwood, N.Y.: SVSP, 1981.

# BIRTH AND DEATH

From the great sufferings of Job to Dostoyevsky's impassioned questions, from the unjust poisoning of Socrates to our time in which injustice and the absurd have become the singular measure of things, a question has been lifted toward heaven. And it falls back to us again, without answer. It has been raised by thinkers, philosophers, and theologians. How, in a world created by God, can we understand and justify the existence of evil and suffering? How can we reconcile divine justice and gentleness with the injustice that surrounds us, with the cruelty of history, with the death of this and that person, with the world's misery and our sense of being orphans condemned to separation and death?

The many attempts to establish a theodicy, a justification of divine action, are so many signs of the passionate human desire to find an answer, to find on this earth a harmony like that of heaven. All of these efforts fall flat, without any intellectual scope. They are fragmentary, completely unsatisfying.

Thus, Lev Shestov's article is quite relevant to what has been said here ("Nicholas Berdiaev," *Annales Contemporaines*, no. 67, October 1938, pp. 196–229). He presents two diametrically opposed answers, two forms of theodicy antagonistic to one another, those of Shestov himself and of Berdiaev. Their positions seem so distant from each other that all the other systems and attempts to create a theodicy could be placed somewhere between them.

First published in Mat' Maria, *Souvenirs articles essais*, vol. 2 (Paris: YMCA Press, 1992) in Russian and in *Le Sacrement du frère*, trans. Hélène Arjalcousky–Kléipinine, Françoise Lhoest, Claire Vajou (Paris–Pully: cerf/Le Sel de la terre, 2001), new editon. Trans. by Michael Plekon.

For Shestov, what is most important is the conviction that every injustice, every evil, every despair can be rendered nonexistent by God's almighty, superrational will. He therefore thinks of suffering and evil as something which by divine will alone, and despite our limited reason and our human blindness, can be transformed as a delusion and disappear. As nowhere else, one feels in this perspective that human destiny is in a blind alley, in endless despair. But at the same time, one can recognize a faith stretched beyond its limits, a faith to the end in spite of everything. Now whatever the substance and honesty of this position, one cannot accept it, for this would amount to increasing the blindness. The inability to see obliterates the very object one is considering.

Berdiaev follows a completely different path. For him freedom extends beyond the limits of the world created by God. This freedom has a wholly other genealogy, for it is not created at all but is pre-eternal. Also, its bearing frees from every evil everything created by God, freeing us ipso facto from the necessity of establishing a theodicy. Thus God is not responsible for the manner in which humankind uses its freedom. Neither is God responsible for the evil and suffering that result from it. In himself God is unable to do anything against evil, which is outside of himself. Only man—who is at the same time made in the image of God and the product of this pre-eternal freedom—is able to dominate and bring evil to submission to God, therefore it is not evil but divine goodness freely chosen that is victorious in man. Thus defined, we have, on the one hand, the tragic fragility of humanity abandoned to itself and, on the other, humanity's formidable mystical and cosmic destiny at the heart of the world created by God.

By its rigorous logic, Berdiaev's approach is both tempting and troubling. Everything is, to put it this way, named and structured in a new way. Yet, nothing changes at the heart of the problem.

This is why in order to resolve this problem we need neither philosophy nor theoretical schemas, but just the modest and intimate experience of our own small lives. We are tempted to turn in on ourselves and attempt to circumvent things in order to justify them. Is it necessary to prevent this introspection from resulting in a failed search? In reality there is no answer to the problem.

The question nevertheless remains. Not long ago the mathematician Lagrange put to the scientific world a series of problems with the obligation to solve them even though he showed the impossibility of a solution. Our task here is very much the same. With regard to the nature of evil and suffering, the meaning of everything, and theodicy, we should be able to furnish a solution even if the problem is unsolvable. Personally, all the attempts to solve it, including those which we will bring forward seem to me insufficient, hardly convincing. It is as if one had lined up a series of absolutely correct mathematical demonstrations, which were then unable to result in proving that $X=A$.

For myself, I want to try the exact inverse operation, to demonstrate that it is impossible to know what is equal to X. All the meaning is right here.

I want to imagine a world that is composed of souls not yet born, a kind of humanity in utero, yet endowed with consciousness. Thus, we imagine that each infant in the womb of its mother is conscious of what surrounds him or her and even has some grasp of the meaning of his or her uterine life. Furthermore, let us imagine that these uterine infants have a collective consciousness. They are able to experience themselves growing larger and developing. They are nourished. They move around. They experience the fatigue and the sickness of their mothers. Their uterine life progresses more or less well. Certain inequalities appear. One group feels itself better than the others, another is more badly off. But they have one thing in common. All are going to know the same destiny. The same tragedy is going to end their uterine life—they are going to be born. And they know what this implies. In the limits of their life it is, first of all, a totally unmerited suffering. If for a healthy mother, strong and well prepared, it is painful to give birth, only the absence of consciousness prevents the newborn from experiencing his birth as atrocious pain, for the bones of the newborn's skull are distended, he is choking, and his first breath seems to tear his lungs out. Here too, this expulsion can vary, can be more or less easy from one case to another. One thing nevertheless is certain. This experience of life in the womb is going to open upon the unknown, perhaps even nothing. What proof is there for the infant, at the beginning of his uterine life, that anything existed other than a black hole? What proof that he would be born to a new life and not just die in his life in the womb?

Moreover, if these uterine infants truly had a collective consciousness, would they not imagine the birth of one of their number as a leave-taking, a definitive departure, in sum, as a death? The newborn is dead to his uterine life—it is no more. The uterine society to which he belonged has suffered a loss and for it the beyond cannot but be the subject of hypothesis. This newborn has perhaps acquired another form of existence; at least he had not faded into nothingness.

Now let us imagine that one conducts a moral inventory of this uterine world, that one lists in two columns the losses and the gains. The balance sheet would indicate that there are many sufferings, that the end had been painful but that the reason escapes us and that there was without doubt no sense to this, no justification for this suffering that amounts to anything. From this might arise the same temptation as for Ivan Karamazov, to very respectfully return one's ticket to God, and in renouncing it to accept the presumed happiness of an eternal life at the price of the sufferings endured in order to be born.

Saint Paul has said, "A natural body is sown, but a spiritual body is raised" (1 Cor. 16: 42). In paraphrasing this, one could say in the present case, "A body of flesh is sown, a natural body is raised." But one is projected into the same unknown, the same nothing, through the same vice of birth-death. The only difference is that we have imagined a consciousness of the uterine world that does not exist in reality, no more than the meaning of evil and suffering. The natural body submits to its birth-death without having consciousness and consequently without questions, without undergoing either conflict or tragedy. Nevertheless in reality the tragedy is the same.

But we who have been born or, which is the same, we who are dead to uterine life from the height of this new stage of our existence, from the greater depth of our natural body, we consider our birth differently. It ceases to appear to us as a death to our uterine life. We do not see it except as a birth to our earthly life. It is not here that we are going to find the source of our problems, for we ignore the evil and the suffering of the period preceding our birth. This period did nothing but prepare us, nourish us, give us an entrance into life.

And now we are on the earth. We begin our earthly life. The same moral inventory, this time real and not imaginary, is going as in the preceding to open a new register of assets and liabilities for our life on earth. Tenderly, as it happens, the pages of the costs are filled: small hurts, caprices, the inattention of those close to you, childhood sicknesses, nightmares. At the start, by contrast the page of receipts is enormous: there is written down little by little all of divine creation, the colors, sounds, all the transparent happiness of infancy. But here the costs surpass the receipts, for they are going to amplify the feeling of injustice that rules here in the world, its ugliness, poverty, our impotence, the progressive collapse of our hopes. Our consciousness becomes extreme. We will come to know it all, that Socrates was poisoned and that nothing justified this crime. We discover the tears of the child. We begin to rebel, to suffer from this terrible knowledge. We then seek our own theodicy, to justify God's ways and, if we cannot succeed in this, terrified, desperate, full of anger, we will cry out "God does not exist!" Our hatred will be directed at the very One whose existence we deny. In such a tragic atheism, growing out of a failed theodicy, God's absence becomes the absence of peace and of meaning. Everything becomes indefinite, nothing seems right, the soul is plunged into night's darkness.

It is there, at the moment when all seems lost, when we cannot see any way out, that the human soul will encounter a terrible thing: death. In this cruel and unjust world, the only things to which we can cling are those close to us, those who give so freely this human warmth distributed in so stingy a manner, those we hold tenderly, in sacrificial love. For in our solitude and night, we find no comfort except in contact with this warmth, from our being warmly touched and comforted by each other. And now these beings, whom we love, are going to be suddenly taken from this world. They will undergo sufferings, illness, agony, abandonment, and then they will disappear. Where to? To a life eternal? To nothingness?

We find ourselves by their deathbed, without any power to help them, we cannot take upon ourselves their sufferings. They have no need any longer of our affection and warmth, for it can no longer console them. They have known here below joy and sadness, reflected on them, they have loved and now, they are gone! For them there is no longer a life here on this terrestrial globe. O Lord, before this horror which is their death, what are the reasons for their dying, why have they been poisoned, torn apart by dogs, or run over by a car! Faced with the stark reality of their death, the reasons for this are nothing but details.

If our soul, as Ivan Karamazov, is filled with the desire to return to God our ticket of entry to the heavenly Kingdom, this is not because of repulsion in the face of a particularly tragic death. No, it is simply because death exists and that humankind is mortal that this person existed and is no more, that with him also goes his love and tenderness, that our warmth and love are left orphans, shivering in the cold of their uselessness. It is precisely the loss of this intimacy and affection that the soul cannot accept. Then we seek to justify God's action, for if we cannot understand any longer and if we cannot find any justification for it, we cannot live any longer either.

There is, it seems to me, something particularly horrific and incomprehensible for us in the last chapter of the Book of Job, at the moment where his contention with God ends and when he receives again his health, his cattle and camels, and his new children—seven sons and three daughters. How could those seven and these three, and even if there were thousands more children, ever replace one of those who were taken? They were unique, those who disappeared, and these new ones are not the same, they are others. The person who has disappeared is never replaceable. Moreover, my grief does not stem uniquely from the loss provoked by their death but from the fact that a life has been cut off, that he or she will never again see the sun, that they are no longer here on this earth. I suffer as much because of my loss as because of their disappearance, I suffer as I feel for them.

When Shestov says that God is able to render inexistent that which exists, I think of my memory, this function that is so noble, so human, so divine. How can this memory accept being forgotten, removed, being made to disappear? What's more, the suffering does not only wound, but enriches memory considerably. What is to become of the wealth of experience then? How can one simply be rid of it? How can I remain a person if God has removed my entire path of life and its experiences? How could I experience the joy of God's divine power, this victory of the divine absurd over my poor reason? No extreme faith in the absurd can save me. It cannot secure me any kind of reasonable equilibrium between good and evil, freedom and necessity, the divine and the pre-eternal.

My conviction is both clear and simple. Within the limits of the three dimensions of our psychological life, within the limits of our earthly life, there is no response, no truth, no justice either human or divine. No balm will be able to heal the wound of a bleeding heart. Every such balm or therapy is ineffective. I consider life as a dagger that pierces me, a poison that consumes me. I see it as Job's destiny, to be delivered over to the devil for a time, the devil who has permission to submit me to anything he wants, the only condition being that he cannot take my soul.

The words of Jeremiah return to me there: "And you, you who claimed great things for yourself. Do not so demand. For see, it is I who bring unhappiness

to all flesh, says the Lord. But you, I grant you life as plunder wherever you go."
To what end? So that there might be someone to take upon himself, to comprehend these miseries which befall all humanity. Without this one remaining
soul saved, the miseries would not be miseries, for there would be no one to see
and understand them.

Such is the law for this natural soul that has been sown. All the world's truth
crashes down and bruises him. The communists in what is today the Soviet
Union, are happy to declare, in their naïve candor, that they have solved all the
central problems, but this does not affect the matter at all. For such is this law:
today humanity has solved everything, the solutions are just and equitable, but
tomorrow we will be run over by a car or poisoned by rotten fish, and what else
is there to this justice but the tomb in the cemetery or the pile of ash in the cre-
matorium. For whom is there justice, when one's death is the only gift for his
neighbors? This insoluble question demolishes all the responses to the preceding questions. It makes consciousness swing in endless despair of the absurd.
Then humanity rejects God, the world, and itself. And destroys itself.

Thus there is no answer. In the perspective of the great mathematician the
problem is declared insoluble. Beneath the canopy of low heaven, murky, in the
fog, all is given up to the absurd if . . . one thinks that death is death.

So Shestov is right on this point. Euclidian reason cannot resolve anything.
Only faith is able to furnish an answer, a response. But not this faith, which consists in saying that God renders inexistent what exists. Neither is it the desperate faith, which collides with the coffin and our earthly heaven; but it is the faith
that suppresses death.

"One is sown a natural body, but raised as a spiritual body" (1 Cor. 16: 44).
But to what is one raised? By what birth is one called to into being?

I imagine this material universe as an enormous womb that carries us, nourishes us, and makes us grow. We are sustained, not yet born to eternal life. The
long years of our earthly existence pass by in suffering, injustice, evil, and spiritual blindness, in total ignorance of the hour of our birth, or perhaps of our
nonbirth, of our eternal death. What tortures us the most is precisely this consciousness of our mortal condition, our impossibility of escaping death. Those
close to us disappear, we find ourselves orphans and, in our turn, prepare ourselves for the great exodus. We are fearful. We feel our bodies aging. And if our
souls were also to age and weaken? We know that our bodies are going to perish, that our coffins will be narrow and be covered by a black, cold earth.

But we have faith. And here is the only power of this faith: we sense that
death ceases to be death, that rather it becomes the birth into eternity, that the
earthly sufferings are only those of our being born. And it comes to us, that so
well-imagined and desired coming hour of our birth that we are able to say to
our sorrows: "Increase, become unsupportable and unbearable, transform me
into ashes for my spiritual body will rise, and I am going to be born into eternity. I am in the confines of this earthly womb. I will accomplish what is pre-

destined for me. I hasten to return to the house of the Father! And I am ready to give all, to pay whatever sufferings it might take to enter this home of my Father and of eternity."

It is not only the Father whom I will encounter again in eternity. There I will also rejoin my dear brothers and sisters and children already born to death and to eternity. I ardently desire to rejoin them, radiant and limitless.

Then, if these meetings have taken place, and I know that they will, the rest is of little importance. The inventory of my life will not occur here, where it is not yet finished, but over there. The page of losses will consist of only two items: two births, or rather, two deaths. The page of gains will contain but one word: "eternity."

Curiously, if one reasons thus, the last chapter of the Book of Job becomes clear in another, different sense. Job has not gained new children. Nothing is returned to him here below, on this earth. But after the long sufferings endured by his soul, which the devil was not able to destroy or disturb, after his sufferings of death-birth, he is finally born to eternity. In the Father's house he finds his loved ones, his children born to eternity with him. Then he is overjoyed that their death was not death but a birth. He rejoices too in being born to eternity. In his earthly life, all seemed to be a mystery, to be absurd. In his eternal life, all he had hoped became reality, most definitively. His faith, thereafter, was useless, for in place of conjecturing or having just an inkling of things through despair, he sees them now face to face.

The prophet says to us: "Death, where is your sting?" At Easter we sing, "By his death, he has destroyed death." Two thousand years have passed since Christ's resurrection, yet human beings continue to die. Would it then not seem as though death has kept its sting, that it has not been vanquished? From the perspective of our earthly existence, the answer is yes, for those close to us disappear and we ourselves, we too come closer all the time, little by little, to our death, when the sting will pierce us through.

Nevertheless, our faith not only compels us to dream that this death is in reality a birth, it also shows us how to realize this being born, how the physical body is raised as the spiritual body, how the Son of God returns to the house of the Father, how from his temporary annihilation he is born to eternity by the power of his being born on Golgotha. And not only him—the Son of God, the Son of David—but in him all of humanity (which he assumes, takes upon himself), is born in its turn to eternal life, to which we were all predestined. There death truly loses its sting. For death becomes birth and all of our earthly sufferings, all the evil and the nails of Golgotha are the sorrows of coming to birth that opens to us the doors of our heavenly and eternal home, the house of the Father.

In this perspective, the theodicy of faith is simple. It is summarized in the Creed in which we confess the faith: "I look for the resurrection of the dead and the life of the world to come." I await the resurrection of the beings whom I love, already born to eternity. I await my own birth, that of all humanity, of all people already dead and of those who are no longer living. And in order to be able to enter the Father's house and dwell there with all those already dead and who have already endured or who are going to endure these sorrows of being born, I am ready to pay whatever earthly sufferings there may be to my earthly body and my soul. I am ready to accept the pains of being born and I am jubilant in the very thought of having to endure the necessity of this suffering and pain. It is of no significance.

My theodicy is simple: "I await, I look for, I expect the resurrection of the dead and the life of the world to come." For me it is the measure of the life of this present world and time.

Anton Vladimirovich Kartashev (1875–1960) came from Kistim in the Urals, and from very humble origins—his father was a miner who became a government clerk. He went from being a schoolteacher to graduating from the prestigious St. Petersburg Ecclesiastical Academy and then teaching there. He was the last procurator and first minister of religion in the provisional Russian government in 1917, and a participant in the Great Council of the Russian Church in 1917–1918. He left Russia after arrest, settling in Paris. From 1925 until his death in 1960 he taught church history at the St. Sergius Institute, being one of the original faculty members and having many important later figures as students, among these Frs. Schmemann and Meyendorff, and Paul Evdokimov. Like his later colleague Fr. Afanasiev, Kartashev was resolute in examining the church and faith in terms of human history. The result of this is evident in their work, particularly here in Kartashev's perspective on dogmatic maximalism and minimalism. So aware was he of the actual situation in the ancient and patristic eras, Kartashev was able to distinguish between what still united and that which divided the churches. The clear and imposing preponderance of the former, that which was still held in unity prompted him and Fr. Bulgakov to not only become deeply committed to ecumenical work (study, discussion, and fellowship), but also to propose that the Eucharist was the sacrament of unity rather than division. Paul Evdokimov described him as coming from the same "prophetic" line as Gogol, Khomiakohv, Soloviev, and Dostoyevsky. To downplay or denigrate the human reality of the Church and the need for living out the Gospel in the concrete tasks of one's society and culture were for Kartashev detours into almost heretical stances, such as Nestorianism and Monophysitism,

*both of which refuse to accept the truly human will and person of Christ, hence
the entry of God into human time and material.*


## FOR FURTHER READING

Anton Kartashev. *On the the Biblical Criticism of the Old Testament.* Paris: YMCA
    Press, 1947.
———. *Way to Eucunemical Council.* Paris: YMCA Press, 1932.
———. *The Restoration of Holy Russia.* Paris: YMCA Press, 1956.
———. *History of the Russian Church,* 2 vols. Paris: YMCA Press, 1959.
———. *The Commercial Councils.* Paris: YMCA Press, 1963.

# THE PATHS TOWARD THE
# REUNION OF THE CHURCHES

The problem of the reunion of the churches belongs to a category of problems insoluble in the ordinary way.

The consciousness and tradition of every church declares itself to be the best, the most perfect and absolute. Therefore a reunion of the churches can either be regarded as an "absorption." of one church by another—of the erring church by the true church—or else as a mutual recognition of the same common truth in one another, expressed in two different ways. But even so, mutual sacrifices are inevitable. Psychologically, this is all very difficult, even for the small elect minority, and for the wide masses of church members it is, generally speaking, impossible.

Therefore all the numerous "unias" or unions between the Roman Church and sections of the Eastern Churches have always been based on a principle of "absorption." In all unias Eastern dogmatic teaching has been replaced in toto by Roman dogmatic teaching. The members of these unias have only been allowed to preserve their ceremonies and rites, and even these have been modified.

Modern history gives us no example of a reunion of churches based on an understanding that results from an agreement between two parties possessing equal rights. The churches have wandered so far apart from one another that this has become impossible for them. Single cases of external reunion between certain Protestant churches, mutually akin to one another, such as, for instance,

Originally published in *The Journal of the Fellowship of St. Alban and St. Sergius*, no. 26 (December 1934).

an administrative union between the Lutheran and the Reformed churches in Prussia, or experiments in reunion between certain churches in England and America, stand quite outside this tragic problem of the reunion of the Orthodox and Catholic churches. Even the most recent case of hierarchical communion between the Anglican and the Old Catholic churches does not present an entirely different case, although it is a promising sign of growing daring among Christians along paths of reconciliation. The Old Catholic Church, after a comparatively recent separation from Rome, finds itself in perpetual restlessness and seeking for some immovable basis. It is similarly not burdened by consciousness of its self-sufficiency, which separates the other great churches, divorced since ancient times from one another. Putting it shortly, a willingness of two churches to recognize *in each other parts of the one, undivided, and true Church*, and to enter into sacramental communion, *while admitting mutual differences* of theology and devotional life, represents a spiritual feat far beyond the psychology of the Church collectively. Perhaps the only instance of this kind we see is in the Anglican Church, which has included within its fold such a wide range of religious divergencies. But this experience, which is also not devoid of inner tragedy, could be only realized within the heart of a *single nation*, and it is impossible to imagine such a thing taking place among historically and nationally estranged churches.

Many hope to overcome the dramatic difficulty of this problem through lengthy discussions and agreement between hierarchs and theologians, trusting that both parties will mutually convince one another of their own truth and will cooperate together in drawing up a creed that will unite them. What would this mean? That one of the churches would reject its own defects and would amend itself in accordance with a standard set up by the other church? Or, would both renounce some of their defects and mutually appropriate certain values? In this "diplomatic" method we must frankly admit a premise that is usually silently evaded. Of course we Easterns usually think that any other side should set itself right according to the measure of our dogmatic infallibility, and that only in this case can a reconciliation be accepted by our faithful. In other words, we presuppose here the "uniting" of the erring church to the true church, the "absorption" of a defective dogmatic by an infallible one. It does happen that numerically, small churches or parts of churches, in humility and sacrifice, follow along this path of reconciliation. But it is psychologically improbable for churches that are great both in the qualitative and in the quantitative sense. And thus when we argue in a positive, sane, and realistic way, we are forced to conclude that the usual "diplomatic" plan for the reunion of the churches leads us to a tragic blind alley whenever we try to realize its fulfillment; or, alternatively it leads us to a bad infinity, to a lack of concrete results, when we allow it to drag on for centuries.

What, then, are we to do? First of all, pray without ceasing, pray for a miracle. Because "what is impossible with men is possible with God" (Mt. 26: 19).

Second, work persistently toward reconciliation and rapprochement between the churches, so that the scandal of strife between churches should be no more. Finally, we must permeate the wide masses of church people in all the churches with a consciousness *of their mystical unity within the fold of the one, invisible, and only universal Church of Christ.* All these paths are accessible to methodic, calculated work of an evolutionary character. But no tragedy has ever been resolved along evolutionary paths. And the psychological blind alley of the problem of the reunion of the churches represents a real tragedy. *A tragedy can only be overcome by a creative act, which adds something new.* In the social sphere this is termed a revolutionary moment. In the religious sphere it is the prophetic breath of God's Spirit, which enriches the treasury of revelation.

Who and what constitute an organ for such revelation? In a church that is quickened by the Holy Spirit—*all and everything* constitutes such an organ, starting with the ecumenical councils, which declare "what seemed good to the Holy Spirit and to us" (Acts 15:28), and ending with "the mouths of babes and sucklings" whom "God hath perfected in praise" (Ps 8:2; Mt 21:16), and "your sons and your daughters, your old men and your young men, your servants and your handmaids" (Acts 2:17, 18; Jl 2:28, 29). The revelation of the Holy Spirit resounds within the Church in small and in great: in the heroic feats of the saints, in the wisdom of the Holy Fathers and elders (*startzi*), in liturgical hymns and acts of brotherly love performed by one of "these little ones." "The Spirit bloweth where it listeth" (Jn 3:8). A word or an act that is born in one part of the Church is later complied with by the whole Church, while, on the contrary, sometimes a resolution passed by a formal ecumenical council is rejected by the very life of the Church, as something that cannot be accepted. A selection of the true from the false, the Catholic from the heretical, takes place in the living experience of the entire Church. This is what is meant by its *soborny* (ecumenical) *receptivity*—that is, avowing, "churchifying" of teaching and fact, their canonization. It is frequently sealed from above, in the solemn declarations of hierarchs and councils, but it is not obligatory for it to begin there. On the contrary, most frequently it begins in the lower depths of the Church, sometimes even on its extreme limits. This is most obvious and typical in the canonization and glorification of saints. A saint is first accepted by the common people and only then, sometimes only because of this, he is canonized by the hierarchy.

Perhaps the simplest and the most natural way for the church to overcome this tragedy of Church division will actually come to be revealed by this unofficial, nonjudicial, spiritual path. But if we admit that this is, predominantly, a spiritual path, we cannot imagine our progress along it as something as clearly defined and as regular as progress along the "diplomatic" path. The diplomatic path leads from above, from the center of hierarchical authority in the Church, and proclaims the union attained from above as obligatory for the whole body of the two churches that have come to an understanding. But the path about which we are now speaking and thinking is one that ascends toward the highest hierarchical center of the Church, from various points in the churches. The first path is one that in its very nature can be planned beforehand, which is easily directed, and subject to artificial acceleration and retardation. The second way by its very nature again is nearer to a spontaneous process, self-begotten, which either spreads with elemental power or is temporarily submerged. This path can, least of all, be preconceived, or subjected to artificial acceleration or fulfillment. But when this way emerges through an actual, burning need in the life of the Church, and when it is accompanied invisibly by the power of the grace of God's Spirit, then we can surely describe it as a path that is, in truth, both Catholic and *soborny*, the inevitable consummation of which will take place at an official council.

Ultimately all that has been accepted by the Church is Catholic and *soborny*, even though very few actual points of the Church's teaching have passed through the filter of official councils.

Here we will allow ourselves to make a somewhat crude comparison, which, perhaps, awakens especially painful reminiscences among us Russians. How do wars end? Officially and regularly by an agreement between the leaders of the respective armies when they send messengers with a white flag of truce to the enemy's camp, or, in more significant cases, by an unconditional signing of the peace treaty in cases of decisive victory. But sometimes wars end in an irregular manner, when the fighting mass is carried away by elemental forces, when it refuses to fight, and breaks up the front by opening up anarchic and friendly relations with the enemy. Why should we not be able to assume that the division of the churches also may cease to exist—first at certain points in the front line—through similar spontaneous breaks? I foresee that such an analogy may evoke a protest among theologians. There is nothing easier than to prove that anarchy cannot exist in the Church and that it is for this reason that canonical law exists, so as to check up formally what is of the Church, what is Catholic, what is obligatory, and conversely, determine what is particular, haphazard, and possibly inadmissible from the point of view of the Church—what is schismatical and heretic. I am ready to lay down arms immediately in the face of such a general, irrefutable argument. Yet, even so, I continue to insist that no ordinary acting instances of Church authority are able to pronounce a *final* judgment as to the Catholicity of certain, separate, partial stages of church reunion, until such a process has attained to its consummation.

In the course of such a process the originally negative reaction of certain church authorities may come to be replaced by a general positive approval of the entire Church. We observe such a process, for instance, in the attitude of the Eastern churches toward the question of the validity of Anglican ordination. Some of them deny the validity, others keep a doubtful silence on the point; others still recognize it. Yet we have grounds for supposing that the decisive moment is at hand when all will recognize the validity of Anglican orders. Of a similar nature is the temporary disagreement concerning the Bulgarian Church. The Greek churches proclaimed the Bulgarian Church schismatic for its "Philetism," that is, its nationalism, at the Council of Constantinople in 1872. But the non-Greek Orthodox churches persist in their communion with the Bulgarian Church, recognizing it as Orthodox. We already know of instances of joint celebration of divine services by Greek and Bulgarian priests in 1912. Let us hope, therefore, that the time is near when the Greeks also will decide to annul this painful schism. Separate instances of its nonacceptance only destroy its obligatory nature for the whole of Orthodoxy, which was the original aim of the Greeks.

We observe similar instances in ancient times when the annihilation of Church separations often followed in the wake of partial and local instances of reconciliation between Catholic parishes and dioceses and certain schismatic parishes that had forsaken the fold of the Church. Such a case took place, for instance, in Africa when the Donatists returned to the Catholic Church. But especially edifying is a case that took place in the East in 358–381, and was submitted to the Second Ecumenical Council. It was a case of reunion within an integral organism of the Catholic Church, when its various fragments, which had come to be separated and had mutually excommunicated one another, came together again. No central authority existed at that time. Rome blindly recognized only one small single church—that of Paulinus of Antioch. Then St. Basil the Great and his confederates—the creators of the Neo-Nicaean theology—began to collect into the fold of the Catholic Church one church after another, one diocese after another. They suggested to Rome that it should recognize this so-called molecular partial recovery of the Church from the Arian heresy. Rome, full of its own pride of authority, for a long time, could not come to understand how the Orthodox faith could exist anywhere without its knowledge and without communion with it. But bitter mistakes at last taught Rome something. It came to understand that its recommendations did not protect Marcellus from the guilt of heresy.

It came to comprehend likewise that Vitalius, similarly recommended by Rome, was discovered to be a new heretic, a follower of Apollinarius. Only after all this did Rome declare that the "Neo-Nicaean " group was an Orthodox one. Then, in its turn, the Neo-Nicaean group, at the Council of Antioch in 397, under the chairmanship of Meletius, proclaimed its agreement with Rome. In this way the main, healthy nucleus of the Orthodox Church, which served as a center of attraction, was consolidated. Partial initiative combined to produce and crystallize the general, which was sought. An integral whole was built from fragments. That which neither Rome, nor Alexandria, nor Constantinople could achieve was built up on the circumference. It only remained to proclaim this "molecularly" united nucleus as the leading center of Eastern Orthodoxy. This was done by the Emperor Theodosius the Great when he assembled the Council of Constantinople of 381. Thus the local and partial led to the universal and

Catholic in the life of the Church. It was as a result of this that the local Eastern Council of 381 acquired the authority and the name of an ecumenical council.

I admit that the examples of ancient times do not equal the difficulties of the contemporary problem—that of the rebuilding of the external unity of the Church. But the lessons of antiquity witness to the variety of paths chosen by the Church in actual life. They all urge us not to rely exclusively on ready-made, formally canonical recipes for the solving of this problem, but to seek for paths that would be the most effective ones for our time. He alone who does not feel the tragic weakness of the contemporary divided Church (which is faced with the hostile forces of secularized culture), to whom all eschatological perspectives appear as something infinitely remote, will be reconciled to the generally accepted method of diplomatic negotiations, which deal with the possibilities of a general and solemn reunion at some remotely unknown date. On the contrary, he who is convinced of the century-old slowness and hopelessness of such a (too promising and smooth) solution of the problem, and who is eschatologically worried by this prolonged separation of the churches, will seek elsewhere for more effective and real paths of partial attainments of church unity, in instances where this is possible.

Men differ, so do methods of their activity. Our compatriot, Vladimir Soloviev, has given us a striking example of such eschatological daring. Worn out by a thirst for the unity of the Church, he dared, against the discipline of the church, on his own authority, to unite in his own heart the Orthodox and the Roman churches. He became a Roman Catholic, without leaving his own Orthodox church. He took Holy Communion from the hands of a uniate priest, and before death he accepted Communion from an Orthodox priest. The gesture of Vladimir Soloviev makes almost a caricature of methods of partial union in seeking for the unity of the church. But who knows the destiny or the manner in which the reunion of the churches will develop even in the coming years? Perhaps Soloviev's formally anarchic act will be one of a series of similar acts, which will no longer be isolated. And may not his act, in some sense, become prophetic?

If groups of people in two churches (for example, the Anglican and the Orthodox, or the Old Catholic and the Orthodox) were to dedicate themselves for a heroic feat of complete church communion in the sacraments—having first agreed, of course, with a pure conscience as to the identity of their faith in all essentials with a divergence only in secondary points—the only thing they would lack for their work so that it could be recognized as fully of the Church and Catholic would be the consent and blessing of the respective bishops from both sides. If such bishops were to be found, then the line separating the two churches would be broken at this part of the front. A kernel of unity would be formed, one which might attract others to itself. The front would come to be broken at other points as well. Partitions of a thousand years' standing would begin to disappear, and all this would take place without doing any violence to

a majority or a minority that might object to entering on this path. This movement, so to speak, "from below" would accelerate the movement from "above."
The general diplomatic discussions as to the reunion of the churches, which, up
to now, have been barren and hopeless, *would encounter the actual fact* of partial reunion. A fruitful meeting of the two movements would take place, their
actual synthesis would be achieved. The heroic and dramatic path of "direct action" adopted in partial reunion, which from the formal point of view appears
as anti-Catholic, anti-*sobornal*, would receive a *formal sanction* and a solemn
*sobornal* vindication.

This is why the path of the partial realization of this great ecumenical act of
the unity of the church of Christ is at present the only path open to men who
are not only Christians in thought but also in *deed*. The time has come when we
are forced to abandon contemplation for action. The problem is no longer a
dogmatic one. It is pragmatic and *a problem of the will*.

# INTERCOMMUNION AND
# DOGMATIC AGREEMENT

From our Eastern Orthodox standpoint there exists virtually no difference between the relationship of dogmatic agreement to the problem of reunion, or to that of intercommunion alone.

Let us disregard for the present exceptional cases of intercommunion *in extremis* and consider intercommunion as the normal practice of participating from the same cup. For us Orthodox such fellowship would imply a full basis for—and an actual realization of—the reunion of the churches. If members of two confessions mutually partake of the eucharistic cup it follows that external unity has already been re-established between their churches. Consequently, the reunion of the churches has actually taken place within their boundaries. For us this is obvious. *In the cup of the Eucharist is to be found the whole mystery of the unity of the church.* Union through the cup solves the problem completely. Outside the cup there remain only questions of secondary importance, however numerous or practically important they may appear.

It follows, therefore, that whenever two confessions seek dogmatic agreement—whether for purposes of intercommunion, or the reunion of their churches—the meaning, the extent, and the quality of such an agreement would remain the same. In other words we, Eastern Orthodox, in all such cases would have to speak always of a complete *dogmatic agreement* which ultimately resolves the problem in its totality.

First published in *Sobornost': The Journal of the Fellowship of St. Alban and St. Sergius* 4 (December 1935): 41–48 (translator unknown).

What then are the limits of a dogmatic agreement that would be sufficient for church unity and consequently for the reunion of a divided church? This raises the eternal question of *unitas in necessariis*. What constitutes a *necessarium*? How can we define it? Is it a question here of distinguishing between the absolutely essential and the relatively important? Is it lawful to apply a certain degree of relativism?

We reply in the affirmative: yes, this is permissible. In defining the limits of that which is absolutely essential—the *necessarium*—there is room for relativism in two senses: in a static sense and in a dynamic sense.

From the Orthodox point of view there exist external, objectively defined, static boundaries of the dogmatic minimum required. The content of this minimum is well known. It constitutes the faith of the ancient undivided church, as expressed in the Nicene Creed, in the pronouncements of the seven ecumenical councils, and in the ritual of the sacraments of the church. The ritual of the holy liturgy—the mass—alone would suffice to exhaust all the other formulae. Anyone who accepts our holy liturgy is accepted by us as a fellow-believer. We know that this "minimum " of ours sounds like a maximum to many who are outsiders. But we who are here without any hesitation describe it as a minimum, because with us, even up to the present day, the majority are inclined to demand the acceptance of far more than this—of the *whole* of our tradition—before intercommunion can take place, or the reunion of our churches become possible. In this case tradition is ambiguously interpreted as something that includes far more than the minimum given above. This minimum, undoubtedly, is preserved and handed down to us by the tradition of the church and represents its main formulated content. But those of us who are conservative include in the bulk of tradition the entire content of our religious life, all the various forms and expressions of our devotional life, the theological opinions acceptable to us, and even the changing theories of our scholars! Such maximalistic traditionalism is in this case an illegitimate pretension. Under cover of the one word "tradition" it confuses different values by blurring the limits of a dogmatic minimum of the *necessarium*. Therefore we would contrast our principle of a "dogmatic minimum" with such incorrectly interpreted traditionalism. Our minimum is the absolutely necessary—the *necessarium*. Beyond it lies the boundary only of the relatively valuable, the relatively necessary where the criteria of relativism may be applied. Thus, for example, the apostolic succession of the episcopate constitutes a *necessarium* for all. Unless it is accepted the reunion of the churches is impossible. But the absence of secret individual confession before a priest does not represent an *impedimentum derimens* to reunion. Or, to take another instance, the veneration of the saints, of the Blessed Virgin, and of their icons comprises a *necessarium*, while the veneration of relics and miraculous images can never be an absolute requirement for unity, however closely these two moments may be interconnected in our own opinion. For further purposes of clarification let us allow ourselves a terminological liberty, and let us describe these distinctions by the arbitrary and artificial definitions of *necessarium absolutum* and *necessarium relativum*.

The whole of the local tradition of the East (*necessarium relativum*) is obligatory for the East. It is therefore inseparable in the religious life of the East from the absolutely essential dogmatic kernel of "tradition" (the *necessarium absolutum*). But the Western church as a whole and in its parts possesses its own relative values and local traditions (*necessarium relativum*). They are inseparable in a similar way from the life of the Western churches from a dogmatic absolute minimum which is like ours (*necessarium absolutum*), yet these are not binding for us, just as our own relative values are not obligatory for them (*necessarium relativum*).

In a similar way, let us attempt to disentangle the misunderstanding that exists with the term "tradition." We must admit that it exists in two senses. Here again we must introduce the criterion of relativity, without disintegrating within any church the concrete unity of its religious values as true to the particular experience of that church, nor classifying them in a scholastic fashion as primary, secondary, and so on. The psychology of religious experience is such that everything that comes in contact with the church—with its basic, absolute truths, its mystical holies, and even with all within it which is humanly imperfect and defective—acquires a reflected holiness. It thus becomes sanctified, revered, and dear to our heart. And this explains why we are all of us so much attached to the details of these particular traditions of ours, which, when we consider them objectively, possess only a relative value. This accounts for our love of them. They constitute, so to speak, the living flesh of divine revelation, which, if we are true to our experience, can never be severed from its spirit. In this particular realm every confession and every single church stand in contrast to each other, and yet each one is right in its own way. Nevertheless, every single church justifies only itself, not other churches. This is the significance of *in omnibus caritas*—"in all things, love"—of a mutual acceptance of one another in love. In this way we define the static boundary between the absolute and the relative in these relationships.

The well-known formula that naturally comes to our mind at this stage, contains yet another point—*in dubiis libertas*—"in things that are debatable, freedom." Where do we actually make use of *dubia*, and is this legitimate? I would reply, "Yes, *dubia* are legitimate," and would add that they are applicable in several instances. Firstly, all the traditions or some of the particular traditions of a certain local church may remain as *dubia*, temporarily or even permanently, in the eyes of another local church. For instance monasticism for a long period constituted a *dubium* for the church of England. Now this has ceased. The Roman teaching with regard to the Pope has always represented a *dubium* to the Eastern church and will probably continue being so. Secondly, the *theologumena* (private theological opinions) of any one church may be *dubia* in the eyes of another church. This applies to the Western *filioque* from the point of view of the Orthodox church. The same would be true of the doctrine of purgatory and of the immaculate conception of Mary. Thirdly, the theological interpretations of some church, even its mystical experiences of the most fundamental dogma (*necessaria absoluta*), which are embraced by the existent unity and are even expressed by a common formula, may form *dubia* for another local church. This is true, for example, of the divergencies in opinion that exist between the Roman Catholics and ourselves as regards the conception of the authority of the church, of its infallibility, of salvation by grace through faith. This would apply similarly to certain differences between ourselves and the Protestants: different interpretations of the Eucharist as a sacrifice, of Holy Scripture as the limit of Revelation. Does this mean that in some way or another the criterion of the "relative" enters within the precincts of what we have described as the "absolute" (*necessaria absoluta*)? Yes, this is precisely the case.

This whole process not only further reveals the limits of the static and immobile boundary, but similarly discloses the dynamic, mobile boundary between the "necessaria" and the "dubia." This boundary may change and move in so far as it affects particular dogmas and traditions in the process of a mutual rapprochement between the churches, according to the measure in which they penetrate more deeply into the spiritual life of each other.

First, it is possible for certain churches that are drawing close to one another to be faced with the experience that separate dogmas and traditions are becoming transferred from the realm of *dubia* in the direct sense, so that they no longer serve to divide, but to unite. If, for instance, a church that does not comprehend the cult of relics, ultimately accepts it, psychologically this tradition becomes merged with its worship and devotion—with the highest category of *necessaria*. Second, dynamic relativity may find expression even within the static limits of the *necessaria absoluta* in a growing similarity in the interpretation of dogmas. Let us take another example. Supposing that the Anglican church, which regards extreme unction and matrimony as "sacramentalia," were to accept them fully as sacraments, and together with the Easterns would tend to encourage a growth in the number of sacraments, a richer sacramentalism, instead of encouraging a minimum of sacraments and an impoverished sacramental life, some of the obstacles which exist between the two churches would be removed and the measure of absolute dogmatic agreement which exists between Anglicanism and Orthodoxy would be increased. Historical evidence favours our hope that what was still impossible a hundred years ago is now becoming a reality. As regards the future, even greater possibilities for mutual enrichment are in store, not only of the West by the East, but likewise of the East by the West.

Having thus begun the reunion of the churches on the basis of a minimum dogmatic agreement (viz., on a foundation of static relativity), we have hopes of passing beyond it. We find that at least the way is open to us for going further and for bringing about the desired maximum on the basis of dynamic relativity. The closed circle, thanks to dynamic relativity, opens again. Relativity in the process instead of being a dogmatic vice becomes transformed into a dogmatic virtue.

We might add here that the historical relativism seen within the church serves especially to save us from despair when we consider the tragedy of the division of the church. The secret of this relativism lies in the fact that the church from the very beginning, in spite of the declared unity of its dogmatic faith, actually combined and embraced within itself different types of understanding and spiritual experience of the faith. This was inevitable at the time and is in its very essence inevitable, owing to the differences of language, culture, race, as well as the individual differences of the human type. Greek and Romans, East and West, have at all times thought in different ways of God, of the Trinity, of salvation, of holiness. All the great heresies and the great divisions of the church originated as a result of this. Every local church succumbed to the temptation of the tower of Babel. Each imagined that its belfry was the only one which rose as high as the heavens, and that its neighbour's did not. And so God punished the churches, as in the book of Genesis of old, by a confusion of tongues. For already a thousand years the churches speak in different tongues and fail to understand each other. Half of their whole history has passed in division. And by now their inborn and inevitable human differences have become so deeply rooted in their actual systems that it almost seems that nothing can be changed and remedied. It is impossible to alleviate or overcome this curse of Babel without applying the minimum described above, which comprises the "absolutely necessary" dogmatic agreement. But this very minimum cannot be determined apart from the principle of partial relativism in the sense described.

Let no one imagine that in this theory we are led by any spirit of liberalism, by any desire to make concessions to the more feeble at the expense of the absolute truth of the Christian revelation. One need only begin to understand how wide, how all-embracing in its dogmatic richness and mystical depth, is our so-called minimum of faith, to be able to dispel entirely any idea of any kind of diplomatically attractive "concession" made in connection with the mysteries of the faith. *Our minimum means the whole dogma of the universal church.* For the disobedient the tradition of the universal church represents an intolerable "maximum." In order to make this minimum acceptable the churches must manifest a profound feeling of corporate repentance, and sacrificially recognize and admit all their historical failures. In another way, this may be described as the *pium desiderium*, of the reunion of the churches. Indeed it is far easier for separate individuals to recognize in full another church in place of their own, than for a wholly "other" church to accept the dogmatic minimum of the Catholic church. It is completely out of place, therefore, to talk about liberalism.

We must be guided in this not by the antiquated liberalism of our great-grandfathers, but by a sober acknowledgment of the sins of our churches (in the light of history) and of the special problems of our particular epoch in the life of the church. We therefore advocate this principle of relativism in the dynamic sense which guides us from a minimum to the absolute maximum.

What are the general features of this minimum of dogmatic agreement for the reunion of the churches round the one cup of the eucharist?

All the churches reorganized during the Reformation must recognize and restore the apostolic succession to their priesthood by acquiring it from those churches which possess it indisputably, or by getting their priesthood confirmed by such churches. They should further admit that baptism, confirmation, and the eucharist have the full power and significance of sacraments—a fact which has been borne out by the teaching of the Eastern church from the earliest times of primitive Christianity. They should acknowledge in principle the sacramental teaching of the church, which regards the sacraments as channels through which special gifts of the Holy Spirit are conferred, as we see in penance, matrimony, extreme unction, according to the teaching of the Orthodox and Roman churches. The Eastern church in particular sees a special gift also in the blessing of the waters and in. the consecration of churches.

We Orthodox, on our part, should recognize for Protestants the right to a special type of theology and worship, to their enthusiasm for the doctrine of salvation by faith, to a special veneration of the written Word of God, to their arid and impoverished forms of divine worship. We cannot expect of them the acceptance of a cult of relics and icons. But nevertheless they should certainly accept the actual dogmas of the veneration of icons, of the saints, and of the Blessed Virgin. And once and for all they should abandon any hostility they have toward these dogmas and toward our forms of worship. Apart from this there is no room for a union of love, for the existence of the one church.

The Roman Catholics should cease to claim just one thing—namely, the *universality* of the Papal authority. While the Orthodox should recognize the new Roman dogmas (such as the *Filioque*, the immaculate conception, purgatory) as Roman *theologumena*, not binding for the Orthodox church. Papacy is profoundly and inseparably welded with the mysticism of Latin ecclesiology, which regards the pope as the heart of the church. If we were to take this from the Latins it would mean a desire on our part to destroy the character of their devotion. The Orthodox church should recognize the papacy, *but for the Roman church alone*. It should be content to regard the Pope only as the first in honour among the, autocephalous patriarchs. This is quite obvious to all parties concerned. It should also regard him as the mystical Pope of the Latins, as a personal organ of the supreme authority and infallibility of the church, according to their Latin interpretation. Of course all the above would actually work only within the limits of the Roman patriarchate, would only apply to the needs and requirements of the internal; local devotion of the Latins.

If we can interpret in this way the supreme authority of the pope within the precincts of the Roman church, then all the other churches must abide in a Catholic union of love and in a fellowship of faith with such a papal church.

None of the other churches (with the exception of the Roman) wish to have such an absolute monarch, but there is no reason why we should oppose a part of the church universal which retained such a system.

The Anglican church, so far as it shares points of doctrine that are definitely Protestant, should shed them, if we are to follow the scheme that has been outlined.

What sort of picture, then, do we get of a reunited church according to our plan? We repeat that the picture here presented is in essence identical both for intercommunion and for complete reunion. It obviously includes an element of federation. Unity in diversity is alone possible. Although a state of federation may appear defective when contrasted with the ideal of church unity (our liturgy says: "with one mouth, with one heart . . ."), nevertheless we should courageously accept this defectiveness and regard it as inevitable, as just payment for the churches' sin of mutual division, which had been allowed and deepened by the church. It is simply unnatural to expect a reunion on a uniform basis, after a thousand years of separation. Such a desire might even be interpreted as an evasion of the issue—that of the restoration of the external unity of the church.

Lev Alexandrovich Zander (1893–1964) was born in St. Petersburg and educated at the law faculty of that city's university. After further graduate work in Germany he served in the army from 1914 to 1917, leaving for China after the revolution. At the momentous meeting of the Russian Christian Students Association in Pecherov, Slovakia, in 1923, he met Fr. Sergius Bulgakov, who became both his teacher and spiritual father. Teaching on the faculty of St. Sergius Theological Institute in Paris from late 1925 on, he regularly traveled with its choir on concert tours throughout Europe. Zander lectured on Orthodox spirituality and theology on these tours and was a member of Berdiaev's Religious Philosophical Association, as well as the fraternity of the Holy Trinity, along with Paul Evdokimov, the future Fr. Sophrony Sakharov, Fr. Basil Zenkovsky, Fr. Bulgakov, Sister Joanna Reitlinger, Mother Maria Skobtsova, and many others. From the mid-1930s he was also active in the Fellowship of Sts. Alban and Sergius and what would later be the World Council of Churches. During World War II, as the secretary of the student movement, he was imprisoned by the occupying Germans along with Fr. Zenkovsky. In the postwar years he wrote God and the World, *a two-volume study of Fr. Bulgakov's thought, to date the single most comprehensive study. He continued to be active in ecumenical work and was one of the cofounders of Syndesmos, the Orthodox international youth movement, in 1953 along with, among others, Frs. Schmemann and Meyendorff, and Paul Evdokimov. With Evdokimov he organized courses in Orthodox theology for Western Christians in Paris, as well as at the Ecumenical Institute in Bossey along with Fr. Lev Gillet and Olivier Clement, while remaining affiliated with St. Sergius. Zander's ecumenical openness was viciously attacked by*

*Fr. George Florovsky, particularly in a review of the latter's* Vision and Action, *published in 1952. He died suddenly on the train returning to Paris on 17 December 1964.*

## FOR FURTHER READING

Lev Zander. *Dostoevsky*. London, 1988.
———. *God and the World*, 2 vols. Paris: YMCA Press, 1948.
———. *Vision and Action*. Translated by Natalie Duddington. London: Victor Gollancz, 1952.

# ON THE ESSENCE OF
# ECUMENICAL PARTICIPATION

*To my spiritual father and teacher, protopresbyter Sergius Bulgakov*

"And together let us glorify the most-Holy Spirit."

The question of unity of the Christian world and of the reunion of churches confronts us as the most difficult and important theological problem, whose resolution naturally acquires one or another dogmatic formulation. However, alongside the theoretical resolution of the issue, contemporary church life has supplied us with a series of facts which theological thought cannot dismiss with indifference. For these facts are not accidental occurrences, but acts of the Church, which demand the attention of anyone who sees in church action not simply the presence of some theoretical truths, but the concrete, though mystical, life of the Body of Christ.

This present study is dedicated to the examination of these facts, which fall under the rubric of the ecumenical movement. Our goal is not to preach an agenda, but to understand what is already placed before us.

However, what can we legitimately examine as given? What are the boundaries of our investigation in terms of the objective ecclesial reality?

The answer to these questions will determine both subject and method of our analysis. The subject, at first glance, seems quite unclear, and cannot be defined by the simple statement of goals. For if the whole history of Christianity testifies to the attempts at rapprochement of various Christian confessions and

Originally published in *Zhivoe predanie*. Paris: YMCA Press, 1937. Translated by Alexis Vinogradov.

the reunification of churches, then it is rather evident that during these latter years a new era has begun, which we can generally characterize as the time of great conciliarity among Christians of various confessions.

The unprecedented aspect of this era is the fact that in the Christian consciousness of various churches, the fragmented state of the Christian world has begun to be regarded as a sin, whereas previously this sorry state was considered almost normal. This is now the source of the thirst for unity, of those efforts at rapprochement, which find their place in the so-called ecumenical movement, which embraces many and often disparate organizations, sustained by one spirit and direction. Such are: the work of reuniting churches in matters of mutual aid and love ("Practical Christianity" or "Life and Work," briefly referred to as the Stockholm movement); the efforts at unity on the dogmatic level ("Faith and Order," or the Lausanne Movement); the work of disseminating Christian principles in international relations (the worldwide union for mutual friendship of nations through the work of churches); and various Christian youth organizations (the Worldwide Christian Student Federation, and Christian councils of young people and young women), etc.

Despite the variety of methods and the difference in immediate goals, all these organizations must be seen as a single whole. For even if they are not united on the organizational level, there is nevertheless a spiritual unity among them, which permits us to speak of them as diverse manifestations of a single movement. Incidentally, this is also confirmed by the fact that the same individuals participate simultaneously in several movements, as well as by the fact (as demonstrated historically) that the majority of older activists in various associations received their internship in corresponding youth organizations.

The boundaries of the ecumenical movement are nebulous, for if in certain circumstances participation demands a high dogmatic consciousness and ecclesial responsibility, in others the sole criterion of membership is the simple desire to take part in the work that bears Christ's name. This is why the roster of participants in the ecumenical movement is kaleidoscopic, and entering it we should expect to encounter not only an Orthodox hierarch, an Anglican bishop, and a Protestant pastor, but also a representative of "liberal" theology who rejects the divinity of Jesus Christ, or a Unitarian who rejects the dogma of the Trinity[1], or a Quaker, who in general rejects any church regulations. Thus, it is entirely understandable and natural that many representatives of various churches of a strict mindset reject the very possibility of ecumenical dialogue, and see in it the danger of losing dogmatic precision and the dissolution of ecclesiology. The facts, however, testify to the contrary: for the Protestant world, which is involved in the ecumenical movement, this participation will certainly signify its own ecclesiological development and a more refined and responsible attitude to the truths of faith; whereas the Orthodox consciousness in the encounter with heterodoxy regularly forces it to provide a more grounded and solid answer regarding its own particular "hope," which usually serves to evoke a greater awareness of its fathomless riches and a more responsible handling of its sacred tradition.

But in addition to this ecclesial/catechetical character of the ecumenical movement, which justifies it in the scheme of the ecclesiological-historical process, we cannot be indifferent to the fact that the movement has already become an established fact of Orthodox church life; for if the initiative in this work always belonged to the Protestants, then the Orthodox Church, by virtue simply of the presence of its hierarchs in ecumenical gatherings and the regular participation of its representatives in general ecumenical work, gave this brotherly vocation its positive legitimization. Of course, this participation in the ecumenical movement in no way signifies a religious compromise, or any sort of alliance with ambiguity or heresy. But it signifies a positive attitude to this initiative as a whole, places a church blessing upon it, acknowledges it as a good, and supports a conscious participation in the reunification and mutual understanding of Christians of various confessions. By participating in ecumenical gatherings, in blessing their members, in praying together with them, Orthodox hierarchs did not first scrutinize the Orthodoxy of the participants, nor set conditions for them. By this they determined the nature of the Orthodox attitude to the ecumenical movement and simultaneously placed on all Orthodox participants the task of not alienating the heterodox by the rigidity of their own beliefs. On the contrary, it required of them the search for those paths by which Orthodox faith and piety would be a factor in the deepening of spiritual life in general, the uplifting of ecclesial consciousness, and strengthening of the piety of the entire Christian world.

This initial and defining moment of the participation of the Orthodox Church in the ecumenical movement, this positive answer of the church of tradition to the problem of total ambiguity and indecision, seems to us to be a new revelation of the deep intuition of Orthodoxy, humbling her wisdom before the unfathomable providence of God, and seeing in the life of the Church not only the immutable forms of worship, but the ineffable mystery of the prophetic voices of the Holy Spirit.

The vagueness of dogmatic consciousness characterizing the ecumenical movement nonetheless finds its limits in the confession of Christ's name. In this regard even the left-most ecumenical initiatives are fundamentally different from so-called religious conferences and movements, which convene in "faith in God," the "primacy of spirit," "moral unity," and similar general attempts to bring together and unite various faiths, irrespective of their relation to Christ. The ecumenical movement is a Christian movement—and in this particularity finds not only the basis of positive possibilities of its development and deepening, but also the essential condition for our own religious participation in it. For if eucharistic fellowship is conceivable only in the framework of a single church, unity in the Lord's Prayer is possible and natural for all Christians who were taught by the Son to pray to the Father. Spiritual fellowship with non-Christians can be many things: deeper self-awareness, meditation, growth in intuitiveness, but not prayer, for there is no One to whom this prayer can be addressed. This difference, which can appear gratuitous and theoretical in Europe, takes on a monumental significance in the sphere of missionary work, which must be most assiduously freed from any religious syncretism. And if the representatives of Orthodoxy can fearlessly meet with Protestants, then in regard to the relation of Christianity with paganism, there can only be one criterion, which is expressed in the first verse of the first Psalm: "Happy are those who do not follow the advice of the wicked, or take the path that sinners tread or sit in the seats of scoffers" (Ps. 1: 1).

Moving from these general remarks to an analysis of the facts in ecumenical action, we encounter two methodological dangers. If we simply focus on the coincidence of external factors, we can easily narrow the field of our inquiry to a chronicle of assemblies, discussions, resolutions, etc. All these facts, however important in themselves, in no way express the goal of the ecumenical movement, inasmuch as the latter is already a religious reality, and not a testimony to the weakness of human debate to make this reality concrete. On the other hand, turning from the historical facts to those psychological processes that accompany them, we can fall into the opposite danger and enlarge our field to such an extent that it will accommodate even our subjective aspirations, idealistic dreams, and unattainable projects.

The answer to the question, I believe, lies in the need, in each concrete case, to determine the ecclesiological significance of the given fact. Thus, the efforts of any gathering can be a turning point in the history of church consciousness, but they can also simply remain a big pile of papers. So, the religious experience that accompanies an ecumenical gathering can remain a subjective feeling, which dissipates over time without a trace, or it can develop into a conscious act of will, into a creative factor in church life. In each case, it is not the isolated fact that matters, but its ecclesial coefficient in its significance and influence within the system as a whole. From this point of view, the subject of our analysis should not be the external facts of ecumenical history, but the spiritual reality underlying them that defines their essence and concretely finds expression in human experience without being exhausted on subjective grounds.

In the testimony of representatives of the ecumenical movement we constantly find the same conclusion: there is an amazingly high and exuberant evaluation of the experience itself in remarkable contrast to the utter poverty of its contents, or in any event, with the complete helplessness to express its fullness in verbal form. The ecumenical experience is described as miraculous, as a revelation, almost as a new birth; but to the question of the contents of this revelation, the usual answers point to general or self-evident truths. And when as a result of very intensive common spiritual work capable theologians joyfully testify that "they have found Christians among their heterodox brothers," then it is evident they are speaking of certain deeper realities, and not the simple assertion that members of other churches[2] also confess the Christian faith.

This dichotomy in the assessment and content of the ecumenical experience puts us face-to-face with the core essence of the ecumenical movement, which in the future we will call the "ecumenical process," by which we refer not to the historical or psychological phenomena, but to that spiritual reality that lies at their roots.

What is the kernel of this process, what is its content, what does it give us? In order to answer these questions, let us turn to the various possibilities in the mutual relations among Christians of varying confessions. These can be formulated along three lines.

First, one can acknowledge the Christianity of the other (more accurately, that the other calls himself a Christian) while remaining utterly indifferent toward him. In that case, this Christianity of the other is regarded only as an external sign, a sort of etiquette, which, remaining on the intellectual plane, in no way affects our spiritual life and elicits in us no emotional response. There is no living relationship between us; we remain strangers to each other; nothing in common unites us. However troubling or sinful such a situation, it must be openly admitted that this is precisely the most common attitude among Christians of various confessions who, as Christians, are totally indifferent to each other. In the language of hypocrisy this spiritual wasteland is generally labeled "toleration."

In the second place, we can acknowledge the Christianity of the other, and treat him negatively. In those circumstances when the differences between confessions are placed in the forefront and are regarded as fundamental and determinative marks, heterodox Christianity becomes "heresy" and prompts alienation and conflict. In comparison to indifference it may appear as a sort of progress, because it presupposes a kind of indirect, albeit negative, affirmation: in order to be a heretic, one must be a Christian—a pagan can't be a heretic. In church history this attitude (not less common than the first) found expression in religious wars and mutual persecutions; today, it finds expression in various forms of proselytism.

Finally, a third type of attitude exists in which heterodox Christianity is seen not as some theoretical formulation and not as a perversion of truth, but as a living and real connection of man with God, as his personal commitment to the Lord Jesus Christ; such a perception must certainly elicit in us a profound sympathy, which we cannot consider as a normal subjective feeling or as an isolated phenomenon. If a Christian—whatever his affiliation and whatever his errors in relation to the true teaching—personally turns to Christ in a living relationship, then according to the word of the Lord he becomes a son of God and, therefore, our brother; and this brotherliness does not depend on our understanding, agreement, or feelings. It is given to us as most fundamental in the spiritual order of things, in that the one and the same Spirit of sonship calls forth in us the "Abba, Father," and testifies to our spirit that we are children of God (Rom 8:15)—that is, brothers to each other. The external confession of this brotherliness is the Lord's Prayer, common to all Christians, in which we name God as our Father.

However, the brotherliness of Christians is not restricted to acknowledging them as members of one family, of one sheepfold of Christ. It also includes other objective moments, which give it the quality of a living unity.

Every Christian having a living connection with Christ, and fulfilling his commandments, renders Christ's face in his own person, is a bearer of his image (Jn 14:20–24; Rv 2:20; 1 Cor 15:4). In this sense we can say that all Christians are "Christ-bearers." This realization of Christ's face can be more or less full and depends both on the personal aspects of one's spirituality, as well as on the objective facts of doctrine, sacraments[3], and all that which affects a person's participation in one or another ecclesial organism. But it is always a fact of spiritual reality and to negate it means to quench the freedom of the Holy Spirit, to limit the love of Christ toward those who call upon him (Jn 3:8; 6:37).

Every Christian realizes in himself the image of Christ; we must acknowledge this truth not as a theoretical postulate of faith, but as a concrete manifestation of the face of Christ in our brother. But, to see the face of Christ in another means to love him; and this love is directed to the very depths of a person's being, to the metaphysical point where a person becomes godlike—this is no longer a sentiment, but an aspect of deeper revelations, of the vision of that which is normally concealed from us by the sinful cloak of our life as well as by the perversions of our confessional structures.

These observations can help us understand the more profound meaning of those initially incomprehensible affirmations by which participants of the ecumenical movement describe their spiritual experience. For if the richness of all these experiences is realized in the simple affirmation that "they have seen Christians," then these words must be accepted as true. They saw that which was hidden from them; with a new insight they saw that living connection which joins their brothers with God; they understood their prayer, felt the fervor of their hearts; and in place of catechetical formulas of comparative theology they were illumined by eyes filled with love and hearts full faith. And this vision filled their souls with great blessedness and joy; for there is no greater joy for man than to see his brother in God.

Christ-bearing becomes the epiphany of Christ[4]; the bearing in oneself of the image of Christ—the manifestation of him for the other—this is the short formula that defines the heart of the ecumenical process.

If these observations are correct, then the following question naturally arises: What is the ecclesiological significance of these experiences? Are they not purely individualistic, and is not their sphere, albeit objective, limited to the individual—that is, in essence nonecclesial self-righteousness of isolated Christians? We must answer the question in the negative, not because we insist on the ecclesiological basis of our affirmation, but because of the very nature of things. In religious life the church is never a product or result of combining individual justifications. Precisely the opposite: the church precedes the individual, it nurtures and forms his spiritual character; in that sense every Christian bears within himself the church's foundation, manifesting in himself the face of his church. This follows from the mystical understanding about the essence of Christianity as well as the psychosociological facts of basic anthropology. This is why in principle we can affirm that there is no nonecclesial Christianity. Individual Christians can reject their own churchliness, can even aim at a pure individualism, but they are powerless to change the laws of nature and grace, which unanimously affirm the primacy of the church over the person, the whole over the parts, the Body of Christ over its members.

Concerning the themes of Christ's image in man, this must be understood in the sense that Christ's face is manifested in each Christian in relation to those possibilities that are given to him in his ecclesial life. And in the same manner as we can speak of the "Russian Christ," we can also speak of the German Christ or the Dutch Christ, the Protestant, Anglican, or Catholic Christ—the history of art and mysticism is its most certain proof.

Such expressions should not cause us any misunderstanding. It is self-evident that the Lord Jesus Christ himself is the same at all times and for all people. But the forms of the manifestations of his face can change relative to a particular era, place, people, confession, etc. If someone will contend that, together with the positive gifts by which the Lord differentiated all peoples, heterodox confessions suffer from one or another perversion of Christ's face based on the errors of their doctrine, then we will respond by saying that the face disfigured by scars does not thereby cease to be the image of God; and we can continue to love not only the classic lines of sinless beauty, but the entire fullness of humanity in the various forms of its fallenness, its perversity and suffering. In ecumenical love, through the piety of individual Christians, we glimpse the soul of one or another church, and we acknowledge in her the higher and eternal, which she bears within herself—in her active love for Christ, in her effort to incarnate his divine image in herself.

But speaking about the ecclesiological character of the object of ecumenical love, we must apply this analysis also to its subject—that is, to ourselves. For, insofar as we are rooted in the church in our religious life, we are not isolated units but bearers of the church's consciousness, since the revelation and love—which are given to us in ecumenical fellowship—belong not to us, but to our church. And this ecclesial character of our ecumenical relations is at the same time given to us as an incontrovertible fact and posited as the highest goal. It is a fact, since outside the church there is not, nor can be, any Christian life, and therefore to be with Christ, to know and to love his face, means to be already in the Church, to be a participant in the love of the Bride of Christ for her divine groom (Rv 22:17). But this manifestation by us of the church's initiative can always be distorted by private deviations, by individualistic theories, self-assertion, and sin. Here becomes evident the supreme goal of ecclesiological responsibility, of the most rigorous examination of convictions, struggles, and feelings—the will that all the manifestations of my spiritual life would express the wisdom and will of the church.

Thus, we can say that in the ecumenical movement there is a profound meeting of the churches: they acknowledge each other in the fullness of their earthly manifestations and differences, and find themselves rooted in one initiative of divine Love. This does not yet signify their unification, for all the conditions which separate them remain in force, but there is no doubt that in this fellowship is realized the commandment of the Lord about love for one another and about being in him through this love.

And in this lies the absolute value of the ecumenical movement, which in a sense gives it its own inherent value, entirely independent of whether it leads to some general historical-ecclesiological achievement or whether it will remain among the events in which the unity of the heavenly Jerusalem is anticipated in the various versions of the face of Christ, manifest in the individual churches.

And it is in this sense that the ecumenical fellowship is on an eschatological path and moves toward that moment when God will be all in all. Regardless of our future hopes, it is already eschatological by its nature, for it sees the churches of Christ and those belonging to them as radiant with the glory of God, and the power and beauty of Christ's image, foreshadowing that hidden time when we will be "like God" (1 Jn 3:2). And in this sense it deeply corresponds to the spirit of Orthodoxy, which more than any church sees the manifest beauty of God's creation and exalts the image of God, imprinted in man. The glory of the age to come already illumines our fragmented world, and one needs eyes that see and ears that hear, in order that hearing this heavenly prelude in this joyous vision we can celebrate the eternal blessedness of the coming age.

o

Ecumenical love, understood as the reality of church relations, must have its own theological and existential conditions for its realization. To these belong certain principles: the antinomical relation between confessionalism and the restraint of proselytism, which can only be resolved by the reality of the ecumenical miracle.

The creedal initiative cannot be understood as a simple differentiation of Christianity. We must decisively and categorically discard the so-called branch theory, according to which all churches are simply one expression of a global Christianity, whose objective reality can only be regarded within their unity; for this conception devalues dogmatic consciousness, relativizes church doctrine, and essentially equates confusion with truth. In response to this, we must decisively confess our faith in the fact that Orthodoxy contains the absolute truth, and that any deviations from it are perversions of Christian teaching. However, concurrently we cannot for one instant lose sight of the fact that other confessions hold precisely to the same point of view regarding their own teachings, and that this is absolutely legitimate and normal, if in the first place we acknowledge their existence. A Protestant who is not convinced of the absolute truth and rightness of the "Reform" is no longer a representative of his church and cannot have a significant role in the ecumenical process. The ecumenical agenda thus takes on a paradoxical character in trying to bring together mutually exclusive principles. There appears to be no solution. At the same time any minimalization of the intensity of this problem inevitably results either in the abolition of the very essence of ecumenism, or dissolves its tragic, albeit blessed, problematics in the indifference of superficial aesthetics.

If we reject the right of other confessions to proclaim themselves as the absolute and only true ones, it follows that we will regard them as the object of our influence. In this case, the only possible goal of our fellowship with them will be their conversion to our faith and making them members of our church. So, all of ecumenism is reduced to proselytism.

Now, insofar as other confessions will seek the same goals in regard to us, the field of our communication will naturally devolve into a battlefield, having nothing in common with the mystery of Christian love. Moreover, the thought of the aggressiveness of the opponent will result in paranoia and fear on both sides, and proselytism will assume the hidden shape of a sacred mission. In this case all initiatives will be seen as organized hypocrisy, whose content will be reduced to two goals: first, to outfox one's opponent, concealing from him one's true ambitions; and secondly, to overwhelm him, and having proved to him the instability of his faith, to co-opt him into one's own church. There exist in reality many variants of such tactics, which can in no way be construed as ecumenism.

Equally disruptive to the ecumenical idea is the so-called interconfessional method, which seeks to unite Christians of various confessions on a doctrinal minimalism. Such an approach fails to acknowledge that any confession is an organic and invisible whole, and the attempt to filter out of the entirety certain "minimums" is equivalent to its annihilation. Church life is always whole and integral, and in the encounter one should either embrace it fully, in all the fullness of its manifestation, or pass it by as if it didn't exist. The practical attempts at finding common markers within Christian confessions always result in an unbearable form of half-truths, which in these cases is more insidious than total confusion, for it negates the possibility of rebuttal and satisfies no one with its partialness and inconclusiveness.

A profound ecumenism can only have its basis in a rigorous and systematic confessionalism, where each church brings to it all the fullness of its gifts (regardless of their compatibility with the gifts of other churches). Here all members of such fellowship feel themselves entirely free and, putting aside all considerations of interchurch diplomacy and religious hospitality, act with full honesty and directness, hearkening only to the voice of their own ecclesial conscience.

We don't need to demonstrate the immeasurable difficulty of this approach in practice. In our actual participation in ecumenical work, we constantly slide either to the path of interconfessionalism (when we try to adapt to heterodox thought and piety), or to the practice of proselytism (when we set out to convince the heterodox of our doctrine). But our practical inconsistency does not have any meaning in a given case; for it is important for us here to establish the principle of our attitude and actions, insofar as they flow first of all from the very idea of ecumenical fellowship, and secondly, from the living reality shown in ecumenical love.

A confessional basis is effective not only in regard to the theoretical aspect of doctrinal truths; but it also influences the practical realization of ecumenical unity in the prayerful fellowship of Christians of various confessions. Experience convinces us of the fact that prayerful presence in a heterodox worship service nurtures the soul far more than the so-called ecumenical services,[5] in which the feeling of unity is supposed to arise through a conglomeration of languages and the distribution of functions. Usually, in such cases, there are prayers read from the services of various confessions, excerpts from sacred Scripture, and the Lord's Prayer. However exalted is the experience of these prayerful moments, they can't compare to the effective power and inspiration of authentic church services that express all the fullness of the ecclesial mystery of a given confession.

The unity of Christians should be profound and not symbolic. And it should be sought on the boundaries of greatest resistance, when Christians live a full life, in all the particularity of their church setting. If this is difficult, if this unity is given to us for only brief moments, and we experience it as a foretaste of the kingdom to come, then the tragedy of our divisions should be consciously experienced by us as the cross of our spiritual fragmentation, which we do not have the right to deny in the name of some apparent universal Christian happiness.

There is not, nor can there be, any ecumenical idyll; we must always keep this in mind when we approach this work. Sooner or later it will bring us heartbreak, and this pain will be right and inevitable, insofar as the tragedy of Christianity will cease to be for us an external and peripheral historical fact, but will appear as a spiritual reality in which we ourselves play a living and responsible role. This sadness about the impossibility of approaching the common cup, this pain of seeing the stubbornness in confusion of those whom we love as brothers, cannot be considered by us as, albeit unavoidable, unnecessary and unpleasant factors in ecumenical work. For they are the negative signs of that same ecumenical love, which by their intensity testify to the initial and fundamental unity of Christians—which has become broken and fragmented by the different confessions. Where there is no unity, there is no tragedy over its destruction; and the absence of this ecumenical pain testifies much more about the indifference to the very problem, about the absence of will toward unity, to the habituation toward the sin of fragmentation, than to the spiritual health of such a self-satisfied consciousness.

Humanly, all of ecumenism is a tapestry of investigation, struggle, and doubt; the moments of success are given to it in the order of miracle, vision, and eschatological joy. As the focus of interconfessional relations, which are deepened through personal struggles, it is first of all the experience of life—and as such carries within it all the fullness of joy and suffering, hope and disappointment, exaltation and failure—that we can count on to accompany our earthly path of church service. We have already shown previously that the restraint of proselytism is a constitutive moment of possibility in ecumenical relations, without which the whole essence of ecumenical relations is destroyed. In the context of confessional consciousness this requirement places before us an impossible problem. How can I restrain myself from trying to make my brother a participant in the truth if I believe in its absoluteness and am aware of his confusion? And in such a case is not my "restraint from proselytism" a demand for my disregard of the living soul of the other, a sign of indifference to his spiritual destiny, to the possibility of his salvation?

Apparently we are standing here before a conundrum; for in affirming the one possibility, we simultaneously negate the other; but in accepting the alternative and choosing one as the truth we obliterate the very problem. Confessionalism appears to be incompatible with a-proselytism, but without the presence of both there cannot be a profound ecumenism. We must acknowledge the difficulty of this position in all of its logical lucidity, for here the question is not about the strategy of our dealings, but about the inner determinations of our will. If the ecumenical movement becomes for us a sign of our ecclesial life, then the inner honesty of these relations is connected not with moral duty or with social expediency, but with the awareness that this encounter is taking place before the face of God. This is why our spiritual position here cannot be justified by any peripheral considerations, but must be subject strictly to the voice of our conscience, verified and deepened by the mind of the church.

In the solution of this problem we take into account the following considerations.

In the first place, we believe that the theoretical impossibility of its logical solution cannot serve as the absolute obstacle to its practical realization. If ecumenical love is a miracle, and this must be understood not only in the sense that it occurs regardless of our ambitions and triumphs over our psychology, but in the fact that its reality wins over the logical laws of our reasoning. In this sense the antinomical structure of ecumenical relations only serves to underline its *meta*logical spiritual nature.

In the second place we know that the possibility of ecumenical dialogue is given to us in the real experience of the life of our Church, which assumes a responsible role in the ecumenical movement. Consequently, the question underlying our awareness relates not to the fact of whether our ecumenical relations are possible in the face of the given conundrum, but to how this unity is realized and in what way it removes this logical contradiction.

This problem, which goes to the very essence of ecumenism, has both negative and positive aspects. In sorting out those elements that are incompatible with ecumenism we thereby refine the sphere of our positive concerns and creative hopes. In order to more accurately orient ourselves in these concerns, let us agree to define proselytism as every effort of our will that is directed at the co-opting of a heterodox Christian into our Church. A precondition of the principal of a-proselytism is the awareness that any Christian life is essentially ecclesial, that every Christian is in some sense a leaf, turning green on the branch of his maternal tree, and that his transition to another church is always a rupture of a connection in an organic order, which has fed his religious existence up to that point. This connection is not limited to the age of reason: all the religious experiences of childhood, all the blessed inheritance of family and national piety, all that which is borne by the history of one's mother church—all of this enters into the soul of the Christian as a treasury that he himself did not consciously obtain, that subconsciously nurtures and undergirds his spiritual life. Rejecting all this, he is in a way a branch striving to be severed from his maternal tree, and begins a new life, seeking to be grafted onto another tree; this is why the transition from one confession to another is always tragic; it is a profoundly destructive process, which penetrates into the subconscious corners of the soul, and can lead to a full spiritual catastrophe in the case where the "grafting" is unsuccessful and the new spiritual home does not become one's "native" home. Life's experience demonstrates the danger of such transitions, which acknowledge the truth of another confession without taking into account that the reception of the blessed gifts of the other church does not take place automatically, but is related to a whole list of psychological and historical factors. In the case of such conflicts we consider it far more correct to carry "the cross of the imperfection of one's own church" and to remain her faithful, though ignorant, son, than to abandon her for the sake of an alien perfection, leaving one's maternal nest and being ashamed of the sins of one's fathers, with whom we are connected by an irrevocable unity of organic life.

It goes without saying that we see these considerations as conditions of our ecumenical situation, and not as absolute spiritual laws. If we consider that the transition from one confession to another is unwholesome and dangerous, then it does not mean that there should not be exceptions to the rule—as, for example, when it becomes impossible spiritually to remain in one's church, and a new homeland is seen as the only saving truth. The discrete exceptions do not change our principal point of view, which is derived from the principle of acknowledging any ecclesial initiative, wherever and however it is manifested.

We must clearly differentiate the understanding of proselytism from mission, which consists in confession of one's faith and the preaching of one's truth. Without this there cannot be a confessional structure. And if we participate in ecumenical fellowship as representatives of our church, then the demonstration of her spiritual riches and the communion with them of our heterodox brothers becomes our natural and necessary imperative. Here we encounter the very essence of ecumenical work, inasmuch as its goal is to show the heterodox world the face of Christ, imprinted in the form of our ecclesiology. All the fullness of doctrine, all the beauty of worship, and the full depths of popular piety must find here their place and be adequately expressed in a language that facilitates for our heterodox brothers the possibility of penetrating and being enriched by the treasure of Orthodoxy. Believing in the truth of Orthodoxy, we look forward to the day that it will reign in the hearts of our brothers, and our "togetherness" with them opens the path to this victory. "May your right spirit set us on a level path."

This desire to enrich and to deepen the spiritual life of another is fundamentally different from the desire to convert him to one's own faith, to enlist him in membership in one's own church; it does not disrupt the organic nature of his church life, it nourishes without destroying, it enriches without rupturing; and its wholesomeness is proven and demonstrated by the application of this principle to one's self. For if from the outset I reject any religious fellowship with a person who seeks to uproot me from the heart of my church, then on the contrary, fellowship with a Christian capable of enriching me by the example of his own or of his church's piety and to share with me the accumulated experience of theology and theological thought of his church can be for me only useful and desired.

The factual history of the ecumenical movement of recent years confirms these observations. The Orthodox Church has always witnessed to her faith in these gatherings, not accepting any compromises, without trying to force her own truth on anyone else; the proof of the effectiveness of her preaching is the unquestionable growth of the ecclesial mind of the Protestant world, its acknowledgment of the value of confessional initiatives, the factual disappearance of nonchurchly individualism, and the examination of a whole series of its own worldviews—all this within the parameters of Orthodoxy's own confessional life, without rupturing or forcing its own historical tradition.

We are forced to review a whole series of established understandings, for in the light of ecumenical relations they take on a somewhat different meaning. Here we are first of all concerned with the understanding of heresy, whose conventional usage would render the ecumenical movement impossible. Church canons forbid not only prayer with heretics, but in general any kind of relations. Besides this, all ecumenical gatherings inevitably have in common the universal Christian prayer, which always forms the most meaningful and substantive moment at such gatherings. At the conference in Lausanne—one of the most responsible and substantive in dogmatic terms—there was even a place for a particular Orthodox service, in which heterodox delegates were present. It is a given that the service would have as its goal communion in prayer with heterodox; otherwise the idea that any of its participants who consciously express, or who receive as inspired, the words of Orthodox prayers without a corresponding movement of the soul toward God sounds as an unbearable and perverse falsehood.

The same thing takes place at other ecumenical conferences, and often the service is the Divine Liturgy, in which heterodox brothers participate in a conscious and responsible way. For a prayerful presence in the Liturgy means participation in it, and in that condition heterodox Christians cannot approach the chalice; they are witnesses to the fragmentation of the Christian world, but not to the impossibility of participation in prayer in the context of a heterodox mystery. Thus, a gathering of heterodox which, in a rigorous application of canons should be considered a gathering of heretics, is in fact thought of as a gathering of church people with whom the Orthodox Church prays together, offers blessings, and so forth. What conclusions can be drawn from this fact?

On the one hand, it is evident from a dogmatic consciousness and confessional principle that the understanding of heresy as something which occludes the true confession of faith must be fully preserved (and this becomes in practice self-evident in the encounter with certain sectarians, with whom it is impossible to have any prayerful relations: in such situations the ancient canon takes on the full power of its dogmatic specificity and psychological impossibility, thereby proving its essential immutability). On the other hand, it is equally evident in the case of ecumenical relations that the Orthodox Church does not consider heterodox Christians to be heretics, and that this is understood not as a form of diplomatic compromise or irresponsible sentimentality, but consciously and substantively. From these two conditions there is only one logical conclusion, to wit, that the very fundamental understanding of heresy has changed and is seen as something more complicated than the simple clash of confessional formulas. Although we cannot enter here into the discussion of this complex and difficult theological problem, we take the liberty of making one observation that seems to us to come out of the facts of church and ecumenical life.

Heresy can be understood logically and statically, as a certain immutable spiritual condition, which is expressed in precise and eternal dogmatic formulas. Such an understanding is applicable where there exists a fully established church life, where, so to speak, in churchly terms, "nothing takes place." But there where we find great spiritual upheavals, where there is a process of the inner development of ecclesial consciousness, where unity grows and fragmentation is overcome, the heretic becomes not the one whose faith in a given moment does not correspond to the teaching of the Orthodox Church, but rather the one who rejects this process of unification, who stands in the opposite stream: that of disunity, of irreconcilability, of opposition to unity, and in the preservation of the fragmented state of the Christian world. One's self-affirmation in a heresy consequently becomes a dynamic understanding and is defined not by its intellectual content in a given moment, but rather by partic-

ipation in one or another ecclesial process—in the mutual unification or disunity; its basis in such a case is not so much its intellectual framework, as its effort of will. And those who want fellowship in prayer and unity in love, while
confessing their own faith without rejecting others, who belong with their
whole being to their own church, and who can acknowledge the face of Christ
imprinted in other churches—can no longer consider each other "heretics," but
become brothers, united in love, even though divided in faith.

Equally difficult and responsible is the examination in the light of the ecumenical reality of such concepts as the church and sacraments (or mysteries).
In the context of historical ecclesial development these concepts have lost their
solid clarity and have expanded their boundaries. But this transformation does
not imply their relativization (for this would mean the very destruction of
Christianity and the Church), but more specifically the transition from logical
formulas to ontological realities, which are always infinitely richer, more full
and actual, than their intellectual formulations.

A detailed analysis of those meanings, which is essential to consider within
these conceptualizations, in the light of the experience of the ecumenical
movement, would require a whole theological treatise; therefore we will limit
ourselves here to some brief remarks concerning the more pressing problems,
which arise in this context before the church's consciousness.

In determining the boundaries of the Church we encounter an enormous
difficulty in applying the dictum: "outside the Church there is no salvation."
For on the one hand we reject the branch theory and believe in one true Orthodoxy; on the other hand, acknowledging the principle of a-proselytism and,
consequently, postulating the possibility of salvation in the loins of heterodoxy,
we thereby include it in the understanding of the term "Church." Therefore
there arises the most difficult problem about how and in what sense and to
what degree do we consider as churches those communities which do not belong (at least according to their confession of faith) to the one, holy, catholic,
and apostolic Church—that is, the Orthodox Church. This difficulty is experienced equally with churches that accept the apostolic creed, as well as in relation to communities with a poorly developed or absent church consciousness.
In regard to the latter the only way out of the situation is the hope that, even
if an ecclesial consciousness is lacking for one or another of their representatives, then their desire for ecumenical fellowship is evidence of the fact that
they already have this consciousness in a hidden form and it can develop to a
normal level. Within such an understanding the very desire for ecumenical
unity can be regarded as a kind of minimum of churchliness, and the ecumenical movement, therefore, seen as a singular spiritual organization, in
which the question about the catholicity (in a sense of universality in the precise meaning of this word) of the Church is put seriously and responsibly. For
we must frankly acknowledge that the principle of universality is completely
obscured in contemporary Christianity by the deep provincialism of individual

churches, which—even if they are expanding beyond national boundaries—
are concerned primarily about the preservation of their own truth and are not
suffering over the fact that this truth currently belongs only to an insignificant
part of the Christian world.

Similar problems attend the understanding of sacraments. For if in Orthodox understanding it is in principle entirely unacceptable to participate in
heterodox sacraments (for this would mean the acknowledgment of fullness
in heterodox church life and would consequently imply a rejection of one's
own ecclesiology, and in any event, its relativization), then the rejection of its
mystical power and the power of its piety for those to whom it is given is also
entirely impossible. This would be to limit divine Love, to deprive the Holy
Spirit of the possibility of acting where there is faith, sincere prayer, and profound piety.

Heterodox Christianity, participating in the ecumenical movement, finds itself today within a great and creative work. Its general direction can be characterized as a growth of ecclesiology, which in one or another degree has always
been there in a concealed form. In relation to this process Orthodox consciousness begins to reexamine its relationship to heterodoxy and finds therein
religious realities that were hidden from it by a range of creedal formulas and
pronouncements of academic theology. In this renewal of relationships we find
Dostoyevsky's rule about the fact that one must trust life much more than logic,
and then the dearly departed, who perhaps were never dying, will resurrect.

We can, of course, follow another path and not leave our rigorism and the
subsequent dogmatic assessments of heterodoxy; but then the ecumenical fellowship will be spiritual nonsense or blasphemous hypocrisy, and all those who
take part in it will be detractors from Orthodoxy who have been tempted by the
new "heresy of ecumenism."

Such is the clear and consequent ideology of the Roman Church, which sees
the unification of Christians as possible only in the form of their indisputable
subjection to Rome; any other fellowship of Christians is regarded as the harmful and criminal efforts of heedless children to connect truth with confusion.
The ideology of the Roman Church on this question is marked by irrefutable
systematics and a steely logic, and the conflict between her and the point of
view (or more precisely, the line of conduct) of the Orthodox Church can deal
not with the formal side of dogmatic or canonical consciousness, but only with
the boundaries of acceptable legal norms.

Honesty demands, however, that we notice that the official irreconcilability
with which the Roman Church sees the ecumenical movement does not determine the mind and will of all the members of the Catholic Church. And the ecumenical movement, understood as a fellowship of Christians, coming together
in the fullness of their own confessions and learning to see within them the ra-
diance of the face of Christ, is actually indebted to Roman Catholicism in a

much larger way than one would surmise, judging by the literature and by official documents and statements.

Finally, we must make a few concluding remarks about the religious nature of the ecumenical movement, and about its place among other spiritual realities.

Any religious phenomenon is necessarily determined by one or another article of the Creed, which embraces the fullness of spiritual accomplishments. In the ecumenical movement such a religious category should seem to be faith in the one, holy, Catholic, and apostolic Church, for the ecclesial initiative appears as the foundational as well as the end point of this process.

However, upon closer examination, we see that it is only the ideal of an ecumenical Church that is the determining moment of ecumenical relations, and can be understood as the inspirational force of ecumenical love. In its historical existence the Church is always a reality in which the grace of the Holy Spirit is given to the faithful in specific forms of sacraments and worship. This is why the dogmatic, canonical, and liturgical rules—the formality of religious life—are characteristic signs of ecclesial life.

In the ecumenical reality these categories are almost inapplicable. Its fundamental mark is freedom; not that superficial freedom, which considers itself not subject to the law and is therefore called liberation; but rather that inner freedom, which seeks the voice of God there where the power of law recedes. If they had adhered only to their own canonical norms, the Protestant churches would never have invited those of different faiths who are frequently even hostile to them. If it would have followed only its canons, the Orthodox Church would never have heeded this call. In order for the ecumenical fellowship to have become possible it needed creative daring and inspiration, the power of which is Christian freedom—the true evidence of the wafting of the Holy Spirit (2 Cor 3:17).

The bishops and the presbyters and the laypeople taking part in the ecumenical movement reveal the more prophetic, rather than the hierarchical, face of the Church. It is of course self-evident that the priesthood is inseparable from its bearers; but in the ecumenical work they act not as representatives of church authority and not as distributors of grace, but as authoritative preachers and elected confessors, freely proclaiming the church's truth. Prophetic ministry—not antithetical to the hierarchical, but fulfilling it—is revealed here with particular force. It is nourished by the depths of church life, it is formed by the wealth of sacred tradition, but in its essence remains a free and creative response to the Holy Spirit, who renews the Church with new accomplishments.

And the ecumenical movement, in its faithfulness to the church's past and with reverent anticipation of new revelations, always stands under the sign of the living words of the Creed: "I believe in the Holy Spirit, the Lord, the Giver of life, who proceeds from the Father…, who spoke by"—and is speaking by—"the prophets."

## NOTES

1. Such opinions are rarely expressed officially, but are present nevertheless in conscious, or more often, in subtle forms. The encounter with Orthodox participants always puts the question of faith in the center of religious consciousness, and helps overcome these confusions.

2. We use the term "church" here and further in its general sense—that is, meaning a religious community united in oneness of prayer, faith, and mysteries—notwithstanding the nature of its relationship with the one, Catholic, and apostolic Church.

3. We use "mysteries" and "sacraments" interchangeably for the Russian word "таинство" in the present translation (translator's note).

4. Literally "christophory" becomes "christophany" (translator's note).

5. *Culte oecumenique*—cited in original Russian text (translator's note).

*Alexander Schmemann (1921–1983) was born in Talinn, Estonia, and died in Crestwood, New York. In between there was a life of priestly service, teaching, and seminary administration, but this does not begin to account for the impact he left on this world in so many ways. There would not be an autocephalous (self-governing and independent) Orthodox Church in America (OCA) without his efforts over many years. The beauty of the Liturgy in the Eastern Church was both restored and shared with many by his lectures and books. Growing up in the Russian emigration in Paris, he experienced the cultural world of this community in a Russian military school and then gimnaziya, or high school. He also was educated in a French lycée and at the University of Paris. Perhaps it was the genius of Metropolitan Evlogy, or other experiences, but his love for the Liturgy, in which he participated at the cathedral on Rue Darue, led him to theological studies at St. Sergius Institute in Paris, where many of the other authors in this collection (Frs. Bulgakov, Kern, Afanasiev, and Anton Kartashev) became his teachers. Each left their imprint on him. Clearly a leader in that emigration community, he nevertheless left it for teaching and pastoral service in America at St. Vladimir's Seminary in 1951. He later served as dean there from 1962 to his death in 1983. Both in the United States and internationally, he became a spokesman for Orthodox Christianity, lecturing at many universities and theological schools. His writings on the Liturgy and "liturgical theology" enshrined him in the modern history of liturgical scholarship and renewal. But he was always first a priest, a celebrant of the liturgical services, a much sought after confessor, and a great teacher of the faith. He prepared and taped for broadcast hundreds of talks for Radio Liberty.*

*The following is one of Fr. Schmemann's numerous weekly radio broadcasts made over a ten-year period through Radio Liberty in New York to Europe and the former Soviet Union. Despite its brevity and simplicity (or more accurately, perhaps due to these virtues), this particular broadcast has a twofold significance in our time. It addresses, on the one hand, the issue of human authority and power, familiar to us in its various manifestations: political, economic, religious, social. And on the other hand, it addresses the perennial aspirations of religion, which so often are also allied with notions of victory over oppression and the triumph of some benevolent form of power, manifested archetypically by an all-powerful divinity, who delegates it subsequently to his faithful devotees. Both these notions are examined in the light of the nature of Christ's "power" and the revelation of his own Person as the antithesis of religious expectations, both then and now. Both aspects of our lives—of power and of religion—are on an unprecedented and perilous historical brink of disaster, and it seems that preceding civilizations have failed in a positive understanding of these fundamental human categories to evolve toward a more "civilized" world. Sometimes it doesn't take a sophisticated sociological treatise to examine and understand the roots and pitfalls of this tragedy. Sometimes it suffices to stop at one moment in one Person's earthly life, to meditate on that moment as a defining moment in history. In his characteristically accessible and direct style, Fr. Alexander looks both at the question of authority and divinity in such a unique Person—Jesus Christ—as they are historically revealed in this timeless moment of the Christian calendar, Palm Sunday. With equally characteristic candor, he shows how in the humbled "king" riding on an ass, these fundamental issues of human culture—power and religion—are flipped on their proverbial heads. What always gives Fr. Schmemann's works their engaging and transformative power, and sets them apart from the typical dead letter of modern theological speculations, is his consistent faithfulness to the church's kerygma: the transmission of the biblical Word into the living word of the contemporary human condition. The other two selections are also Radio Liberty talks, and they close this anthology with direct, simple, and beautiful words about faith and the experience of God. [Alexis Vinogradov, translator]*

## FOR FURTHER READING

Schmemann, Alexander. *A Celebration of Faith*, 3 volumes. Translated by John Jillions. Crestwood, N.Y.: St. Vladimir's Seminary Press, 1991, 1994, 1995.
———. *The Lord's Prayer.* Translated by Alexis Vino-Gradov. Crestwood, N.Y.: St. Vladimir's Seminary Press, 2001.
———. *O Death Where Is Thy Sting?* Translated by Alexis Vino-Gradov. Crestwood, N.Y.: St. Vladimir's Seminary Press, 2003.
———. *Freedom and Conscience.* Translated by Alexis Vino-Gradov. Crestwood, N.Y.: St. Vladimir's Seminary Press, 2003.

————. *Introduction to Liturgical Theology*. Crestwood, N.Y.: St. Vladimir's Seminary Press, 1966.

————. *For the Life of the World*. Crestwood, N.Y.: St. Vladimir's Seminary Press, 1972.

————. *Of Water and the Spirit*. Crestwood, N.Y.: St. Vladimir's Seminary Press, 1974.

————. *Great Lent*. Crestwood, N.Y.: St. Vladimir's Seminary Press, 1974.

————. *The Historical Road of Eastern Orthodoxy*. Crestwood, N.Y.: St. Vladimir's Seminary Press, 1977.

————. *Ultimate Questions: An Anthology of Modern Russian Religious Thought*. Crestwood, N.Y.: St. Vladimir's Seminary Press, 1977.

————. *Church, World, Mission*. Crestwood, N.Y.: St. Vladimir's Seminary Press, 1979.

————. *Liturgy and Life*. Crestwood, N.Y.: St. Vladimir's Seminary Press, 1983.

————. *The Eucharist: Sacrament of the Kingdom*. Translated by Paul Kachur. Crestwood, N.Y.: St. Vladimir's Seminary Press, 1988.

————. *Liturgy and Tradition*. Crestwood, N.Y.: St. Vladimir's Seminary Press, 1990.

*The Journals of Father Alexander Schmemann 1973–1983*. Translated by Julianna Schmemann. Crestwood, N.Y.: St. Vladimir's Seminary Press, 2001.

# PALM SUNDAY

In the Christian world the last Sunday before Easter is called Palm Sunday. On this day the faithful remember how six days before his sufferings and death Christ entered the Holy City and was greeted by a victorious crowd.

Here is the Gospel account:

And when they drew near to Jerusalem and came to Bethpage, the Mount of Olives, then Jesus sent two disciples, saying to them, "Go into the village opposite you, and immediately you will find an ass tied, and a colt with her; untie them and bring them to me. If anyone says anything to you, you shall say, 'the Lord has need of them,' and he will send them immediately." This took place to fulfill what was spoken by the prophet, saying, "Tell the daughter of Zion, behold, your king is coming to you, humble, and mounted on an ass, and on a colt, the foal of an ass." The disciples went and did as Jesus had directed them; they brought the ass and the colt, and put their garments on them, and he sat thereon. Most of the crowd spread their garments on the road, and others cut branches from the trees and spread them on the road. And the crowds that went before him and that followed him shouted, "Hosanna to the son of David! Blessed is he who comes in the name of the Lord! Hosanna in the highest!" And when he entered Jerusalem, all the city was stirred, saying, "Who is this?" And the crowds said, "This is the prophet Jesus from Nazareth of Galilee." And Jesus entered the temple of God and drove out all who sold and bought in the temple, and he overturned the tables of the money changers and the seats of those who sold pigeons. He said to them, It is written,

Translated by Alexis Vinogrador. Originally published in Sermons and Conversations, edited by Serge A. Schmemann and Fr. Alexander Piskunov. Moscow: Palomink, 2000.

"My house shall be called a house of prayer; but you made it a den of robbers." And
the blind and the lame came to him in the temple and he healed them. But when
the chief priests and scribes saw the wonderful things that he did, and the children
crying out in the temple, "Hosanna to the son of David!" they were indignant; and
said to him, "Do you hear what these are saying?" And Jesus said to them, "Yes;
and have you never read, 'Out of the mouth of babes and sucklings thou has
brought perfect praise?'" And leaving them he went out of the city to Bethany and
lodged there (Mt 21:1–17).

In order to appreciate the full depth of this text, in order to feel the joy of this
annual feast, the feast of Palms, it is important for us to remember, first of all,
that this victorious entry into Jerusalem was the only evident victory in the
course of Christ's earthly life. Nowhere and at no time did he ever seek fame,
or power, or glory, he never even asked for the most basic comforts of life.
"Foxes have holes,"—he would say—"and the birds of the air have their nests,
but the Son of Man has nowhere to lay down his head" (Mt 8:20). He rebuffed
all attempts to glorify him, and his whole teaching was about humility and
meekness: "[L]earn from me for I am meek and humble of heart, and you will
find rest for your souls" (Mt 11:29). From our earthly human point of view his
whole life, from the moment of his birth in a cave to his shameful death on a
cross beside condemned criminals, was a complete and tragic failure. And by
the end even those crowds that followed him, expecting miracles and healings,
abandoned him, and all finally ran away.

It is important to understand that at the heart and very core of the Christian
faith there really is earthly disappointment, tragedy, and failure. And it is this
fact that evoked the scorn of the opponents of Christianity, beginning with
those who stood by the cross and derided the suffering Man: "Save yourself! If
you are indeed the Son of God, come down from the cross" (Mt 27:40). But he
refused to come down, he answered them nothing. In later history he was the
scorn of Voltaire and the representatives of the so-called Enlightenment, and
later on by Nietzsche and his followers, promoters of the idea of the Superman.
Finally, in our day, he is derided by various candidates of philosophical sciences,
by those who keep obediently producing the requisite antireligious pamphlets.

It is important to add that at times the faithful themselves forget about the
central paradox of their faith, and assign to Christ that same power, strength,
authority, and success that he so decisively rejected. They forget so readily the
words of the Gospel: "and he began to be sorrowful even unto death" (Mt
26:37). But then this unique earthly victory, this glorification of Christ, which
he himself evoked, which he himself desired, takes on an incomparable and
specific meaning—"the whole town gathered around" (Mt 21:10). We know
that the words shouted by the crowd, "Hosanna to the son of David," we know
that those symbols by which they surrounded Christ, palm branches—all of this
"smelled" of a political insurrection, all of these were traditional symbols for
greeting a king, they signified the recognition of Christ as a king and the rejec-

tion of the incumbent authority. "Do you not hear how many are witnessing against you?" (Mt 27:13)—this is how the authorities interrogated Christ. And at this point Christ did not reject such praise, he did not answer that this was a mistake; and so it is clear that he accepted this celebration on the eve of his betrayal, suffering, and death. He had wished that even for a few moments, even if only in one city, people would see and recognize and proclaim the truth, that genuine authority and glory cannot reside with those who acquire it through external force and power but with the One who taught nothing except love, profound freedom, and subjection only to the higher and divine law of conscience.

This entry into Jerusalem signified the unmasking, for all time, of power based on force and obligation, of power that demands for its existence continual self-adulation. For a few hours in the Holy City there prevailed the kingdom of light and of love, and people recognized and received it. And what is most important, they were never able to forget about it. Huge empires rose and fell, whole governments came to power and declined; they achieved unprecedented power, the unprecedented glory of all sorts of leaders and lords who just as readily vanished, faded into dark nonexistence. "What earthly glory remains strong and immutable?" asks the poet,[1] and we answer—None. But the kingdom of this impoverished and homeless teacher remains and shines with that very joy, with that same hope. And not only once a year on Palm Sunday, but always, truly unto ages of ages. "Thy kingdom come" (Mt 6:10)—this is the prayer of Christians that is still heard, which still triumphs, however unnoticed or imperceptible its victory in the noise of earthly and transitory glories.

## NOTE

1. From the hymns of St. John of Damascus, Orthodox funeral service. "Service for Those Fallen Asleep," compiled by Rev. Igor Soroka, p. 56. South Canaan, Pa.: St. Tikhon's Seminary Press, 1992.

# CONCERNING THE PERSONAL NATURE OF FAITH

**S**everal years ago a French publisher approached a mix of well-known personalities—writers, philosophers, artists—with a proposal to write a small book on the theme: "What do I believe?" The majority of these people were believers, mostly members of the same church—the Roman Catholic Church, that is, the church which least tolerates so-called freedom of thought, advocating conformity. And yet, despite this fact, the answers of those questioned turned out to be profoundly different, and we can read each one with engaging interest. One and the same faith, described in light of individual experience, through individual interpretation and understanding, becomes new and personal, and at the same time does not cease to be one and shared.

I'm speaking about this because in our day people often speak about faith, about religion, and about Christianity first of all on the level of something impersonal, objective, and dogmatic. Not only the enemies of religion, but believers themselves have gotten used to talking about the objective teachings of Christianity, about what people in general believe. Yet, by its very nature and essence faith is something deeply personal, and only in the person and in one's personal experience does it have true life. Only when one or another teaching of the church, one or another dogma—that is, an affirmation of a certain truth—becomes *my* faith and *my* experience, and consequently, the very content of my life, only then does this faith truly live.

---

Translated by Alexis Vinogradov. Originally published in *Sermons and Conversations*.

If one considers the question of the transmission of faith from one person to another, it is clear that the only convincing and inspiring experience is the personal one. This is particularly important in Christianity, since in its very essence Christianity is the personal *encounter* with Christ, and not, in the final analysis, the acceptance of one or another teaching or dogma about Christ, but of Christ himself. In other words, Christianity is specifically personal. This does not at all mean that it is individualistic, for people encounter, come to know, and love one and the same Christ. At the same time this means that Christ turns to each one individually, and therefore each discrete faith, the faith of each one, although rooted in a common faith, is at the same time unique.

It is important to emphasize this fact, because in our times the enemies of faith try to reduce the debate over faith and religion to some sort of scientific demonstration, to undermine believers by means of objective arguments. For if one were to reduce the whole content of Christian faith to the level of objectively known facts of nature, then certainly on the scientific, or more accurately, pseudoscientific level, all this is truly unprovable. At the same time, Christians do not demand any proofs. For, for them, this proof lies in their experience. They know the direct reality of this experience, as a person knows in himself the reality of love, of elation, of sympathy, of cosuffering. And this means that faith cannot be proven, it can be related or told.

Such a telling, or an account of the faith, rather than a scientific analysis of facts, is in essence the Gospel itself. This is a telling by those who saw and heard Christ, who believed him, who loved him, for whom he became their life—it is a transmission precisely of their experience. For this is why the Gospel forever remains living, that is why it strikes us directly in our hearts, whereas philosophical and theological treatises so often leave our minds and hearts cold. And what our cold and sterile world needs more than anything else is precisely the living story of the living faith, the transmission not only of knowledge, not only of facts, but the very experience of faith.

Let each one of us believers know with certainty and conviction that even though our faith is weak, insufficient, although the words of Christ are addressed to us—"Oh you of little faith" (Mt 8:26)—nevertheless, in our better moments, we have this experience, which is unique and incomparable, for if it did not exist in hundreds of people before us, where would we have derived this faith, how would we know that 2000 years ago there occurred in this world an event which would have a direct, decisive, significance for our lives today? But this is precisely the content of faith: in the mystical confidence that everything which was done and said by Christ, was done for me, or said for me, that he is not separated from me by centuries, by distance, by nothing short of my own lack of faith, my own confusion, my own innumerable betrayals of him.

And so, I would like to dedicate these conversations to faith, but not simply in its objective and so-called theological content, but first of all in its personal development in our souls. What would I answer if someone were to ask me: What

is the meaning for you of God? What, in fact, do you understand when you proclaim this mystical, and at the same time, familiar and mundane word? Who for
you is Christ? Christians respond, "he died for us, he rose from the dead, in him
death is overcome"; they sing in their churches—"and not one dead remains in
the grave"—and yet all around us death continues to be victorious.

And what does all this mean, not only in words, not only in the conclusions
of sophisticated books, but what does it mean in the real and living life of a single person? You speak to us about the Church—what is its purpose? You speak
to us about the Trinity, about the Holy Spirit, about grace and mysteries, about
the remission of sins, but behind all these words should there not be some sort
of living and personal experience? For otherwise, what do they all mean? At the
same time, in our world, how far it is that we have come away from faith, how
difficult it is to reach toward it, to this experience, how difficult it is to share our
intimate thoughts about this. And so, let us make an attempt.

In the thirty years of my priesthood I understood that the most difficult thing
in the world is to speak about that which is most simple, most essential; that it is
far easier to pontificate on someone else's ideas, to quote someone else's experience, to speak with foreign words, and so difficult to communicate from one
heart to another. And so, let us begin at the beginning of all beginnings with God.

"God exists"—so affirms the believer; "there is no God"—responds the un-
believer; but what is the content, what is the life, what is the reality of this word
in me?[1]

## NOTE

1. Father Alexander develops this theme in further broadcasts, some which will be
published under the title *Freedom and Conscience*, translated and edited by Alexis Vinogradov. Crestwood, N.Y.: SVSP, 2003.

# BE LIKE CHILDREN

How can we find a most simple, usual, conventional way to speak about that which is most important, about that which is most difficult to transmit concerning man—about his religious experience? And here lies the whole problem—that this experience is precisely almost impossible to transmit, that as soon as you try to explain it in words, something strange happens, something cold and abstract. And this is why all the arguments about religion are so frequently boring. At the same time how rarely does either side achieve the essential?

And is this not why we read in the Gospel—"Be like children" (Mt 18:3)?—what can this mean? Is not our whole civilization focused on the task of turning children into adults, of making them as smart, as analytical, and as prosaic beings as we ourselves are? And are not all of our proofs and all of our discussions and arguments directed precisely at the adults for whom childhood is simply a time of development, of preparation, a time precisely for overcoming any childishness in oneself?

And yet, "Be like children," says Christ, and also: "Do not hinder the children to come unto me" (Mt 19:14). And if this is said, then for us believers there is no reason to be ashamed of the unquestionable childlikeness that is connected with religion itself, and to every religious experience. It is not accidental that the first thing we see as we enter a church is the image of a child, the image of a young mother holding a child in her arms; and this is precisely that which is most important in Christ—the Church is concerned with the fact that we

Translated by Alexis Vinogradov. Originally published in *Sermons and Conversations*.

should not forget this first and most important revelation of the divine in the world. For the same Church further affirms that Christ is God, Wisdom, Mind, Truth. But all of this is first of all revealed in the image of this child; it is precisely this revelation that is the key to everything else in religion.

Let us ask ourselves: what do they mean, what can they mean, these words: "Be like children"? Certainly these words cannot refer here first of all to some kind of artificial simplification, the denial of growing, of education, of having the experience of growth, of development—that is, all of which we call in childhood the preparation for life, the mental, emotional, and physical maturation. In the Gospel itself it is said about Christ that he "grew in wisdom" (Lk 2:40).

In addition, "Be like children" in no way signifies some sort of infantilism; it is not a supremacy of childhood over adulthood; it does not mean that in order to receive religion or religious experience one has to become a simpleton, or more crudely—an idiot. I am insisting on this point because this is the attitude, this is the understanding of religion by its opponents. They reduce it to fairy tales, to little stories and riddles, which only children or adult children—undeveloped people—can accept.

What is the meaning of the words of Christ? In order to answer this question it is important first to formulate another question—for the question is not about what a person acquires in becoming an adult, for this is evident even without words, but about that which he loses, as he leaves his childhood. There is no doubt in the fact that he does lose something, something unique and precious, that for the rest of his life he remembers his childhood as a paradise lost, as a kind of golden dream, at the end of which life became sadder, emptier, fearsome.

I believe that if we had to define this in one word that word would be "wholeness." A child does not yet know the fragmentation of life into past, present, and future, the sad experience of vanishing and irretrievable time. He is completely in the present; he is totally in the fullness of everything that is *now*, be it joy, be it grief. He is completely in joy, which is why people speak about "childlike" laughter and about a "childlike" smile; he can be completely in grief and sadness, and this is why we speak about the tears of a child, and thus, why a child so easily and unreservedly cries and laughs.

A child is whole not only in relation to time, but in relation to all of life; he gives himself to everything with his entire being; he does not understand the world by deliberation, through analysis, or through one of his particular emotions, but with his whole being without reservation—and this is why the world is open to him in all of its dimensions. If in his eyes the animals are speaking, the trees are suffering or rejoicing, the sun is smiling, and an empty matchbox can miraculously appear as a car, or a plane, or a house, or whatever, this is not because he is silly or immature, but because open and given to him at the highest level is this feeling of the miraculous depth and connectedness of everything with everything. Because he has the gift of full indwelling with the world and with life. And in growing up, we indeed hopelessly lose all of this.

First of all we lose this very wholeness. In our mind and consciousness the world disintegrates to its constituent parts, and outside of this profound inter-connection all these elements become isolated, and in their isolation become limited, unidimensional, and boring.

We are beginning to *understand* more and more, but less and less to truly *comprehend*, we are beginning to acquire *knowledge* about everything, but no longer have a real *communion* with anything.

But this miraculous connection of everything with everything, this possibility of seeing the other in everything, this possibility of a full giving of oneself and connectedness, this inner openness, this trust in everything, is precisely the very content of religious experience—this is in fact the feeling of divine depth, of divine beauty, of the divine essence of everything, this is in fact the direct experience of God, who is all in all!

The very word "religion" in Latin means "connection." Religion is not simply one area of experience; it is not one category of knowledge or experience; religion is the connection of everything with everything, which is why, in the final analysis, it is the truth about everything. Religion is the depth of things and their height; religion is light, which flows from everything, thereby illuminating everything; religion is the experience of the presence in everything, behind everything, and above everything, of the *final* reality, without which nothing has any meaning. And this whole divine reality can only be perceived with an understanding that is whole, and this is the meaning of "Be like children."

It is to this that Christ calls us when he says "The one who does not receive the kingdom of God like a child, will not enter it" (Mk 10:15). For in order to see, to desire, to feel, to receive the kingdom of God it is necessary precisely to see this depth of things, to see that which in the better moments of our life they proclaim to us, that light which begins to flow from them when we return to our childhood wholeness.

# FREEDOM AND FAITHFULNESS: AN AFTERWORD

The authors represented in this volume all have one thing in common: uprootedness. All but one, Fr. Alexander Men, found themselves exiled from their native Russia, in Paris, during the years before and during the Second World War; some went on to America. Father Men's exile was no less tragic for the fact that it did not involve banishment to another country. A Jewish convert to the Orthodox Church who was as compelled by Dante as he was by the Cappadocians, Men was more eclectic, and altogether larger than so many of the Orthodox of his time and place. His murder was the ultimate sign of his internal exile.

Exiles—internal and external—are faced with different ways of surviving physically and morally, different ways of maintaining their identity. History up to the present day offers many examples of exiles and émigrés who hole up into a ghetto, or into a siege mentality, where identity is established through sharp contrast with the "other." We are familiar with this mindset in Orthodox circles around the world.

Other exiles and émigrés assimilate so totally into their new surroundings that it becomes no longer possible to discern where it was they came from and what they believe.

The approach taken by the authors here represented is altogether different. They preserved their identity in exile, yet never retreated into a ghetto. Their writing arose out of several qualities that forbade—or rendered utterly unnecessary—a siege mentality: *security* in their faith, *love* for their Church, and the *missionary commitment* to convey the Gospel to their time and place.

These people knew who they were, and were utterly secure in their identity as Orthodox Christians. Security of this kind is not the same thing as personal pride.

We witness in these authors a calm certitude in their faith and in their church, which translates into a *freedom* to seek different and new ways of seeing and expressing the timeless faith. They brought a healthily critical spirit to the "earthen vessels" that convey the "treasure" of the Gospel (cf. 2 Cor 4:7). They shunned a fundamentalist reading of Scripture, the Fathers, the canons (doctrinal formulas)—which is often an expression of fear, or the absence of security.

The authors here represented were no doubt aware of the possible imperfections of their lines of thought. Consequently they never expressed their ideas as dogmas, but as theologoumena for the consideration of the wider Church. They knew that if their ideas did contain errors, the Church—the great conciliar body—would surely correct or adjust them in good time. The risk of requiring adjustment or correction was for them worth taking, and certainly less than the opposite risk of falling into a deadening traditionalism, which they saw as facile, infectious, and harder to remedy.

Related to security is love. These authors' love for the Church and for all of its historic means of handing down the gospel led to their conviction that the canonical and conciliar formulas, the liturgical and patristic texts, do not represent dead letter but living spirit. Their love for the traditional sources of theology entailed the most intellectually and spiritually honest encounter with these sources—and their essays call the reader to engage with the Church and with tradition as with a living, cherished, and esteemed being.

Their clear sense of identity, and their love for the Gospel as expressed in its purity through the Orthodox Church, necessitated for these people the struggle to convey that Gospel to the people around them, where they were in space and time. The Christian pluralism of the West—notably Paris and America—did not threaten them in their Orthodoxy. It drove them to engage with Protestants, Anglicans, and Roman Catholics, to seek out Christ wherever he could be found in their respective theologies and spiritualities. Furthermore, Christian pluralism challenged them to express Orthodox faith and life in new languages, and to audiences for whom Orthodoxy was foreign.

Out of these points of origin came a diverse body of essays, not to mention countless unrecorded lectures, sermons, and living room conversations, the spirit of which has been enormously influential on Orthodoxy today, particularly (though not exclusively) in its expression in the West. Two areas may be of particular interest to us in our own day, as we evaluate the contribution of these authors: their approach to Church doctrine, and their approach toward non-Orthodox Christians.

## CHURCH DOCTRINE

Reading today an essay such as Fr. Sergius Bulgakov's "Dogma and Dogmatics"—and taking that essay as representative of the basic theological

hermeneutic which informed nearly all these authors—there is the impression
that its approach is not so new or radical. We are liable to think it quite obvious, for example, that tradition is not a closed book, that there are new theological and ethical challenges presented in each era, which the writers of the
previous era cannot be expected to have addressed, much less to have sealed
with the Church's final word. To us, it is commonplace to say that the Fathers,
in order to be understood properly, must be read with as clear as possible a conception of their context, their "problematics" as Bulgakov likes to put it. In
short, it is easy to forget how new and radical these ideas seemed to many of
Bulgakov's readers. And so we are apt to wonder why he feels the need to come
back to these themes again and again—as if we didn't understand them the first
time around—and why he is at such great pains at every step to qualify his position as one which does not undermine patristic authority, but rather seeks to
uncover and awaken the fullness and meaning of that authority.

If some of the positions of Bulgakov, Kartashev, Afanasiev, and Kern are so
familiar to some of the people who never read them, it is because they were so
thoroughly digested, synthesized, and reexpressed in the persons of their
students—Fr. Alexander Schmemann and Fr. John Meyendorff—who in turn
never failed to acknowledged the importance and influence of their teachers
upon them. And yet, in our time, the reemergence of essays such as these, in
their raw, original form, may well reveal something about Orthodoxy today.
Might they make apparent a rift, which if anything continues to grow ever
deeper since the mid-twentieth century, between those who will leap in welcome recognition at this approach to tradition, and those who will see it as suspect, as modernist, liberal, and Westernized?

## THE ORTHODOX CHURCH AND OTHER CHRISTIANS

The Christian pluralism in which most of these authors found themselves,
prompted, for the first time in centuries, serious Orthodox reflection on the nature of the Church, and more particularly, the nature of the boundaries of the
Church. As Fr. Florovsky liked to point out, there is no "definition" of the Church
that could claim any doctrinal authority[1]—strictly speaking the Church has no
"ecclesiology" in the same sense as it has a Christology and a Trinitarian theology.
Yet once Orthodox Christians are summoned to look around them and discover
others who call on the name of Christ, they are forced to answer how the "separated brethren" relate to the one, holy, Catholic, and apostolic Church, and thus
reflect on the nature and boundaries of the Church, spiritually, canonically, insti-
tutionally. Florovsky's essay on "The Limits of the Church,"[2] represents but one
of the clearest and better known of a series of reflections by several of the émigré authors on the relationship between the Orthodox Church—which they all
saw as the true Church of Christ—and the other Christian bodies.

Without exception, all the authors here published were torn by two convictions that seemed to lead in different directions. On the one hand, their theological and historical integrity led them to assert unwaveringly that the Orthodox Church is the one true Church, in historic and apostolic continuity with the community established by Christ and his apostles. It follows that the Church itself is not divided, but that there are divisions or separations *from* the Church. Yet on the other hand, witnessing the spirituality, the piety, and the theology of the Protestants and Roman Catholics around them, distortions notwithstanding, our authors could not but be stirred to recognize Christian reality outside the canonical boundaries of the Orthodox Church. Thus guided by their minds (but never with a cold intellectualism) and by their hearts (but never in sentimentality) they struggled to find ways both to express the paradox of the Church and the churches, and to relate in a right way with other Christians.

Their theological conclusions did not waver from identifying the Orthodox Church with the *Una Sancta*, even as, on the basis of patristic and historical precedent, they admitted that the Church's charismatic boundaries were not coextensive with its canonical boundaries. Their practical conclusions were not, ultimately, conclusions, but only gropings. There were proposals, particularly within the context of the Fellowship of Sts. Alban and Sergius, for a limited intercommunion between Anglicans and Orthodox, but caution and patience on both sides advised against.[3]

For all of their theological sobriety and ecclesiastical responsibility, it would be no exaggeration to say that our authors were cut to the heart by the divisions of Christians. The newness of their encounter with the Christian West, and the relative newness of the modern ecumenical movement, lent their reflections a sense of urgency and hope, as well as the freedom to put forward—as suggestions—proposals that for most Orthodox today are unthinkable.

Both Orthodoxy and the ecumenical movement today have all but lost this freshness. We Orthodox devour each other through printed and Internet media, as watchdogs of each others' succumbing to the "pan-heresy of ecumenism." The ecumenical movement is becoming ever more institutionalized, shackled by bureaucratic structures and politicized lobbies. Today we do right to follow the caution of the émigré authors, and stop short of any normalized intercommunion between Orthodox and their Protestant and Roman Catholic partners. But is there a way that we can recover their sense of urgency to the problem of divided Christendom, and their creativity in continuing to seek ways of expressing the nature and boundaries of the Church in the pursuit of unity?

## WINNERS AND LOSERS

Particularly as the work of Bulgakov, Afanasiev, Kern, Kartashev, and others begins to resurface in new publications and in translation, several commentators have remarked that these authors lost out to the "neo-Patristic" school, represented by the likes of Florovsky and Vladimir Lossky. Yet these categories are not always easily sustainable. Some figures have indeed been more widely published at this point in history. Yet who are they? Schmemann and Meyendorff freely acknowledged their dependence upon the thought of their professors—especially Bulgakov, Kern, and Kartashev. Florovsky was in an essential unison with the conclusions of the other authors about, for example, the relationship of non-Orthodox churches to the Orthodox Church. What he rejected strenuously was sophiology—primarily in its expression by Soloviev but also in Bulgakov. Indeed, one could fairly say that it wasn't this or that writer and his "school" that was marginalized by subsequent history, it was sophiology. Sophiology formed a critical part of Bulgakov's thought, but cannot be said to be utterly coextensive with the thought of any of the authors here published.

History has yet to pronounce the winners or losers of this period. The publication of this anthology of texts, which have not been seen or considered for some decades, will play an important part in history's evaluation of the theological landscape of the twentieth century. May we reflect on them with the same commitment to faithfulness, the same sense of security, freedom, and panache, which produced them.

—Peter C. Bouteneff, assistant professor in Dogmatic Theology
St. Vladimirs Orthodox Theological Seminary

## NOTES

1. Cf., for example, "The Historical Problem of a Definition of the Church," in volume 14 of *The Collected Works* (Vaduz: Büchervertriebsanstalt, 1989), p. 29.

2. This essay, originally published in *Church Quarterly Review* (1933), was revised and retitled "The Boundaries of the Church" in volume 13 of *The Collected Works* (Vaduz: Büchervertriebsanstalt, 1989). The same line of thinking is expressed in Florovsky's later essay, "The Doctrine of the Church and the Ecumenical Problem," *The Ecumenical Review* 2: 2 (1950): 152–61.

3. See Anastassy Gallaher, "Bulgakov and Intercommunion," in *Sobornost* 24: 2 (2002): 9–28.

# INDEX